DO
TOUCH

DO TOUCH

INSTANT, EASY HANDS-ON LEARNING EXPERIENCES FOR YOUNG CHILDREN

BY LABRITTA GILBERT

ILLUSTRATIONS BY:
LINDA GREIGG

PATTERN ILLUSTRATIONS BY:
CATHI HENRY
MICHAEL GILBERT

gryphon house
Beltsville, Maryland

ACKNOWLEDGEMENTS:
I wish to express special appreciation to my father-in-law Fred and my sons Russell and Michael: to Fred and Russell for long hours spent before computers transforming my very rough copy into a manuscript; to Michael for coming to my rescue many times with graphics which do not appear in the book but were vital to its realization. Thanks also to Kathey Carreiro and Alyne Gilbert for spotting missing and misplaced pieces of the puzzle that was to become this book.
I gratefully recognize contributions of teachers and kids: teachers offered insightful suggestions during workshops, and kids happily tested activities for me, thinking we were having fun, which, in fact, we were.

© 1989 by LaBritta Gilbert

Published by GRYPHON HOUSE, Inc.,
10726 Tucker Street, Beltsville, Maryland 20705.

World Wide Web: http://www.ghbooks.com

All rights reserved. No part of this publication except for patterns which may be copied for classroom use, may be reproduced, stored in a retrieval system, or transmitted in any form or by any means, electronics mechanical, photocopying, recording or otherwise, without the prior written permission of the publisher. Printed in the United States of America.

Library of Congress Catalog Number: 89-84144

Design: Graves Fowler Associates

PROLOGUE

Kids like
mud and noise
and democracy
and experimentation
and wheelbarrows and shovels
and hammocks and wagons
and drums and gongs
and magnets and mirrors
and telescopes and magnifiers
and sticks and timers
and clocks and stopwatches
and spontaneity and unafraid teachers
and visitors and singing
and animals and sand and water
and making things
and coconuts and hammers
and cooking and weighing
and measuring and balancing
and feeling a hundred of something
and climbing trees
and walking in the rain
and play spaces they make for themselves
and umbrellas
and baking their own birthday cakes
and digging holes and being outdoors (without coats)
and soft things for quiet moments
and wondering
and teachers who like them.

PROLOGUE

Teachers like quiet
and clean
and lots of pictures and volunteers
and hatching eggs
and curiosity
and democracy
and sorting and stacking
and shapes and colors
and organizing and classifying and reading aloud
and questions and answers
and recycling
and inspiring
and Fridays
and the sound of their own voices
and progress
and contributing
and a child with a book
and quiet
and mornings
and doing six things at once (doing them well)
and being allowed to say, "I don't know"
and smiles and unexpected hugs
and sitting in a circle
and learning from children
and listening
and cupcake occasions
and glue bottles that work
and quiet
and being surprised
and seeing former students
and the sanctity of children's wonder
and kids to like them.

TABLE OF CONTENTS

INTRODUCTION 9

STICKS
Pairing and puzzling with marker-designed craft sticks ... 15

SET I-BASIC
- ONE-COLOR 18
- TWO-COLOR 19
- WHAT'S MISSING 20
- PATTERNS 21
- DOTS 22
- ARROWS 22
- GEOPUZZLES 23
- HEARTS 24
- LINES 24
- HALVES 25
- STEPS 26
- STRIPES 27
- ICE CREAM CONES 27
- HIGH-LOW 28
- SMILES 29
- STARS 30
- PUZZLES 31
- NAMES/FACES 34
- MUSIC NOTES 35

SET II-ADVANCED
- COLORS/NAMES 36
- NUMBERS/NAMES 36
- GEOSHAPES/NAMES 37
- 1-10 38
- 1-20 39
- ALPHABET (UPPER CASE) 40
- ALPHABET (LOWER CASE) 40
- MEASUREMENTS 41

TABLE OF CONTENTS

SPONGES
Feeling, forming, fitting shapes cut from sponges 43
SET I-THICK SPONGE
    SHAPES FOR BEGINNERS 48
    BEGINNER PUZZLES 49
    WIDTH BARS 50
    LENGTH BARS 52
    COLOR STACKS 53
    SHAPES FOR INTERMEDIATES AND ADVANCED . . . 54
    TOWERS 55
    FEELING SHAPES 57
    TWO-COLOR PUZZLES 58
    OUTLINES 59
    POSITIVE/NEGATIVE BARS 60
    VERTICAL PUZZLE 61
    BUILDING BLOCKS 62
    ONE-COLOR PUZZLES 63
SET II-THIN SPONGE
    PUZZLES 64
    OUTLINES 66
    SQUARES 67
    PATTERNS 68
    LOTTO 70
    ALPHABET (UPPER CASE) 72
    ALPHABET (LOWER CASE) 75
    NUMBERS 78
    GRAPH 80
    FRACTIONS—CIRCLE 83
    FRACTIONS—SQUARE 84
    FRACTIONS—TRIANGLE 85
    FRACTIONS—RECTANGLE 86
    CUTOUTS (ROUND) 87
    CUTOUTS (SQUARE) 88

STICKERS
Grouping and categorizing sticker squares 89

TABLE OF CONTENTS

    SORTING 95
    LEFT/RIGHT 96
    ORIENTATION 97
    PAIRING 98
    LARGE/SMALL 99
    COMPONENTS 100
    CATEGORIES 101

CUPS
Measuring substances, counting trinkets and toys 103
SET I—MEASURING
    DOTS 107
    GRADUATED FILL LINES 108
    NUMBERS 109
    SAME FILL LINES 110
SET II—COUNTING
    HOW MANY NUTS TO FILL? 111
    1-10 (TOYS) 112
    1-10 (FRINGE BALLS) 113
    SETS 113
    HOW MANY CLIPS? 114
    ADVANCED NUMBERS (TWO DIGIT) 114
    MONEY 115

POCKETS
Duplicating the contents of plastic pockets 117
    COINS 119
    SEWING TRIMS 120
    RIBBONS 121
    COUNTERS 121
    WASHERS 122
    MAGNETS 122
    RINGS 123
    CLIPS (PLASTIC) 124
    CLIPS (ASSORTED) 124
    ERASERS 125
    POKER CHIPS 126

TABLE OF CONTENTS

  FELT SHAPES 127
  PAPER MONEY 128
  PEGS 128
  BUTTONS 129
  LACE 129
  TEXTURES 130
  FABRIC TEXTURES 131
  BEANS 132
  RUBBER BANDS 133
  FLAGS 133
  CLIPS (METAL) 134
  FLOWERS/LEAVES 135
  COLOR SHADES 135
  STAMPS 136
  CARDS 136
  SPICES 137
  SPANGLES/BEADS 138
  DOMINOES 139

GADGETS
Tinkering 141
GADGETS AND BAKER'S CLAY
 CUTTERS 147
 CLAY/HANDS 148
 LETTERS 148
 STAMPING TOOLS 149
 STAMPING TOOLS/KNIFE 150
 STAMPING TOOLS/PASTRY WHEEL 150
 FLAT BEADS 151
 ROUND BEADS 152
 NAMES 153
 NUMBERS 154
GADGETS AND SAND
 MEASURING CUPS AND SPOONS 157
 STRAINER/BEANS 158
 FUNNELS/BOTTLES 159
 MOLDS 160

TABLE OF CONTENTS

    VILLAGE 160
GADGETS AND WATER
    FLOATING THINGS 160
    FUNNELS AND BOTTLES 162
    FUNNELS AND TUBES 163
    SQUEEZE, SPRAY, AND SPRINKLE 164
    SIPHON AND SUCTION 165

TRANSPARENCIES
Superimposing outlined transparencies over matching pictures 167
    DIFFERENT SHAPES 171
    DIFFERENT SIZES 179
    RELATED SHAPES 187

RINGS
Sorting little collectibles in six rings 195
    FARM ANIMALS 198
    CORKS 198
    METAL KEY RINGS 199
    FRINGE BALLS (POMPOMS—BY COLOR) 200
    FRINGE BALLS (POMPOMS—BY SIZE) 200
    LARGE/SMALL 201
    BUTTONS (ASSORTED) 202
    PLASTIC EGGS 203
    WASHERS 203
    NUTS 204
    WILD ANIMALS 205
    BOTTLES 205
    BUTTONS (BY COLOR) 206
    BUTTONS (BY SIZE) 206
    BEADS 207
    DINOSAURS 208
    TOYS 209
    MEASURING SPOONS 209
    THREAD 210
    COLORS/OBJECTS 210
    ET CETERA 211

TABLE OF CONTENTS

    METAL, PLASTIC, WOOD, PAPER, FABRIC, RUBBER 212
    LACE 213
    COINS 213
    HARDWARE 214
    FABRIC PATTERNS 215
    MARBLES 215
    PAPER MONEY 216
    SANDPAPER 216
    SHELLS/ROCKS 217
    PEGBOARD HOOKS 218
    PRICING 219
    CORKS/NOT CORKS 219
    FABRIC TEXTURES 220
    COLORED PENCILS 220
    CORNERS/NO CORNERS 221
INDEX 223

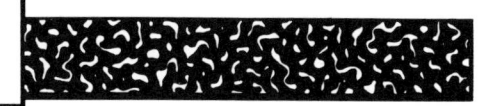

INTRODUCTION

Kids can't keep from learning! It's the happiest of natural consequences. They learn best with things—objects they can hold, control, arrange, and manipulate. If you and your class haven't tried manipulatives, both of you are missing out! Active learning breathes new life into any class. It's an ongoing process—children use activities over and over, seeing new possibilities and sharpening skills with each use. Everybody wins in a switch from passive to active learning: students are freed to do—to participate, to make decisions, to stretch beyond the limitations of teacher-led lessons. Teachers are freed to learn—to observe, to follow children for a change, to enlarge the children's world by enriching the classroom environment.

Why Active Learning?

Actually, there's no other kind. A learner must participate in the learning process, however minimally. But we want maximum learning! To maximize learning, we must maximize participation. Given kids' propensity for exploration, their insatiable curiosity, and their need to do, to find out, to know, all we really need to do is surround them with things to explore, to wonder about, to do, and to discover. Sophisticated learning materials are nice but by no means indispensable. (We might be surprised at how many children learn to read from the backs of cereal boxes, mightn't we?) DO TOUCH! learning materials are blessedly uncomplicated; toys, trinkets and simple materials can be made into activities children can't keep their hands off—and that brings about active learning.

Self-esteem—"I am worthy of knowing this—and much more!"—is the foundation upon which all learning rests. Magazine articles and books offer suggestions to parents for building their children's self-esteem. Actually, allowing it to develop is a more accurate description of what takes place. Children develop it naturally when they believe in themselves, their abilities, their worth. It happens when they are allowed to do many things, and are allowed to make decisions and sometimes mistakes. THE MORE CHILDREN ARE ALLOWED TO DO, THE MORE THEY FEEL THEY CAN DO, AND THE MORE ABLE TO DO THEY BECOME. Conversely, over-controlling robs them of initiative and inhibits the development of self-esteem. This may mean that teachers must take a more passive role to enable children to be more active, and this happens best in a rich, child-active environment. That's where manipulatives—three-dimensional, hands-on, active learning materials—come in! They are the key to transforming a learning environment from passive to active. If you want such a transformation for your classroom, it's easier than you might think.

What You Do

Think TOUCH! Think as children think—that the world is to be seen with the hands as well as the eyes. See objects—even simple things—as if for the first time, as a child sees them: What is this? What can it do? Why is it the way it is? What can I make it do?

What They Do

Become active learners! Touching, interacting, decision-making learners. They switch roles (naturally and easily) from being primarily listeners and followers (passive!) to being doers. They work directly with materials which speak to them in a language they understand, activity.

What You Both Do

Become friends. Listen and learn with and from each other. You will see them differently, admiring ingenuity and originality you never noticed before. They will see you differently, too—as a helper and friend, rather than as a taskmaster. You will appreciate each other as never before.

Activity-centered classes evolve, and no two classes evolve the same way. They continually change! All the participants—teachers and students—become players in an original play—one that has never been played before.

How To Shake Up A Classroom

It's easy! Fill it with things. It has too many things, already, you say? Get rid of some of those things! Use an unjaundiced eye to mercilessly unclutter, tossing out things which haven't been used recently, broken and tired old things, and especially things which enhance neither learning nor the room's appearance. Push aside some paper materials—"dittos" and worksheets—to make room for colorful, child-involving materials. Make lots of room, because a few activities are like a few peanuts—they leave you wanting more! I wanted a roomful of activities when I changed my class from passive to active—and ended up making my own materials to make it possible. Continual streamlining, paring down and simplifying over the years resulted in the activities in this book.

INTRODUCTION

They are so quick and easy to make, you can have a roomful in a hurry—and for an almost unbelievably low cost.

How Active Learning?

Start by starting, as the saying goes. Make the activities and the rest will fall into place. Few rules are needed for using them, but I will share strategies that have worked for me. The most important thing is to begin—just gather and prepare a large supply of one type of material—STICKS, for instance—and start. Wait until you have a sizable number, however, to introduce them to the class so that everyone who wants to is able to use them.

The activities in DO TOUCH! can be made quickly, because all of the activities in one group use the same basic materials and techniques. Some simply require buying or collecting inexpensive items. It's preferable to make all (or as many as you decide to make) from each group before going on to the next group since you'll be familiar with the process of making them and will have the necessary materials assembled. Sources for buying the materials are given in the introduction to each section.

What Now?

Once you have made the DO TOUCH! materials and have a reasonable supply of colorful, new activities, you can't wait to share them with the children. How you do this is an individual matter, but my personal preference in this, as in most things, favors simplicity. The fewer the rules, the better. That way everybody feels relaxed about the classroom's new look and eager to investigate. Keep in mind:

■ You need to demonstrate to the class how the activities are used (more about this later).

■ Most teachers like to have a designated time for manipulative activities; they use them either as primary learning tools or as enrichment.

■ Activities need a place of their own—roomy shelves, accessible to children.

■ Children must be taught to return activities to the shelf in their storage containers—each and every time. You know why.

■ Most of these are single-child activities—not appropriate for use by two or more children, unless specified (in a few cases a friend or two is asked to share the activity.)

■ Activities should never be mixed together or with toys, etc.

INTRODUCTION

Introducing The Activities

Each different type of activity—STICKS, STICKERS, SPONGES, etc.—needs to be carefully demonstrated to the children before they use it. Since all activities of one group are used in essentially the same way, simply demonstrating a sample activity from a group will usually be sufficient—children can then continue on their own with the others in that group. Exceptions are the CUPS and GADGETS activities. You will need to demonstrate each of these individually. After your demonstrations, emphasize your expectations for putting all materials away—and do so yourself in front of the children. Put them back in their containers and return them to their proper storage place.

Storing The Activities

My favorite way to store the activities is in self-closing, freezer weight clear plastic bags. All except the CUPS and GADGETS activities will fit in either the large (gallon) size or the small (pint) size bags. You will want to apply small adhesive labels to the outside of the bags to help teachers identify them. If most of the activities will be stored with only a few in use at any given time, and you or another adult will be taking the materials out of and returning them to the bags, you can self-seal the bags, which can then be stored in plastic dishpans or crates. If the activities are to be displayed for children to make their own choices, don't depend on them to be able to self-seal the bags; this is too tricky an operation for most children. You can display them by using a paper punch to make a hole in both thicknesses of the bag just above the "zipper," and hanging them on hooks (cup, magnetic, suction, or pegboard) at child level. The bags will automatically be closed as they are hung on the hooks.

Of course, plastic bags are not the only way to store the materials. Disposable plastic tumblers (shatter-resistant) make attractive holders for the STICKS, and reusable plastic food containers (with labels removed) and pre-moistened towelette containers make good storage containers for the CUPS activities and others, and are free. Suggestions for storing the GADGETS are given in that section. Skip lids or use them as you see fit. Practical and pretty small baskets are widely available; not free, but inexpensive. Number or letter coding is essential for the STICKS, STICKERS, and TRANSPARENCIES activities to enable adults to quickly identify misplaced pieces. For instance, all the pieces of one activity could have the same code letter on the back of each piece, to quickly identify them as part of the same activity.

INTRODUCTION

You can store these activities with commercial materials such as puzzles, etc., or they can have their own space. If your room has learning centers, you can add the activities to them or create new centers—one center for each type of activity. You can store all of one type together or mix them; it really makes no difference.

Levels Of Difficulty

These materials are designated as BEGINNING, INTERMEDIATE, and ADVANCED. As a general rule, those listed as BEGINNING are appropriate for two and a half to three year-olds, INTERMEDIATE for four year-olds, and ADVANCED for five year-olds and older. However, you know your own class—ignore the levels if an activity seems to fit your group's skill level, or you think you can modify it to make it fit.

STICKS

Pairing and Puzzling

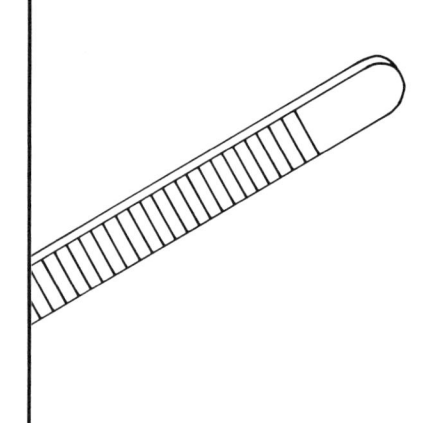

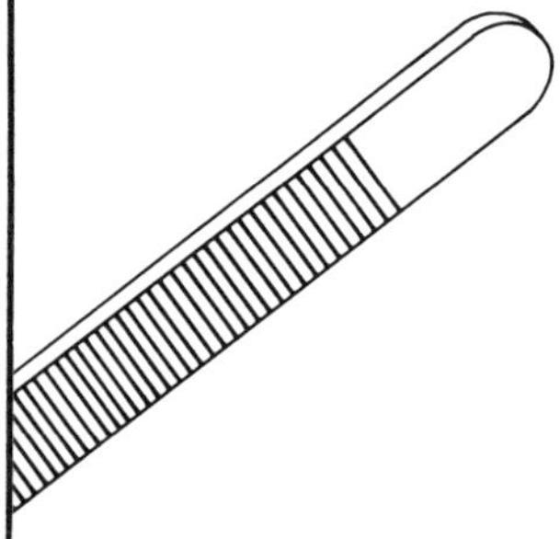

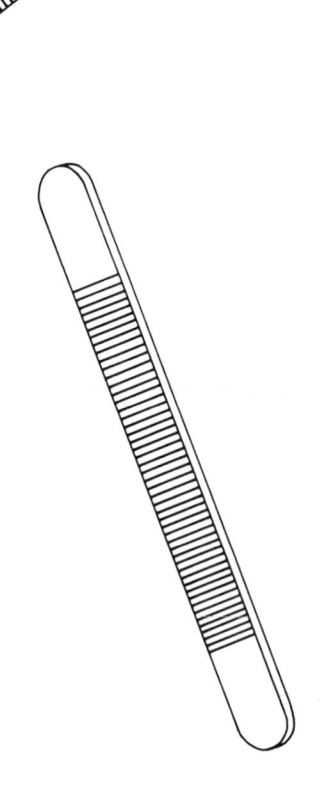

STICKS

What kids do

Match pairs of sticks. They appear deceptively simple, yet they require quite a lot of concentration and reasoning.

Kids place a matching pair of sticks side by side; sometimes they like to stack the two matching sticks, which is also acceptable, but side-by-side pairing is probably preferable because seeing the two together visually reinforces, and proves, the match. However, stacking is a good idea if workspace is limited, and is certainly better than crowding the sticks so that separate pairs can't be distinguished.

What teachers do

STICKS are quick to make and quite cheap. In fact, a complete activity costs only a few cents and takes just minutes to make. They are made with tongue depressors and markers.

What you will need

■ TONGUE DEPRESSORS—called "Jumbo Craft Sticks" in hobby and handicraft stores, and some school supply catalogues, but are much less expensive from a pharmacy. They may be a bit of a problem to find, but a box of five hundred is very inexpensive, and usually a pharmacist will order a box for you, or sell you fewer than a box.

■ MARKERS—only the permanent kind will do as water based ones will smear with use. Paint pens (both water and oil base) work beautifully, come in a wider range of colors than markers and are opaque, which is an advantage. Find them in handicraft or office supply stores. Broad-tip or chisel-tip permanent markers are sold as school supplies (individually, not as a set). Magic Marker and Sanford's Sharpie are two brands. Both work well and make either fine or broad lines. Initially, you will need at least the four basic colors—red, blue, green, and yellow—plus black. These will be sufficient to make most of the activities, but for those specifying more colors, you will need others—purple, orange, and brown.

Drawing STICKS designs is simple. They can be done freehand; no need to draw them first with pencil. Have some extra tongue depressors so you can toss out mistakes. Have a ruler, pencil, and masking or clear tape on hand.

STICKS

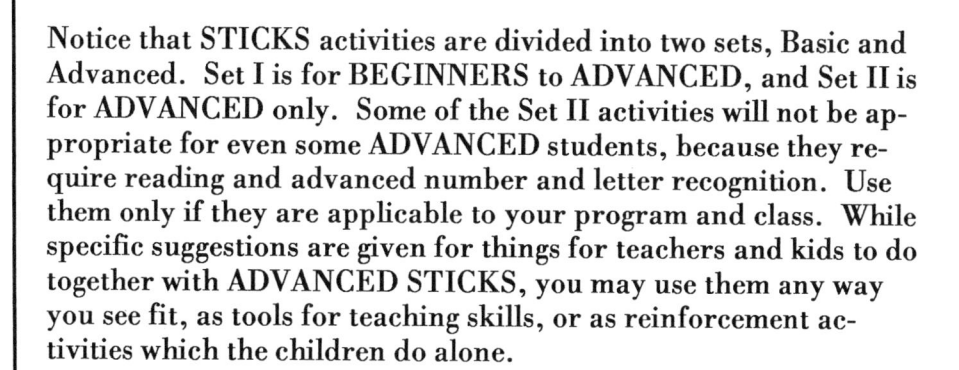

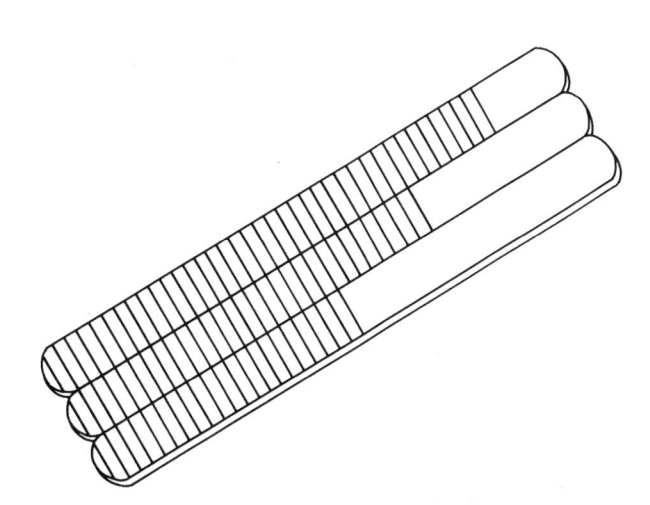

Notice that STICKS activities are divided into two sets, Basic and Advanced. Set I is for BEGINNERS to ADVANCED, and Set II is for ADVANCED only. Some of the Set II activities will not be appropriate for even some ADVANCED students, because they require reading and advanced number and letter recognition. Use them only if they are applicable to your program and class. While specific suggestions are given for things for teachers and kids to do together with ADVANCED STICKS, you may use them any way you see fit, as tools for teaching skills, or as reinforcement activities which the children do alone.

STICKS

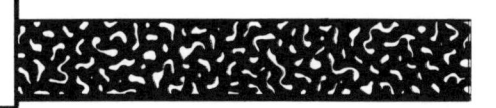

ONE-COLOR

Sticks with a wide band of color are paired.

SET I — BASIC

LEVEL
Beginning

SKILLS:
Color recognition

MATERIALS:
16 sticks

Markers in 8 colors are required for 16, however, fewer colors and sticks may be used

Ruler

Tape

What teachers do

Tape eight sticks together, approximately 1" (2.5 cm) from the top and bottom edges, making two sets. Turn over as one. Use the ruler and pencil to lightly mark a line 1" (2.5 cm) from the top and bottom edges, across all eight sticks. Remove tape, and color the spaces between the marks, making two sticks of each color.

What kids do

Lay the sticks face up. Pair them by placing matching sticks side by side.

What kids and teachers can talk about

Talk about the names of the colors.

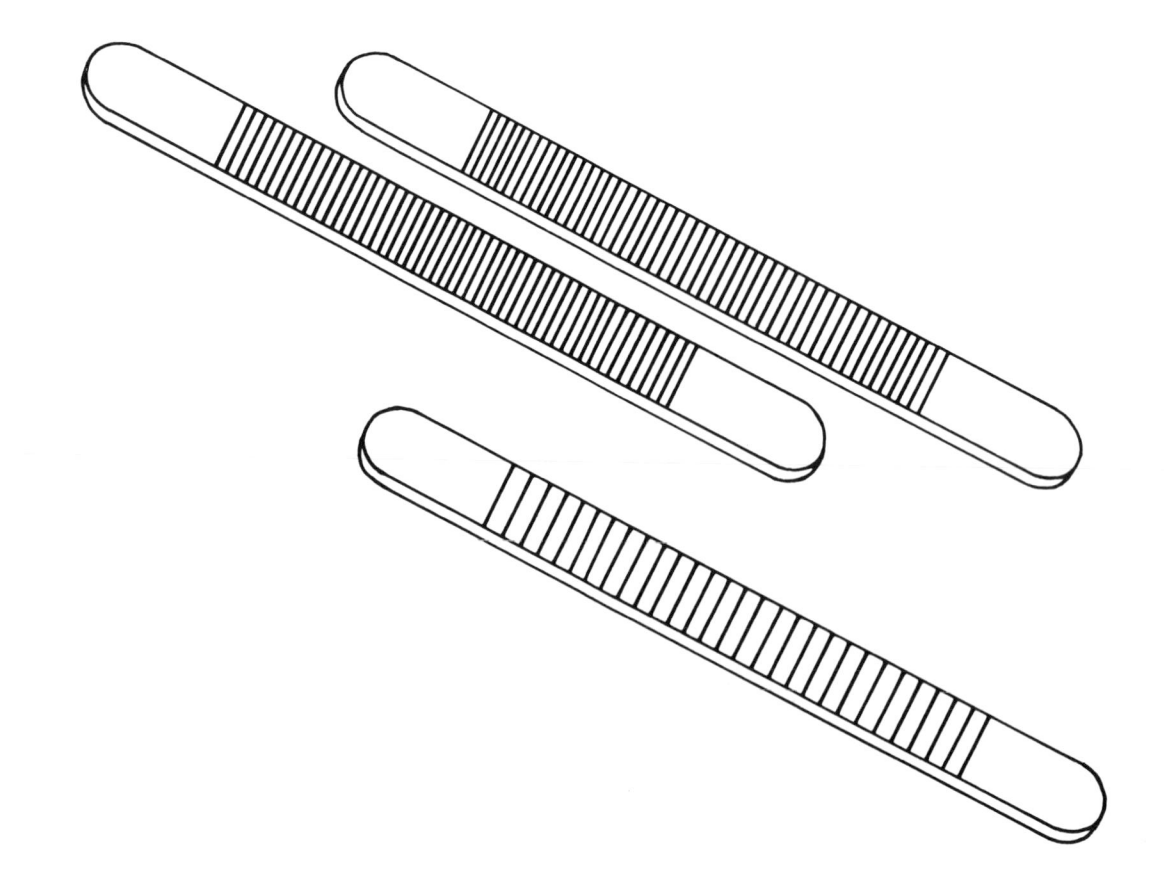

STICKS

TWO-COLOR

These sticks with two bands of differing colors are paired.

What teachers do

Tape eight sticks together, approximately 1" (2.5 cm) from the top and bottom edges, making two sets. Turn over as one. Use the ruler and pencil to lightly mark lines 1" (2.5 cm) from the top and bottom edges, and again 2 1/2" (7.5 cm) from the top and bottom edges. Remove tape, color the two spaces on each stick, leaving the space between the colors and at the ends blank. Use two different colors for each pair. Make one set of eight, and then a duplicate set exactly like it.

What kids do

Lay the sticks face up. Pair them by placing matching sticks side by side.

What kids and teachers can talk about

Talk about why it's important to pay attention to both colors on the sticks.

SET I — BASIC

LEVEL:
Beginning-Advanced

SKILLS:
Color recognition

MATERIALS:
16 sticks

Markers in 8 colors are required for 16; fewer colors and sticks may be used

STICKS

WHAT'S MISSING?

SET I — BASIC

LEVEL:
Intermediate

SKILLS:
Abstraction, perception

MATERIALS:
16 sticks

Markers in 4 colors plus black

Each pair of sticks has five different-colored dots; one of each pair has four dots and the fifth dot is on its matching stick.

What teachers do

With sticks placed vertically, space solid-colored dots which are approximately 5/8" (about 1.5 cm) in diameter evenly on half of the sticks, making two dots above and two dots below the center of the sticks, leaving the center space open. Make each of the four dots in a different color. On the matching sticks of each pair, make a dot of the missing color in the center of the sticks. Use the same five colors (four colors plus black) on all pairs, but vary the sequence of the colors.

What kids do

Lay the sticks face up. To find pairs, look carefully at the sticks with four dots, then find the stick which has one dot in the color that is missing from the sticks with four dots. Place the sticks that go together side by side.

What kids and teachers can do

This activity requires close attention to detail, and a teacher's help may be needed, at least initially.

STICKS

PATTERNS

The sticks have two different patterns; pairs with identical patterns are matched.

What teachers do
With sticks placed vertically, make a bold black line across the center of the sticks. Make a different repeating pattern on each half of the sticks of each pair. Use patterns such as dots, stripes (crosswise, lengthwise, and diagonal), plaid, checks, etc., covering the entire topside of the sticks. Use colors as desired; make pairs exactly alike.

What kids do
Lay the sticks face up. Pair them by placing matching sticks side by side.

What teachers and kids can talk about
Talk about the names of the patterns and notice if any of the patterns are visible in the classroom.

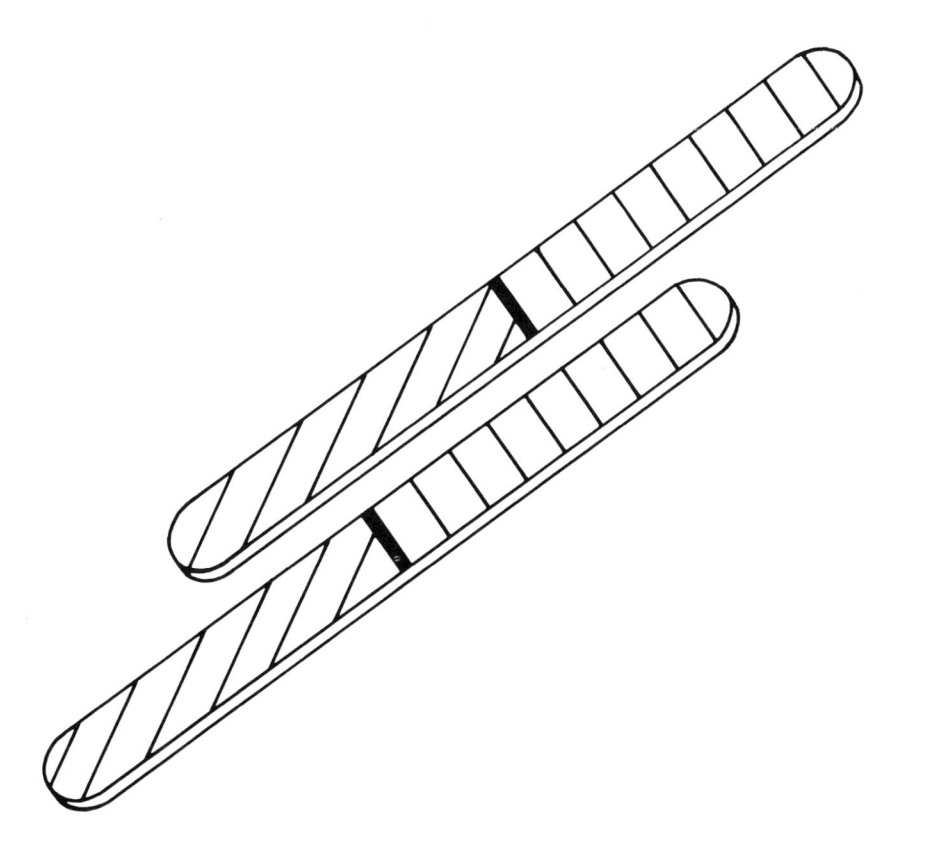

SET I — BASIC

LEVEL:
Intermediate-Advanced

SKILLS:
Visual perception, color distinction

MATERIALS:
Markers in 4 or more colors

16 sticks

STICKS

DOTS

The sticks of each pair have the same number and placement of colored dots.

SET I — BASIC

LEVEL:
Intermediate-Advanced

SKILLS:
Visual perception, quantity recognition

MATERIALS:
16 sticks
Black marker and one colored marker
Ruler

What teachers do
Make two identical sets of eight, one set in black, one set in a color, with one to eight 3/8" (about 9.5 mm) diameter dots on each stick, spacing them in varying ways on the sticks, being sure each matching pair is exactly alike.

What kids do
Lay the sticks face up. Separate the sticks of each color. Pair them by placing matching sticks of each color side by side.

What else kids can do
Find the pair with the most dots, the pair with the fewest dots.

ARROWS

These sticks are paired by the lengths and directions of the arrows they contain.

SET I — BASIC

LEVEL:
Intermediate-Advanced

SKILLS:
Visual perception

MATERIALS:
16 sticks
Marker in 1 color

What teachers do
Using bold lines, approximately 3/8" (about 9.5 mm) wide, make one set of eight sticks; then, placing a blank stick beside each finished one, make its duplicate, so that you will have two identical sets of eight, all in one color. Make two arrows of different lengths on each stick, pointing them in any direction.

What kids do
Lay the sticks face up. Pair them by placing matching sticks side by side.

What kids and teachers can talk about
Talk about directions—up and down, right and left.

STICKS

GEOPUZZLES

These are stick puzzles, each with a different geometric-shaped design.

What teachers do

Lay six sticks vertically side by side, with tops and bottoms even, and tape them together across the top and bottom. Repeat with the remaining sticks to make a total of three sets. Turn the sticks over as one. On the top side, with sticks placed vertically, use the pencil and ruler to make a square with 3 1/2" (about 8.5 cm) sides on one set of sticks, a triangle with 3 1/2" (about 8.5 cm) sides on one set, and a circle approximately 3 1/2" (about 8.5 cm) in diameter on one set. (An easy way to make the circle is to trace around a cup or other round object.) Color inside each shape with markers, using a different color for each shape, and outline the colored shapes with black. Remove the tape. All three puzzles make one activity.

What kids do

Separate the sticks into three groups by color. Place the sticks of each group together side by side to form the three shapes.

What kids and teachers can talk about

Teachers can point out the importance of keeping either the top or bottom edges of the sticks even when putting the puzzles together. A table edge is helpful for this.

SET I — BASIC

LEVEL:
Intermediate-Advanced

SKILLS:
Formation of geometric shapes

MATERIALS:
18 sticks

Markers in 3 colors plus black

Ruler

Pencil

Tape

STICKS

HEARTS

Sticks containing hearts in three colors in varying sequences are paired.

SET I — BASIC

LEVEL:
Intermediate-Advanced

What teachers do

With sticks placed vertically, make two sets of eight pairs using three colors and five hearts on each stick. Make solid-colored hearts, approximately 5/8" (about 1.5 cm) tall, all pointing in the same direction. Use the same three colors on all the sticks, but vary the color arrangement on each pair.

SKILLS:
Color distinction, number distinction, orientation

What kids do

Lay the sticks face up. Pair them by placing matching sticks side by side.

MATERIALS:
16 sticks
Markers in 3 colors

What kids and teachers can talk about

The heart shapes may remind you of a particular holiday—Valentine's Day; you may want to talk about it.

LINES

Each pair of sticks has a different line design; like sticks are matched.

SET I — BASIC

What teachers do

LEVEL:
Intermediate-Advanced

Make one set of eight in one color, the second set in the second color. Make a different line design, from one end of the sticks to the opposite end, on each pair. You can use these suggestions, or lines of your own design: wavy, zig-zag, scallop, dash, loop, dotted, square-wave, straight.

SKILLS:
Pattern distinction

What kids do

Lay the sticks face up. Separate them into two groups by color. Pair them by placing matching sticks side by side.

MATERIALS:
16 sticks
Markers in 2 colors

What else kids can do

Kids may like to make lines like some of these on paper with paint, markers, or crayons.

STICKS

HALVES

One stick of each pair has two halves of a simple shape; sticks of a pair are placed side by side to complete the shapes.

What teachers do

Shapes to be used: circle, square, heart, diamond, oval, triangle, cross and club (three-leaf clover). Make half of a shape in a large size in the upper half of a vertically-placed stick, and a smaller version of the same shape in the lower half, both in the same color, and colored solidly. Place a blank stick close beside the completed stick and make the other shape halves on the blank stick, using the same color. Make the rest of the pairs the same way, using a different shape for each pair. Colors may be used more than once.

What kids do

Lay the sticks face up. Pair them by placing sticks with matching halves side by side.

What kids and teachers can talk about

Talk about the shapes and where you may have seen shapes like them before.

SET I — BASIC

LEVEL:
Intermediate-Advanced

SKILLS:
Abstraction

MATERIALS:
16 sticks

Markers in assorted colors

STICKS

STEPS

SET I — BASIC

LEVEL:
Intermediate-Advanced

SKILLS:
Graduation, progression

MATERIALS:
10 sticks
Marker in 1 color
Ruler
Tape
Pencil

The colored portions of ten sticks, when placed in the proper side by side arrangement, have graduated amounts of color.

What teachers do
Lay sticks vertically side by side, with tops and bottoms even, and tape them together across the top and bottom. Turn them over as one. On the top side of the sticks, use the ruler and pencil to lightly make a diagonal line across the sticks from the top left corner to the bottom right corner. With marker, color the portion of each stick below the line. Remove the tape.

What kids do
It seems to me, as a teacher, that this activity should start with either the stick with the most color, or with the one with the least, and progress from left to right. But children's strategy is sometimes to go from the middle to the ends. Who is to say if one way is better than the other?

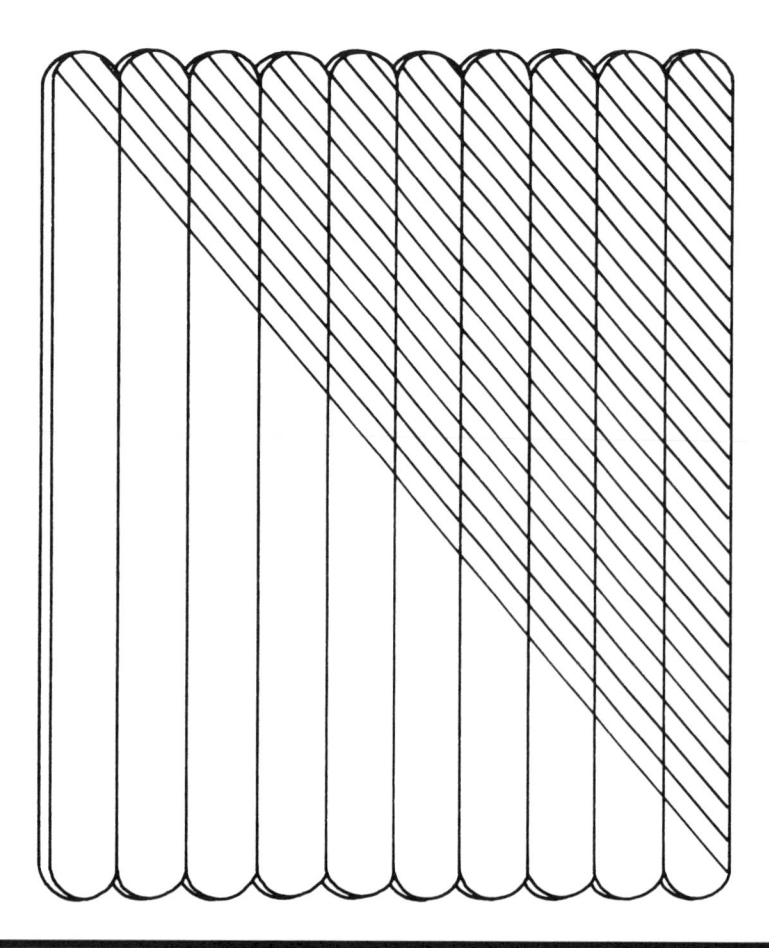

What kids and teachers can talk about
Teachers can point out that a straight edge, such as a table edge, is helpful to align the bottom edges of the sticks to make the design match. Kids and teachers can talk about steps and stairs, and find different ways to start, as mentioned above.

STICKS

STRIPES

Pairs of sticks with five color stripes in the same sequence are matched.

What teachers do

Divide sticks in twos. Place the sticks of each pair side by side, with ends even, and tape the pairs together across the top and bottom. Turn the pairs of sticks over. Using the ruler and markers, with sticks placed vertically, make five broad crosswise lines at 1" (2.5 cm) intervals across both sticks, using a different color for each stripe. Vary the color sequences on each pair.

What kids do

Lay the sticks face up. Pair them by placing them very closely side by side to prove the matches. Look carefully.

What kids and teachers can talk about

Talk about why it's important to have the ends of the sticks of each pair even when matching them.

ICE CREAM CONES

These sticks have cones holding one or more scoops of various "flavors" of ice cream; pairs are matched.

What teachers do

With sticks placed vertically, draw an upright cone near the bottom end of each of the sticks. On each cone, make one to six ice cream balls, alternating solid-colored balls and those with simulated "ripples" and "chips". Make each pair exactly alike.

What kids do

Lay the sticks face up. Find sticks that are exactly alike and place them side by side.

What kids and teachers can talk about

Conversations about ice cream should be easy!

SET I — BASIC

LEVEL:
Intermediate-Advanced

SKILLS:
Color recognition, sequencing, concentration

MATERIALS:
16 sticks

Markers in 5 colors (including black)

Tape

Ruler

Pencil

SET I — BASIC

LEVEL:
Intermediate-Advanced

SKILLS:
Attention to detail

MATERIALS:
16 sticks

Markers in 3 or more colors

STICKS

HIGH-LOW

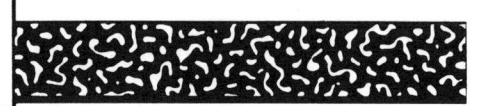

SET I — BASIC

Each of three sets contains five sticks with colored portions which graduate in size.

What teachers do

Make three sets of five sticks each, making each set a different color. For each set, use the ruler and a pencil to make a line 1" (2.5 cm) from one end of the first stick, 2" (5 cm) from one end on the second stick, 3" (7.5 cm) from one end on the third, 4" (10 cm) on the fourth, and 5" (12.5 cm) on the fifth. Color below the lines with the markers. All three sets of sticks make one activity.

LEVEL:
Intermediate-Advanced

SKILLS:
Length comparisons

MATERIALS:
15 sticks
Markers in 3 colors
Ruler

What kids do

Lay the sticks face up. Separate them by color if they like. Put the sticks of each color in order from high to low or from low to high.

What else kids can do

Stack the three sticks that have the same size colored part and perhaps find other ways to arrange the sticks.

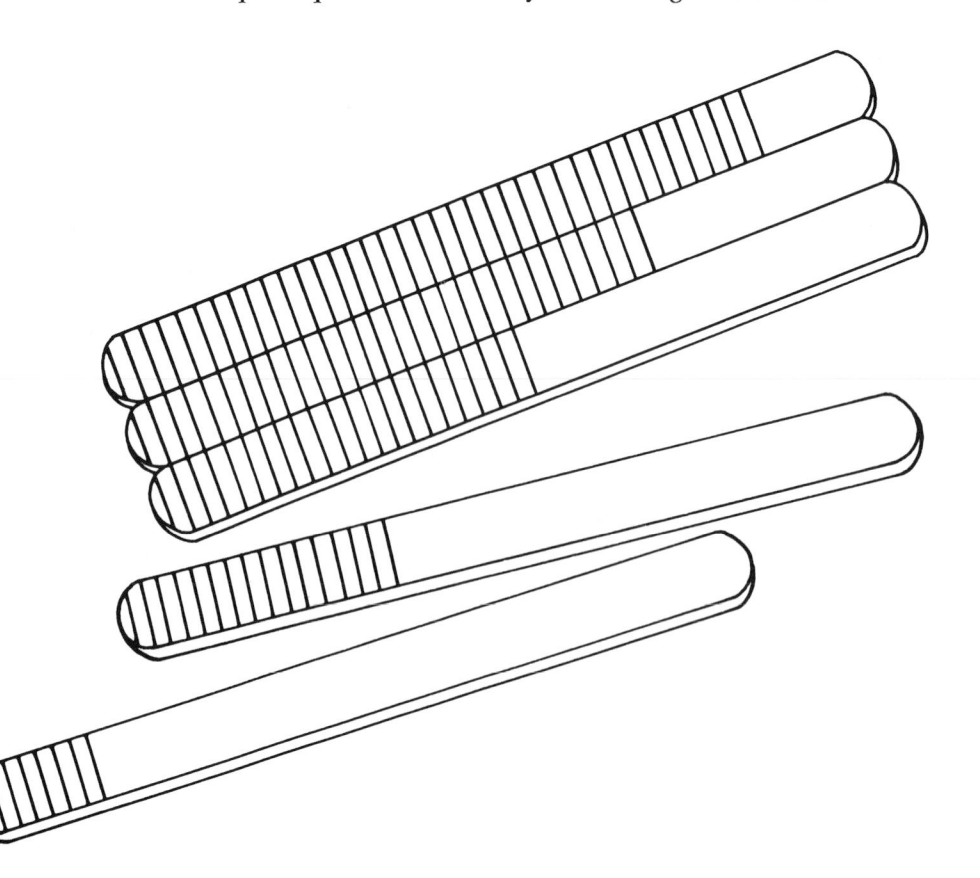

STICKS

SMILES

These pairs of sticks have the same number of smile faces in like sizes and colors.

What teachers do

With sticks placed vertically, make one to six or more "smile faces" on the sticks in varying colors and sizes, making the sticks of each pair exactly alike.

What kids do

Lay the sticks face up. Find the two sticks that are exactly alike and place them side by side.

What else kids can do

This activity may inspire a rash of smiling faces drawn on paper; perhaps some students would like to make SMILES sticks for others to use.

SET I — BASIC

LEVEL:
Intermediate-Advanced

SKILLS:
Size, color distinction

MATERIALS:
16 sticks
Markers in assorted colors

STICKS

STARS

SET I — BASIC

LEVEL:
Intermediate-Advanced

SKILLS:
Attention to detail

MATERIALS:
16 sticks
Markers in 2 colors

These sticks contain eight stars, seven of one color; the odd-colored star is in a different position on each pair. Like sticks are matched.

What teachers do

Make eight stars on each stick, seven of one color and one of a second color. Place the one different-colored star in a different position on each of the eight sticks. Make two identical sets.

What kids do

Lay the sticks face up. Find the two sticks that are exactly alike and place them side by side.

What else kids can do

Some children may like to learn how to draw stars in the "back-and-forth" technique (drawn with one continuous line, with five angles).

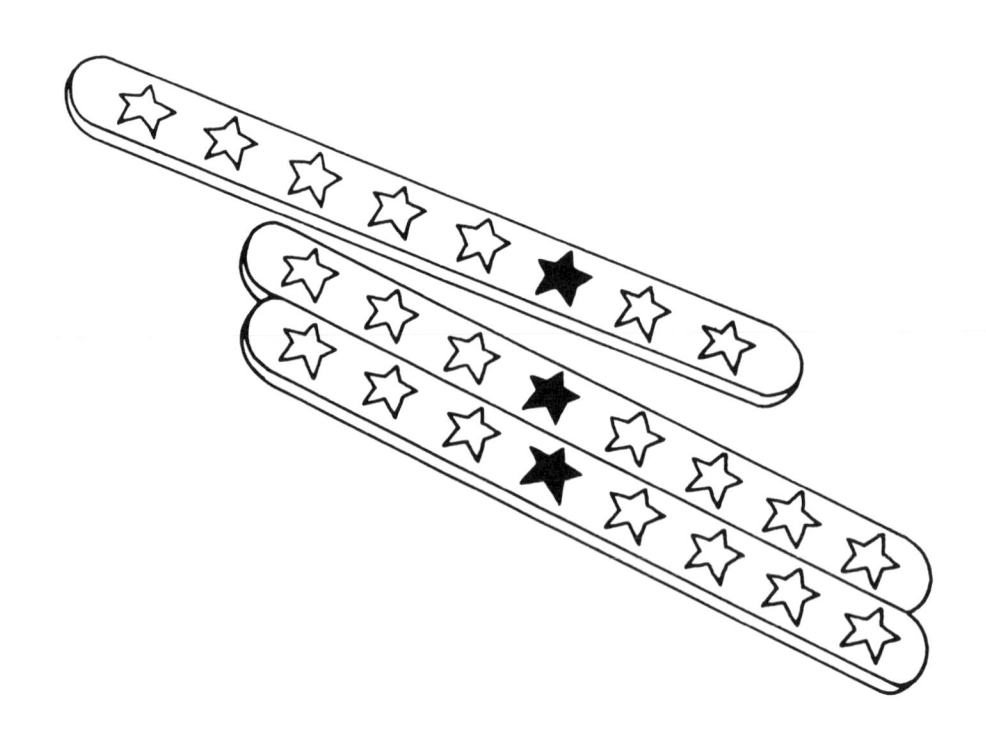

STICKS

PUZZLES

Patterns are given for six different puzzles, each of which contains eight sticks. Puzzles are assembled by placing matching sticks side by side in the order that completes their pictures.

What teachers do

Copy the patterns on a copier, laminate, and cut them out. Place eight sticks side by side for each puzzle, ends even. Tape them together at the top and bottom. Turn over as one. Place the pattern on the sticks and trace around it, being sure part of the pattern is on each stick. Color the designs with markers, outline them with the broad side of the black marker, and add legs and other details shown on the pattern for the CHICK PUZZLE, and wheels and other details shown on the pattern for the TRAIN PUZZLE. Remove the tape.

Each puzzle should be stored as a separate activity when they are new to the children. After they have become proficient at putting them together, you may want to store the pieces of two or three puzzles together. The children can then separate the pieces and put the different puzzles together.

What kids do

Lay the sticks face up. Put the puzzle together by placing the sticks side by side.

What kids and teachers can talk about

Talk about the importance of keeping the ends of the sticks even to make the picture match correctly.

SET I — BASIC

LEVEL:
Intermediate-Advanced

SKILLS:
Completion, perception

MATERIALS:
8 sticks per puzzle

Tape

Colored markers plus black

STICKS VERTICAL

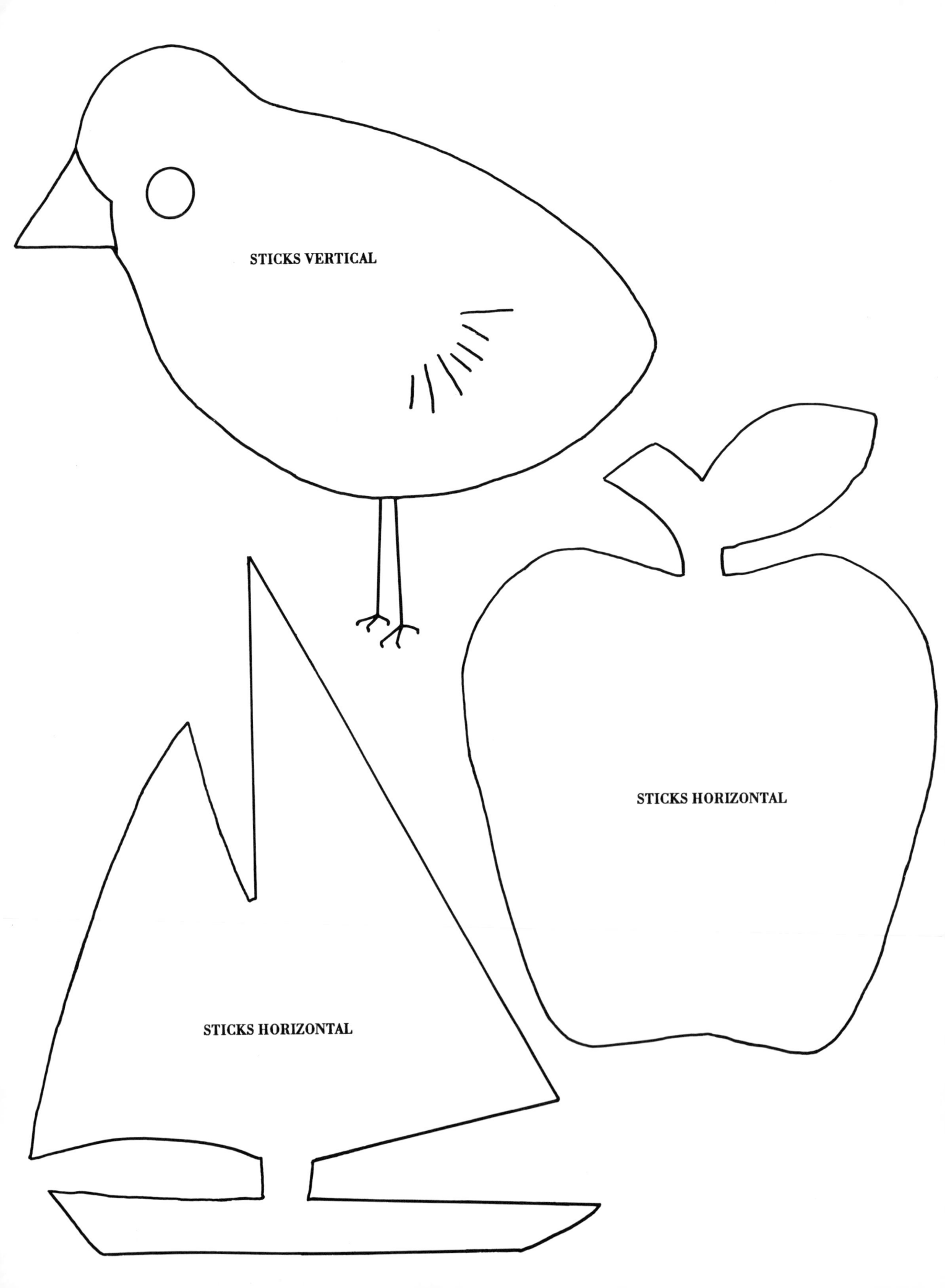

STICKS HORIZONTAL

STICKS HORIZONTAL

STICKS VERTICAL

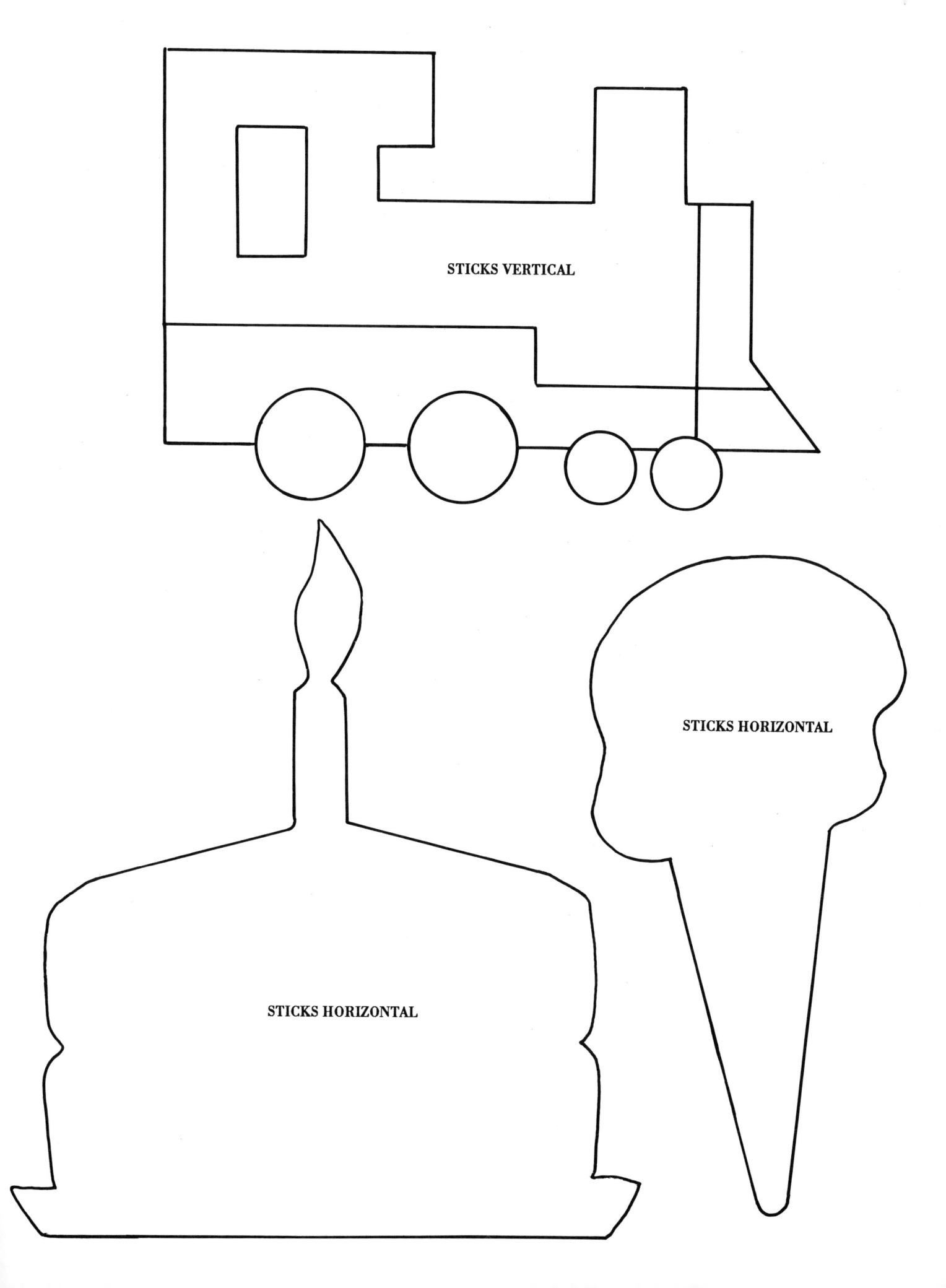

STICKS HORIZONTAL

STICKS HORIZONTAL

STICKS

NAMES/FACES

Sticks with photographs of children in the class are matched with sticks containing the children's names.

SET I — BASIC

LEVEL:
Intermediate-Advanced

SKILLS:
Recognition of classmates, matching names and faces

MATERIALS:

Twice the number of sticks as children in the class

Markers in one or assorted colors

A small picture (face only) of each child (and adults if desired) in the class

What teachers do

Children who are just learning to recognize their own names may match only their own name and picture. Those who are learning to recognize others' names may try to match all the names and faces. They may ask others to help them identify their names if this doesn't prove too disruptive. To make the sticks, print the names on the horizontally placed sticks, using only the first names of the children, and first names and last initials in case of duplicates. Cut the pictures to fit on the matching sticks and glue them on securely.

What kids do

Lay the sticks face up. Look carefully and find their own name and picture. If they know how to match any of the other names and faces, match them, too.

What kids and teachers can do

This activity is ideal for doing together. An adult's help may be necessary and should be given freely—this is not a test.

STICKS

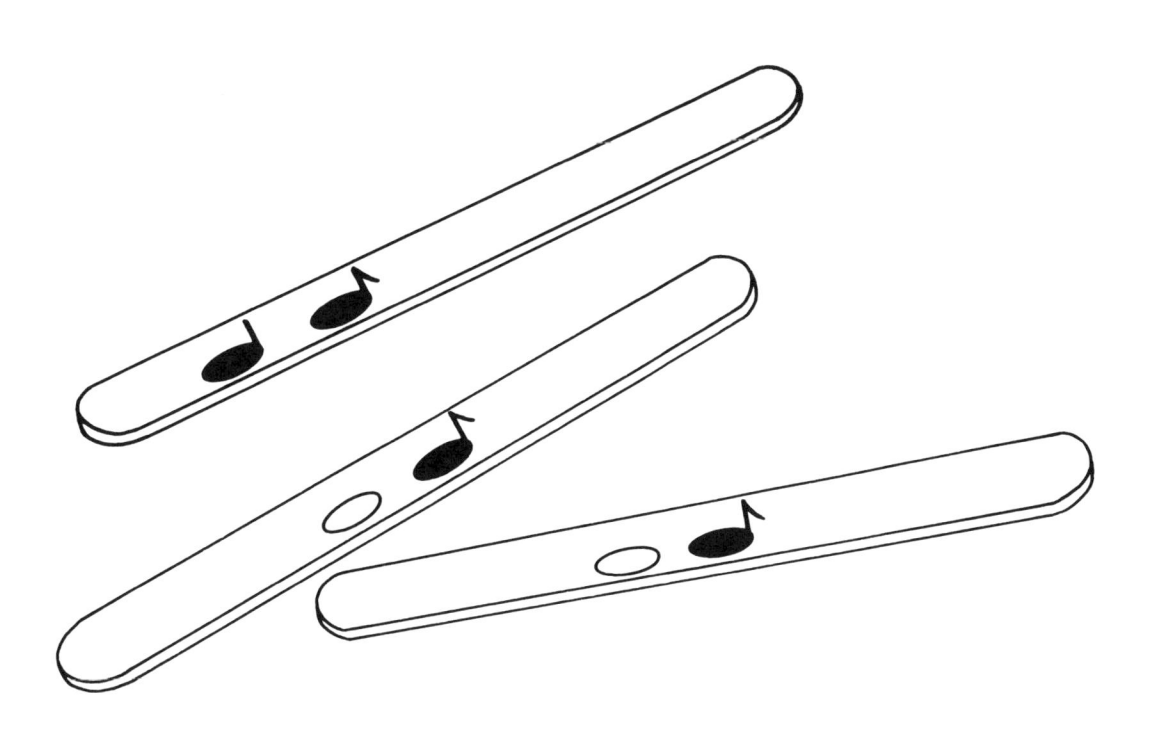

MUSIC NOTES

Pairs of these sticks have identical combinations of music notes.

What teachers do
With sticks placed horizontally, make bold black notes—whole notes, half- quarter- and eighth-notes—in various combinations, making three to five notes on each stick. Make both sticks of each pair exactly alike.

What kids do
Lay the sticks face up. Find the two sticks that are exactly alike and place them side by side.

What kids and teachers can talk about
Talk about these music notes. Look at some real music. Don't talk about the names of the notes unless children happen to know the names from having taken music lessons, or are curious and ask about them.

SET I — BASIC

LEVEL:
Intermediate-Advanced

SKILLS:
Attention to detail

MATERIALS:
16 sticks
Black marker

STICKS

COLORS/NAMES

SET II — ADVANCED

LEVEL:
Advanced

SKILLS:
Recognition of color names

MATERIALS:
14 or more sticks

Markers in a minimum of 7 colors (including black)

These pairs match colored designs with their color names.

Note: This activity is more useful if it contains the basic 4 colors—red, blue, green, yellow—and as many of the other colors as possible—orange, purple, pink, brown, and black, etc.

What teachers do
Choose a simple design for the design sticks—perhaps a looped line, linked squares, etc.—and make it in a repeating pattern on half the sticks, each in a different color. Place the remaining sticks horizontally, and print the color names in black in bold letters. You will probably want to display a chart in the classroom showing the colors and their names for the children to use as a guide.

What kids do
Lay the sticks face up. Pair the color names with their appropriately colored designs.

What kids and teachers can talk about
Talk about the colors and their names.

NUMBERS/NAMES

SET II — ADVANCED

LEVEL:
Advanced

SKILLS:
Recognition of numeral names

MATERIALS:
20 sticks

Black marker and 1 or more colored markers

These stick pairs match numbers and their printed names.

What teachers do
With sticks placed horizontally, print the names of the numbers from one to ten on half the sticks in bold black letters, and the numbers in the centers of the remaining sticks (one number per stick), using colored markers. A chart showing the numbers and their names may be visible in the room for the children to use as a guide.

What kids do
Lay the sticks face up. Pair the names and the numerals.

What else kids can do
Put the paired sticks in order from one to ten or from ten to one.

STICKS

GEOSHAPES/NAMES

Each of these pairs has a stick with a geometric shape and a stick with the name of that shape.

What teachers do
With the sticks placed horizontally, print the geometric shape names in bold black letters on half the sticks, one shape name per stick. On the remaining half of the sticks, also placed horizontally, make three of each geometric shape, all in the same color, solidly-colored, on each stick. Use these shapes: circle, square, rectangle, triangle, diamond, and oval (or ellipse, if your students have been taught that term instead of oval). You will probably want to display a chart showing geometric shapes and their names in the classroom for the children to use as a guide.

What kids do
Lay the sticks face up. Pair the names of geometric shapes with their shapes.

What kids and teachers can talk about
Talk about the geometric shapes on the sticks and about other things that have these shapes.

SET II — ADVANCED

LEVEL:
Advanced

SKILLS:
Recognition of the names of circle, square, rectangle, triangle, diamond, and oval

MATERIALS:
12 sticks

6 or fewer colors plus black

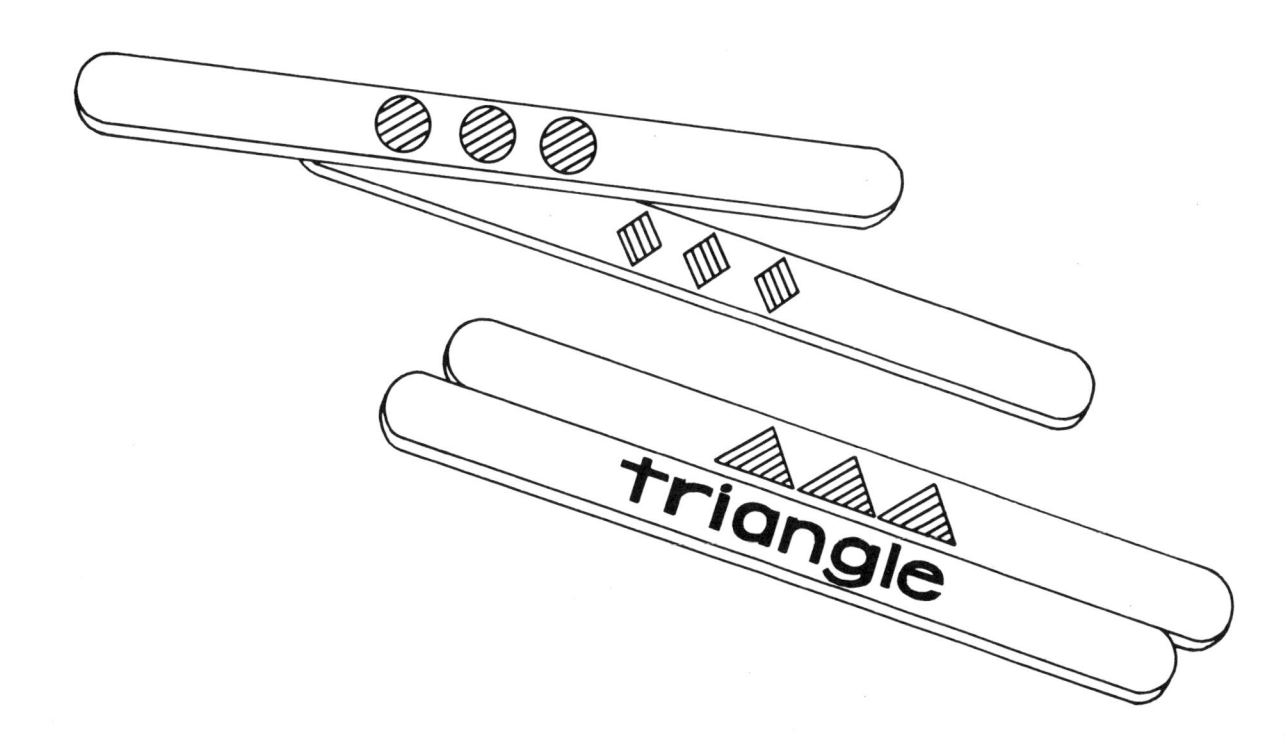

37

STICKS

1-10

SET II — ADVANCED

One of each of these pairs contains a printed number; its matching stick contains the same number of repetitions of a simple design.

LEVEL:
Advanced

What teachers do

With sticks placed vertically, make bold black numbers from 1 to 10, about 1 1/4" (3.5 cm) tall, on half the sticks, one number per stick. With the remaining sticks placed vertically, make one to ten colored designs, one design per stick. Use simple designs such as hearts, flowers, smile faces, crescents, and stars. Shapes can be used on more than one stick if different colors are used.

SKILLS:
Counting, matching numerals 1-10 with the appropriate number of pictured objects.

What kids do

Lay the sticks face up. Pair the numerals and the pictures.

What kids and teachers can do

Talk about the designs on the sticks.

MATERIALS:
20 sticks

Black marker and markers in assorted colors

STICKS

1-20

Each stick has a number from zero to nine; sticks are arranged from one to nine, then two sticks are placed side by side to make the numbers ten to twenty.

What teachers do

With sticks placed vertically, make bold numbers, approximately 1 1/4" (3.5 cm) tall. Make two sticks containing a zero (one for ten, one for twenty); make eleven ones, and two of each of the other numbers. You will probably want to display a chart of numbers from one to twenty in the classroom for the children to use as a guide.

What kids do

Lay the sticks face up. Place sticks one to nine in order, then place two sticks side by side for numbers ten through twenty.

What kids and teachers can talk about

Teachers can help kids understand the decade concept—the numbers from eleven to nineteen are made by preceding the numbers one to nine by a one.

SET II — ADVANCED

LEVEL:
Advanced

SKILLS:
Counting to twenty

MATERIALS:
31 sticks

Marker in 1 color or black

STICKS

ALPHABET (UPPER CASE)

SET II — ADVANCED

LEVEL:
Advanced

SKILLS:
Upper case letter recognition

MATERIALS:
26 sticks
Marker in 1 color

Each stick has an upper case letter from A to Z, to be arranged alphabetically, or to be matched with ALPHABET (LOWER CASE). The activity can be shortened to rotated groups of letters, instead of the entire alphabet, if desired: put five or more letters in series to be alphabetized. A chart of the upper case alphabet displayed in the classroom can be used by the children as a guide.

What teachers do

With sticks placed vertically, make one bold capital letter, from A to Z, approximately 1 1/4" (3.5 cm) tall, near the upper end of each stick, using the same color for all letters.

What kids do

Lay the sticks face up and put them in alphabetical order, or match them with ALPHABET (LOWER CASE).

What else kids can do

They may want to find their initials from among the stick letters.

ALPHABET (LOWER CASE)

SET II — ADVANCED

LEVEL:
Advanced

SKILLS:
Lower case letter recognition

MATERIALS:
26 sticks
Marker in 1 color

Sticks containing lower case letters of the alphabet for ordering alphabetically or matching with ALPHABET (UPPER CASE).

What teachers do

Each of these sticks contains a letter of the alphabet in lower case. They can be arranged in alphabetical order or matched with ALPHABET (UPPER CASE). The activity can be shortened to a group of five or more letters in sequence, if desired, with other groups of letters rotated at intervals. A chart of the lower case alphabet displayed in the classroom can be used by the children as a guide. With sticks placed vertically, make one bold lower case letter, from a to z, approximately 1 1/4" (3.5 cm) tall, near the upper end of each stick, using the same color for all letters.

What kids do

Lay the sticks face up and put them in alphabetical order, or match them with ALPHABET (UPPER CASE).

What else kids can do

They may want to find letters that are in their names.

STICKS

MEASUREMENTS

Sticks containing colored lines of various lengths are matched with sticks containing their written lengths.

What teachers do

Kids use the small ruler contained in the activity to measure the lengths of the lines on half of the sticks, then they find the sticks with the written measurements and pair them. Use a ruler to make bold assorted-color, lengthwise stripes on half the sticks, varying the lengths from 1/2" to 5" (1.25 to 12.5 cm). With the remaining sticks placed horizontally, use the black marker to write the measurements in bold numbers and letters, for example, "2 inches," or simply "2". If the small ruler the children will use has metric measurements on one side, cover them with black permanent marker to avoid confusion. Store the ruler with the activity.

What kids do

Lay the sticks face up. Use the ruler to find pairs by measuring the lengths of the stripes on the sticks. Place matching sticks side by side.

What kids and teachers can talk about

Talk about the importance of measuring carefully to obtain accurate matches.

SET II — ADVANCED

LEVEL:
Advanced

SKILLS:
Measuring

MATERIALS:
16 sticks

Markers in assorted colors

6-inch ruler for student use

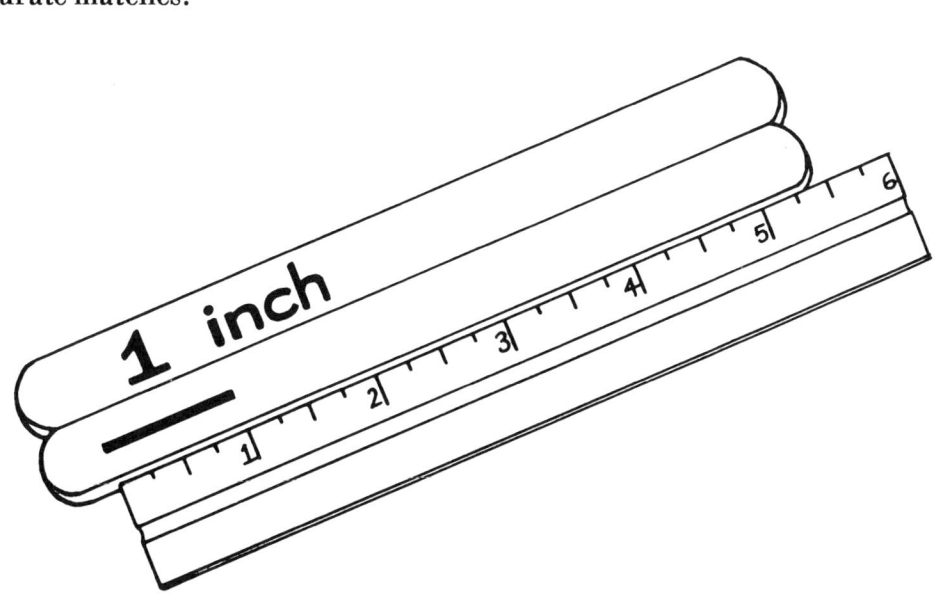

SPONGES

SPONGES

Feeling, Forming, Fitting

SPONGES

What kids do

Explore. Experiment. Discover relationships tactually and visually. THICK SPONGE activities are open-ended, allowing creative thinking and exploration. Their objective is to find out what the sponge pieces will do, discovering the reasons for their shapes, sizes, and colors. In many cases, several different activities are possible with a single set of sponge pieces. When you introduce them to the children, help them to see the different possibilities. Given young children's propensity for bringing order to their environment—categorizing the information they continually receive—these explorative tasks are natural and satisfying.

Kids will know what to do with THIN SPONGE materials. They perform in predetermined ways—puzzle pieces fit together, shapes match outlines, sizes progress. However, these materials are ideal as teacher-assisted activities as well as independent-learning ones because they are so versatile. In some cases, students may need an adult's help to see all the possibilities.

What teachers do

BUY SPONGES

Only one type of sponge will do—the kind made of polyester (polyfoam), not cellulose. The way to tell the difference: the labels on cellulose sponges will say "cellulose," but the labels on polyester sponges will not usually say what they are made of. Rectangular (which I will refer to as "thick") sponges come in pastel colors and are usually packaged in sets of twelve or so. They are the kind that stay soft when dry. The size needed for the THICK SPONGE materials is a common size for household sponges—3" x 5" x 7/8" (7.5 cm x 12.5 cm x 21 mm), but sizes slightly smaller or larger than this can be used. The thin sponges—usually labelled sponge cloths—are approximately 7" x 8" x 1/4" (17.5 cm x 20 cm x 6 mm) and come in a more limited number of colors than thick sponges.

One word of caution about thin sponge (sponge cloths): BUY ONE PACKAGE AND TRY IT BEFORE BUYING MORE. Some brands of sponge cloths are packaged with moisture and become quite different when dry—they may stiffen and curl slightly. Polyester sponge cloths will retain the same texture wet or dry—soft and malleable.

SPONGES

Both kinds of sponges—thick rectangles and thin sheets—are sold in supermarkets, home centers, drug and variety stores. Store managers may order the quantity you need if necessary. I originally found the brand I prefer, Nation/Ruskin, at Woolworth stores; later I contacted the Nation/Ruskin Company and began ordering directly, paying wholesale prices, which they graciously extended to me. They have agreed to the same arrangement for other teachers who wish to order. Over a period of time, I have received at least ten different colors of the thick sponges and four of the thin ones, all beautiful and vibrant. An order of thick sponges usually contains one color combination, four colors to a package, three of each color. All the activities can be made with this combination. However, if you order more than once and receive different color combinations, so much the better, because a wider range adds distinction to the materials, preventing their all looking alike. Orders of thin sponge (sponge cloths) will contain one to four colors. You should be able to obtain four colors, which is ideal, by purchasing several packages, but you can use as few as one or two colors for many of the activities. To order from Nation/Ruskin, call 800-523-2489 and ask for a price list. Be sure to ask about shipping charges. Payment must accompany orders. Their address is P.O. Box 567, Montgomeryville, Pennsylvania 18936.

BUY GLUE

Glue is needed for only two activities—WIDTH BARS and CUTOUTS (SQUARE). Several kinds of glue will adhere to sponge, but ordinary white household glue will not. Craft glues are best and dry clear. Test glue on sponge by letting it dry overnight before trying to pull the glued pieces apart.

MAKE OUTLINE CARDS

The outline cards used for some activities are made of heavy white card or poster board, which should be laminated by machine or covered by hand with clear plastic adhesive such as clear Contact Paper. If you are using a laminator, use the heaviest card stock the machine will accept. Use a wide black marker to make the outlines as directed in the instructions with the activities.

LEARN HOW TO GET ALONG WITH SPONGE— HERE'S HOW:

■ It wants you to be the boss. Decisive cuts produce clean lines, timid cuts produce ragged ones. Hesitancy worries sponge.

■ Make quick, long cuts, over-cutting slightly when necessary to get sharp corners, using long, pointed scissors. Hold scissors straight up and down, not leaning to the side. Whenever possible make cuts in one stroke, as in cutting a sponge in half crosswise.

■ Don't labor over mistakes—reach for a new sponge. Use mistakes for smaller pieces and trial runs.

■ Cut from outside in when possible. Cut, then make a second cut to meet the first. It is easier and cleaner than trying to turn the scissors. Don't be afraid to bend the sponge to get a clean cut.

■ Consider carefully before changing the number of colors suggested: a single color focuses attention on shape or form, avoiding the distraction of too many colors. Conversely, assorted colors emphasize color or add to the activities' attractiveness. But when the same combination of four colors is used too frequently, the materials will tend to all look alike. You may want to limit colors to one or two in any given activity to allow for greater variety and attractiveness overall.

■ To make cutouts within a shape—as in the letters D and O, for instance—use small pointed scissors, such as manicure scissors, to punch a hole in the part to be cut out, then cut out the part, starting from the hole.

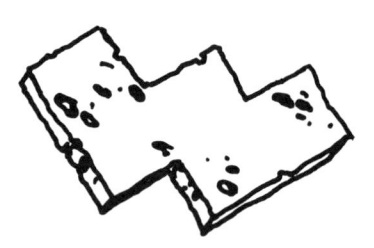

MORE SPONGE TIPS

■ **DEMONSTRATIONS**

Demonstrations are extremely important with SPONGE materials because of their openendedness. The appearance of some, such as LENGTH BARS, belies their complexity—subtleties which children may miss unless a teacher's demonstration has started ideas flowing. Suggestions are given toward this end with each activity.

■ **MEASURING AND CUTTING THICK SPONGE**

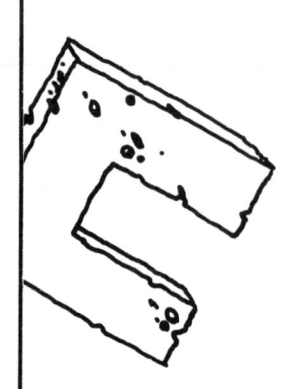

Cutting thick sponge is easier than it looks and no patterns are needed—only a ruler, scissors, and pen. Pieces are either fractions—halves, fourths, etc.—or they require simple measurements with a ruler. To measure and cut sponge pieces, place a ruler on the sponge and mark lines with a felt tip writing pen, following the dimensions given in the activity directions, then cut on the lines. The lines can be easily removed by swishing the pieces in water. Always follow this rule: WHEN CUTTING TWO OR MORE IDENTICAL PIECES, USE THE FIRST PIECE YOU CUT AS A PATTERN FOR CUTTING THE REST. PLACE THE CUT PIECE ON THE NEXT SPONGE, AND, WITHOUT MARKING, CUT CLOSE TO THE EDGES OF THE PATTERN PIECE.

SPONGES

Sponges are rarely exactly the dimensions given on the package. This is not a problem—simply adjust your measurements, making them scant or slightly larger to accommodate. Measurements are not usually critical. It's a good idea to keep a crosswise and lengthwise sponge half (marked "pattern" with pen) as patterns for cutting halves for any activity requiring them, since they are used frequently.

■ MEASURING AND CUTTING THIN SPONGE

Cutting thin sponge requires no special expertise. Just measure with a ruler, mark with a felt tip writing pen and cut with scissors, or use the patterns provided as directed, copying them with a copier and laminating. Marks can be removed from finished pieces by swishing in water.

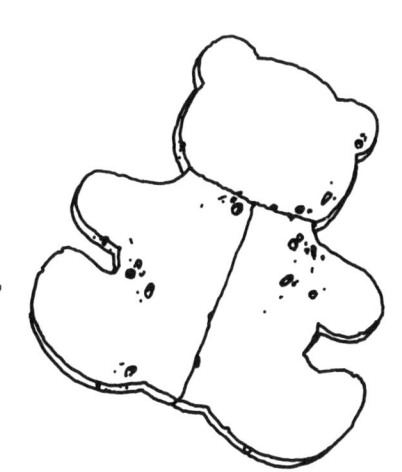

■ STATIC ELECTRICITY

Sometimes sponge pieces seem to take on a life of their own, literally jumping away from one another, because of static electricity. While the children will find this amusing, it makes completing an activity difficult. Static electricity can be easily controlled however—just lightly spray fabric softener on the "jumping" pieces, or rub a fabric softener sheet (or cloth containing the liquid form) inside the activity's storage container to eliminate static build-up in the future.

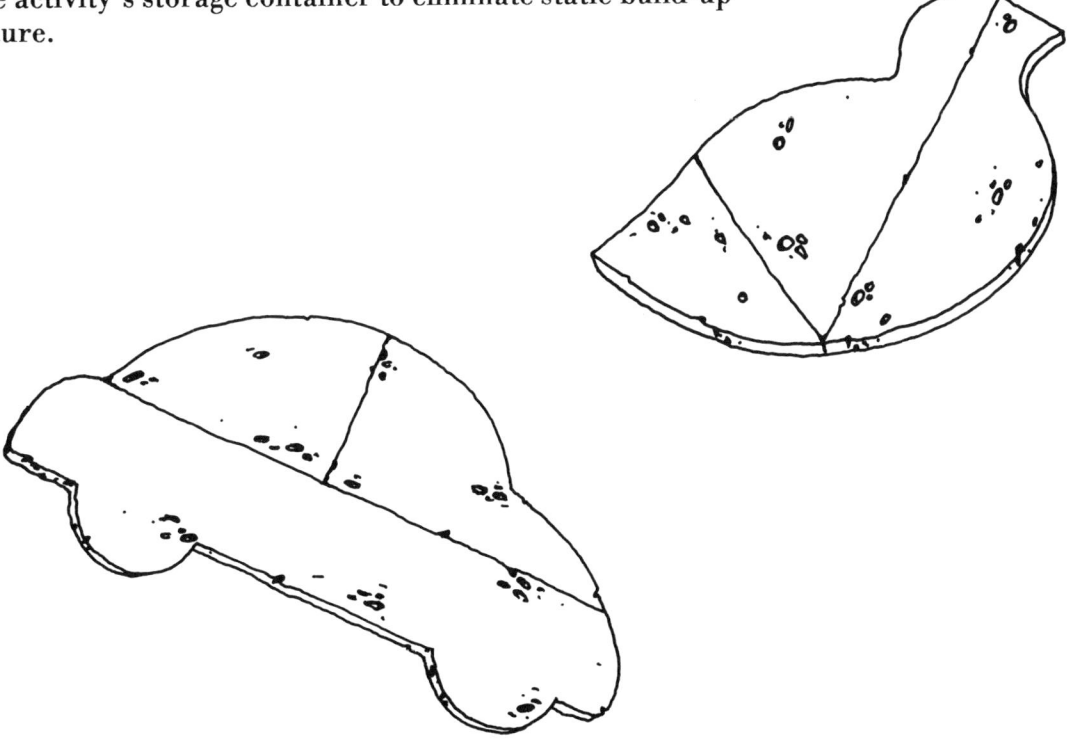

SPONGES

SHAPES FOR BEGINNERS

SET I— THICK SPONGE

Beginners sort and match these large shapes.

What teachers do

Cut all the sponges in half crosswise. Following the cutting directions in the introduction to this section, cut one piece of each color in a different shape, and use it as a pattern to cut the same shape in a piece of the other two colors. Make each shape in each of the three colors. Make the shapes by cutting V-shapes and squared notches of different sizes from the sides, and by cutting off one or more corners, of the half-sponges.

LEVEL:
Beginning

What kids do

Experiment: Will the shapes stand on their edges? Can they be stacked? Sorted by color, by shape? Arrange in any way that comes to mind.

SKILLS:
Shape recognition, color distinction, manual dexterity

What else kids can do

Feel the shapes with closed eyes. Make a sequential pattern using one sponge of each shape. Duplicate the pattern twice, using the other pieces.

MATERIALS:
9 sponges in 3 colors, 3 of each color

SPONGES

BEGINNER PUZZLES

Each of these puzzles, when assembled, reforms a whole sponge. Beginners put them together on outline cards initially; later they probably won't need cards.

What teachers do

■ Measure, mark, and cut one sponge in half crosswise, one in half lengthwise, and one in half diagonally (from any corner to its opposite corner).

■ Measure, mark, and cut one sponge in thirds crosswise, making each piece a bit less than 1 3/4" (about 4 cm) wide.

■ Make outline cards: trace around each puzzle, then outline each individual piece in pencil on the cards. Remove the sponge pieces and trace over the pencil lines with a broad black marker, using a ruler to make straight lines. Laminate the cards.

What kids do

Using the outlined cards as a guide, put the puzzles together.

What else kids can do

After BEGINNING students are well-acquainted with the puzzles, they may want to try putting them together inside a blank outline, which does not have the individual pieces outlined, or without any outline cards.

SET I—THICK SPONGE

LEVEL:
Beginning, Intermediate (if appropriate)

SKILLS:
Abstraction, manual dexterity

MATERIALS:
4 sponges of 4 colors

Four 5" x 7" (12.5 mm x 17.5 mm) white cards

Ruler

Broad black marker

SPONGES

WIDTH BARS

SET I—THICK SPONGE

Kids arrange these bars by width, from the narrowest to the widest and/or in reverse order.

What teachers do

Cut the sponges this way:

LEVEL:
Beginning-Advanced

■ For Bar #1, the widest bar, leave one sponge whole.

■ Measure, mark, and cut 3/4" (about 20 cm) from one end of a sponge. The large piece will be Bar #2, the small piece will be Bar #8.

SKILLS:
Ordering, gradation, width comparisons

■ Measure, mark, and cut 1 1/4" (3.5 cm) from one end of a sponge. The large piece will be Bar #3, the small piece will be Bar #7.

■ Measure, mark, and cut 2" (5 cm) from one end of a sponge. The large piece will be Bar #4, the small piece will be Bar #6.

MATERIALS:
5 sponges of 1 color

Glue (see note on glue in the introduction to this section)

■ Measure, mark, and cut one sponge in half crosswise. One of the halves will be Bar #5; use the remaining half to make lift knobs (Next step).

■ Cut the half-sponge referred to in the previous step into eighths: measure and mark it in half lengthwise or crosswise and cut each half into fourths (no need to measure the exact size of the fourths—just use the ruler and pen to mark them into pieces that appear equal in size.) There should be 8 lift knobs.

■ Glue one lift knob in the approximate center of each Bar (See the reference to GLUE in the introduction to this section.) Don't omit the knobs; they indicate the direction of placement of the bars. Be sure all lift knobs are glued on in the same direction.

SPONGES

What kids do

Order the bars from large to small or from small to large. This activity can be done both horizontally and vertically. A table edge is helpful to align the lower edges.

What kids and teachers can do

Talk about the lift knobs—their function as lifters, and the importance of placing the bars so that all the lift knobs are positioned alike. Find the narrowest or widest bar with closed eyes. By placing them side by side, see how many of the narrowest bars it takes to make the same width as some of the widest ones.

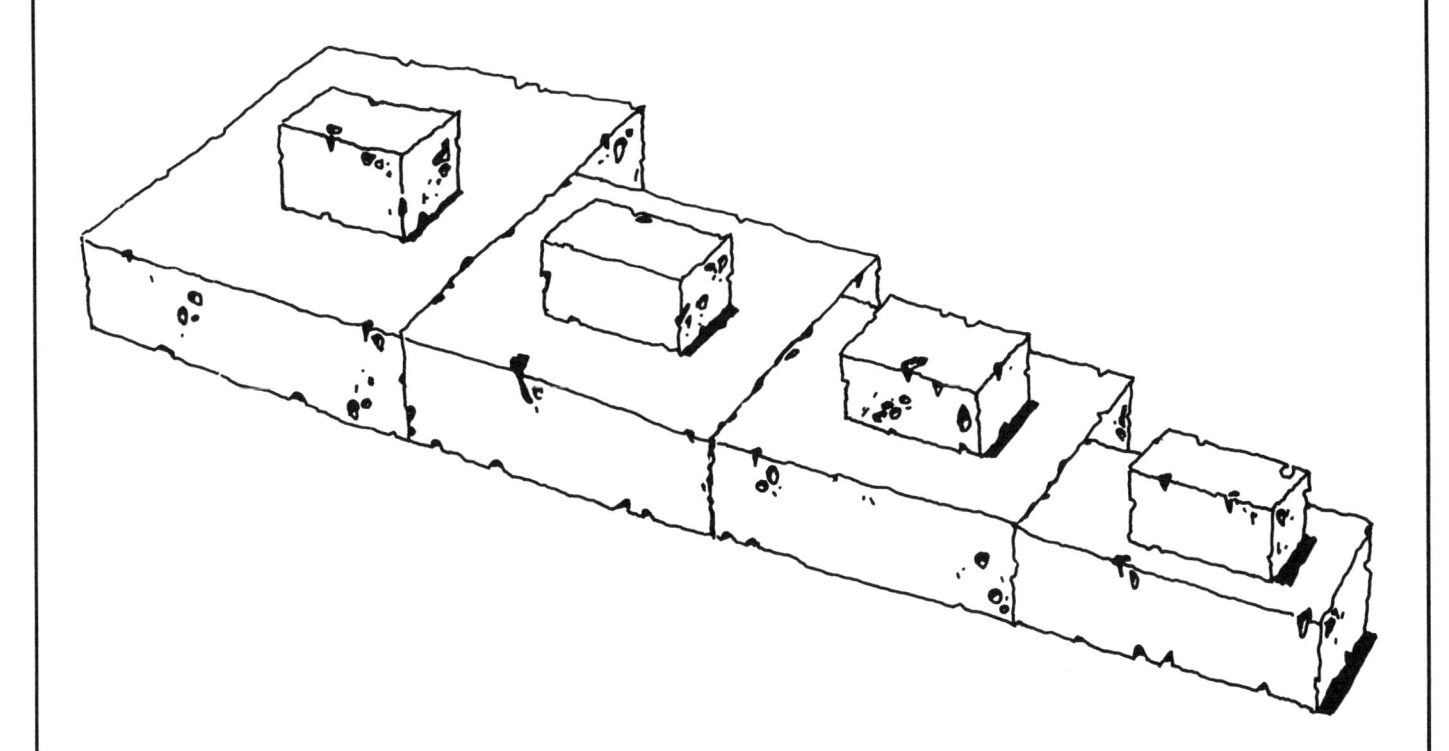

SPONGES

LENGTH BARS

These versatile bars demonstrate length progression when they are arranged in the ways suggested.

What teachers do

Measure, mark, and cut the sponges in half lengthwise, then, cutting carefully to enable the bars to stand on end:

- Leave 5 halves as they are for the longest bars.
- Cut 1 1/2" (3.8 cm) from one end of 5 halves, making bars of two different lengths.
- Cut 3 halves in half crosswise. Use only 5 of these as LENGTH BARS; the leftover pieces can go in your scrap collection. You should have a total of 20 bars, four different lengths, 5 of each length.

What kids do

Stand all the bars in a continuous line, progressing from tall to short or short to tall. Lay them on the table in order, from long to short and short to long. Stack the bars in sets, with the longest bars on the bottom, progressing to the shortest on the top. Sort or stack the bars by length. How far will they reach if you place them all end to end?

What kids and teachers can talk about

Talk about tall and short—what is, what isn't, who is, who isn't. Which are the shortest and tallest bars? Which shorter ones can be placed end to end to equal the length of the longest bar?

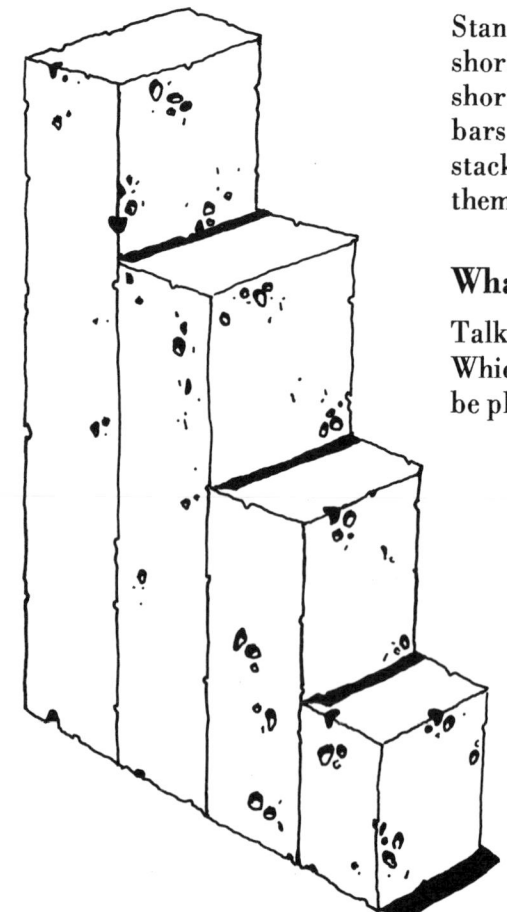

SET I—THICK SPONGE

LEVEL:
Beginning-Advanced

SKILLS:
Length comparisons, gradation

MATERIALS:
7 sponges of 1 color

SPONGES

COLOR STACKS

Sponge squares are stacked on cards containing colored dots to indicate the colors of the squares to be used.

What teachers do

Cut twenty 1 1/2" (about 3.8 cm) squares from the sponge scraps, using the colors randomly. (Measure, mark and cut one square to use as a pattern to cut the others; hold it on a sponge piece, and, without marking, cut close to it on all sides.) Make a 1 1/2" (about 3.8 cm) square outline in the center of each of the cards with black marker. Underneath the outline, make 4 colored dots, about 3/8" (9.5 mm) diameter, making a different combination on each card by repeating or omitting some colors on some cards. Use the same colors as the sponge squares.

What kids do

Find the colored sponge pieces to match the dots on the cards. Stack the sponge pieces on the outlines on the cards.

What else kids can do

Kids can stack the squares in the order the dots appear reading from left to right or right to left.

SET I—THICK SPONGE

LEVEL:
Beginning (with help)-Advanced

SKILLS:
Color recognition, manual dexterity

MATERIALS:
Sponge scraps in assorted colors

5 - 4" (10 cm) square white cards and broad marker

Markers or crayons in colors to match the sponges

SPONGES

SET I—THICK SPONGE

LEVEL:
Intermediate-Advanced

SKILLS:
Shape recognition, color distinction, manual dexterity

MATERIALS:
3 sponges in 3 colors

SHAPES FOR INTERMEDIATES AND ADVANCED

Intermediate and advanced students sort and match these shapes.

What teachers do

Cut each sponge in eighths, by cutting in half lengthwise, then cut each half into fourths, by making crosswise cuts every 1 1/4" (3.5 cm). There should be 24 pieces in all, each approximately 1 1/2" x 1 1/4" (3.8 X 3.5 cm). To cut the shapes, cut one piece of each color in a different shape and use it as a pattern to cut the same shape from the other two colors, following the cutting directions in the introduction to this section. Make the shapes by cutting V-shapes and squared notches of different sizes from the sides, and by cutting off one or more corners of the sponge pieces.

What kids do

Find the shapes of each color that are exactly alike and stack them together, being sure they are the same.

What else kids can do

ADVANCED students may be able to match more than three shapes of each color, or sets of the same color.

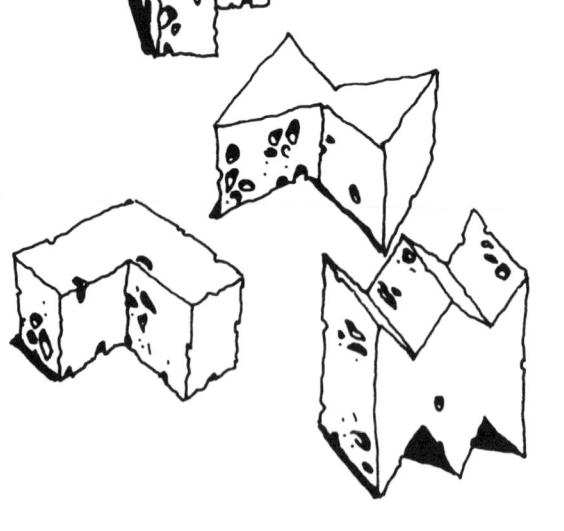

SPONGES

TOWERS

Squares, rectangles, triangles, and diamonds in four sizes can be stacked or placed in graduated order.

What teachers do

The largest and next largest piece of each shape begins with a whole sponge. The rest of the pieces of each shape can be cut from whole sponges or scraps.

Rectangle

■ Leave one sponge whole for the largest one, Rectangle #1.

■ Trim approximately 1/4" (6 mm), without marking, from all sides of a second sponge for Rectangle #2.

■ For Rectangle #3, hold Rectangle #2 on another piece of sponge, and cut close to it on all sides; trim this resulting piece 1/4" (6mm) on all sides.

■ For Rectangle #4, repeat Step 3, making an even smaller rectangle.

Square

■ Measure, mark, and cut 2" (5 cm) from one end of a whole sponge. The larger piece is Square #1, the smaller piece can be used as a scrap.

■ For Squares #2, #3, and #4, follow Step 3 of Rectangle to make progressively smaller squares.

Triangle

■ Using a ruler and felt-tip pen, mark from two corners of one of the long sides of a sponge to the center of the opposite side, and cut on the lines. The large piece is Triangle #1. Use the two small pieces for scraps.

■ Follow Step 3, Rectangle, to make progressively smaller Triangles #2, #3, and #4, using whole sponges or scraps.

Diamond

■ Using a ruler and felt-tip pen, mark from the centers of the long sides to the centers of the ends of a sponge and cut. The large piece is Diamond #1, the small pieces are scraps.

■ Follow Step 3, Rectangle, to make progressively smaller Diamonds #2, #3, and #4, using sponge scraps.

SET I—THICK SPONGE

LEVEL:

Intermediate-Advanced

SKILLS:

Size differentiation, manual dexterity

MATERIALS:

Approximately 10 sponges in 1 color, or 8 whole sponges and sponge scraps, all in 1 color

SPONGES

What kids do

Find many ways to order these pieces. Stack them, stand them on end, arrange them from small to large and any other ways they can invent. Talk about the shapes and where they have seen shapes like them before.

What else kids can do

Play a "Please give me" game with a friend—"Please give me the largest triangle", etc. Take turns being giver and asker.

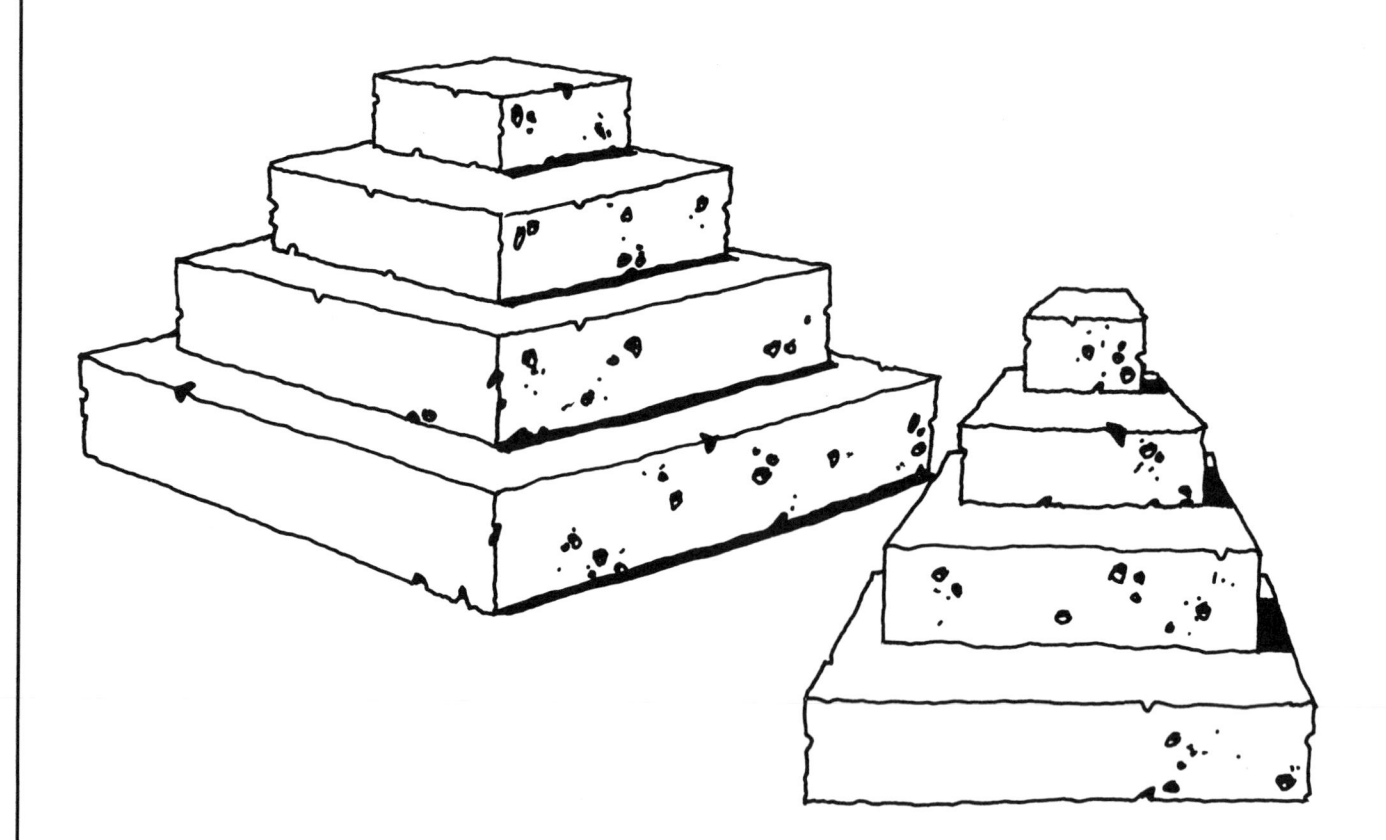

SPONGES

FEELING SHAPES

Kids sort the shapes in three groups by feeling and identifying the pieces with closed eyes.

What teachers do

Measure, mark, and cut the two sponges into fourths, cutting in half both crosswise and lengthwise, making 12 pieces. Using colors randomly, cut three distinct, simple shapes such as an L-shape, T-shape, and U-shape. Use these three cut pieces as patterns to cut two more shapes, making three of each shape. Hold the cut pieces on the uncut pieces, and cut the shapes without marking.

What kids do

Remove all the sponge pieces from the bag, and divide them into three groups on the table, according to their shapes. Now put them back into the bag, and with closed eyes, reach into the bag, pull the shapes out one by one and put them into three groups, according to their shapes.

What else kids can do

Play this game with a friend: place all the pieces on the table. The person who is the "feeler" plays with closed eyes. The "giver" hands the "feeler" two sponge pieces, which may or may not be the same shape. The "feeler" feels the pieces carefully and says "yes" if they are the same shape, "no" if they are not. If "no," the "giver" gives the "feeler" more shapes to try, until a match is made. The game is continued as long as matches can be made.

SET I—THICK SPONGE

LEVEL:
Intermediate-Advanced

SKILLS:
Tactile distinction of shape

MATERIALS:
3 sponges, any color(s)

Small bag made of fabric or opaque plastic

SPONGES

TWO-COLOR PUZZLES

SET I—THICK SPONGE

LEVEL:
Intermediate-Advanced

SKILLS:
Symmetry, logic

MATERIALS:
8 sponges, 2 sponges each of 4 colors

White card and broad marker, optional

Ruler

These two-color puzzles reform to make whole sponges.

What teachers do

Using a ruler, measure, mark, and cut one sponge of each color the following ways:

■ In half lengthwise; combine one piece of each color to form the puzzle.

■ In thirds crosswise, making each third approximately 1 5/8" (4 cm) wide; combine two pieces of one color with one piece of the other color to form the puzzle.

■ In fourths diagonally—place the ruler from any two corners to their opposite corners, mark, and cut. Combine two end pieces of one color with two side pieces of the other color to form the puzzle.

You will have two complete sets of puzzles, with each two-color puzzle consisting of half of each color. Keep these sets separate. ADVANCED students will probably be able to put these puzzles together without an outline card, but INTERMEDIATES may need either a detailed outline card of each puzzle, as for BEGINNER puzzles, or a block outline card, as in one-color puzzles. Encourage them to put the puzzles together without a card after a period of time.

What kids do

Put the puzzles together, using an outline card if needed and making sure each puzzle has two colors.

What kids and teachers can talk about

Notice that each puzzle has two colors. Does this make the puzzles easier to put together than if they were all the same color?

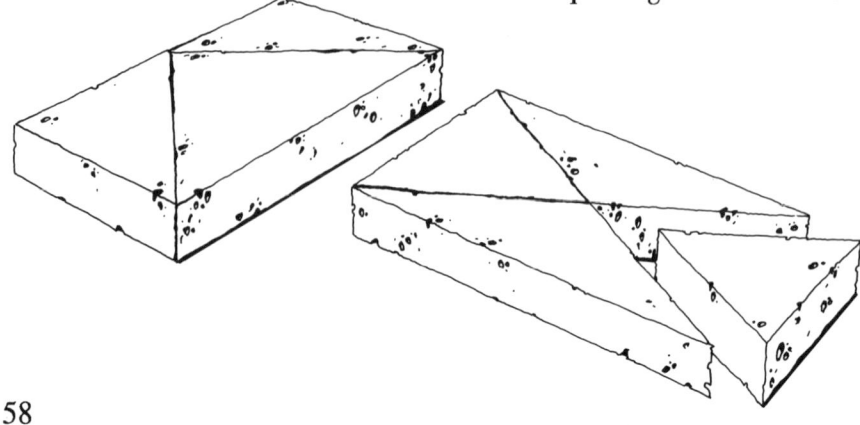

SPONGES

OUTLINES

Different-sized sponge blocks match outlines when they are turned correctly, on ends or sides.

What teachers do

Use sponge scraps or pieces cut from whole sponges to cut eight to ten rectangles of various sizes, with no two being alike. Place them on a suitably-sized card in various positions—broadside, on end, on the side, and mark around them with pencil, making sure no two are the same size. Trace over the pencil lines with marker, using a ruler if necessary. Laminate the card.

What kids do

By turning the blocks in different directions, find the one outline which exactly fits each block. Try all sides and ends. Remove them and do it again.

What kids and teachers talk about

Isn't it funny how such a long block can fit in such a small space if it's turned on its end? Does this outline card with the blocks all in place remind you of city skyscrapers? You may want to do as some kids and I once did—cut large and small "buildings" of sponge, make doors and windows and signs on them with permanent marker, and add little vehicles and people to make a village.

SET I—THICK SPONGE

LEVEL:
Intermediate-Advanced

SKILLS:
Fine spatial distinction, logic, reasoning

MATERIALS:
Sponges and/or scraps of 1 color

White card and broad black marker

SPONGES

POSITIVE/NEGATIVE BARS

When the bars of each color are assembled in progressive order by length, they form a rectangle, with the spaces left by the bars of one color filled by the bars of the other color, creating a positive/negative pattern.

LEVEL:
Intermediate-Advanced

SKILLS:
Positive/negative concept, graduated sizes

MATERIALS:
2 sponges, 1 each of 2 colors

7" x 8" (17.5 cm x 20 cm) white card and broad marker

What teachers do

Cut the sponges in thirds lengthwise, making 1" (2.5 cm) wide bars. Leave one bar of each color as is. Shorten one of each color by 1" (2.5 cm), and one of each color by 2" (5 cm). The 1" (2.5 cm) and 2" (5 cm) cut pieces become the two shortest bars. Make a 5" x 6" (12.5 cm x 15 cm) outline on the card. Divide it horizontally in 5 spaces, each space 1" (2.5 cm) wide. Make vertical lines in the appropriate spaces at 1" (2.5 cm), 2" (5 cm), 3" (7.5 cm), and 5" (12.5 cm). Laminate the card.

What kids do

They may want to divide the sponge pieces by color on the table. Start with the longest piece of either color and put it in the space on the outline card it fits exactly. Do the same with the rest of the pieces of that color. Do they see where the pieces of the other color will fit? Try this without the card, if they want.

What kids and teachers can do

A table edge will help to keep the left edges of the bars even if no outline card is used. Help kids to see that a straight edge is important to making all the pieces fit.

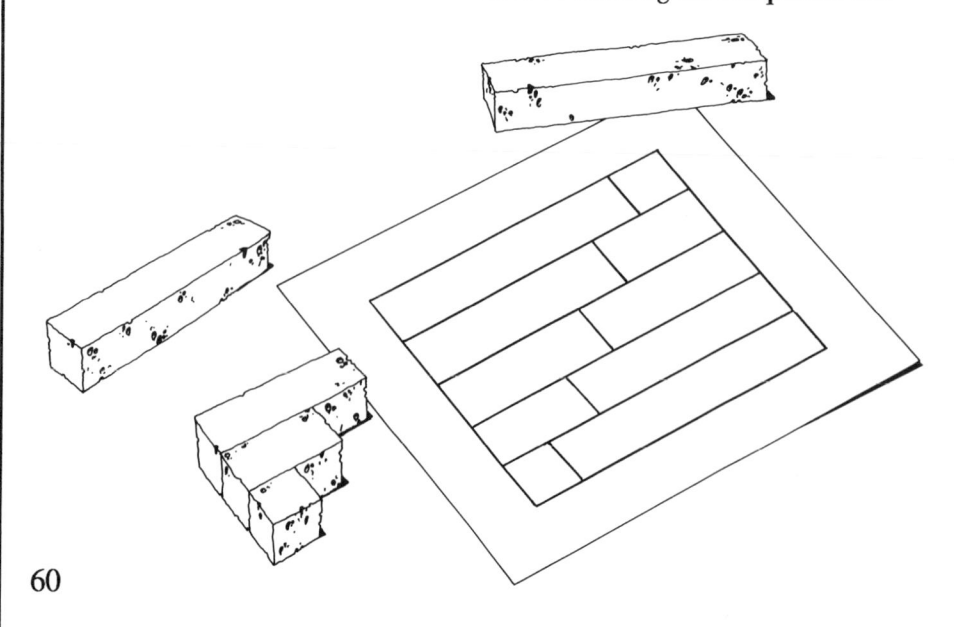

SPONGES

VERTICAL PUZZLE

A puzzle assembled by stacking sponge pieces on an outline card.

What teachers do

Cut 2" (5 cm) from one end of each of the whole sponges, or cut ten 3" (7.5 cm) squares from scraps. If using whole sponges, use only the larger cut pieces; the smaller pieces can be used as scraps. Cut three of the sponge squares in half across, and three in half diagonally (from any corner to its opposite corner), and leave three squares as they are. Make a 3" (7.5 cm) square outline with the marker in the center of the card, and laminate the card.

What kids do

Stack all the pieces on the outline to make a tower. They may also want to form a large rectangle with sponge pieces on the table.

What kids and teachers can talk about

Teachers can help kids see that two halves cut across or two cut diagonally form a whole.

SET I—THICK SPONGE

LEVEL:
Intermediate-Advanced

SKILLS:
Precision, eye-hand coordination

MATERIALS:
10 whole sponges in assorted colors, or scraps to cut 10 3" (7.5 cm) squares

6" (15 cm) square white card and broad black marker

SPONGES

BUILDING BLOCKS

SET I—THICK SPONGE

LEVEL:
Beginning-Advanced

SKILLS:
Having fun (construction skills, too)

MATERIALS:
Sponges

What teachers do

This activity is not limited to individualized use, although it may be used that way; it can also be a group activity. Sponges make marvelous quiet, safe, and inexpensive blocks for building. Simply pile a huge supply in a laundry basket for a starter set. Double-thick sponges (the same width and length as the usual ones, but twice as thick) make better blocks and jumbo (any size larger than the double thick ones) make the best. To gild the lily even more, cut regular-sized or double-thick sponges in unit block shapes—halves lengthwise, crosswise and diagonally and fourths lengthwise, crosswise and diagonally. The pieces will approximate the shapes and sizes of commercial hardwood unit blocks and can be used the same way. Order all three sizes, regular, double-thick, or jumbo sponges from Nation/Ruskin, whose phone number and address are given in the introduction to this section.

What kids do

Kids are born knowing what to do with blocks!

What else kids can do

This can be a shared activity if the block collection is large enough.

SPONGES

ONE-COLOR PUZZLES

Each of these puzzles, when assembled, reforms a whole sponge.

What teachers do

Measure, mark, and cut:

- One sponge in half lengthwise
- One sponge in fourths (crosswise or lengthwise halves cut in half again)
- One sponge in fourths diagonally (place the ruler from two of the corners to their opposite corners, mark and cut).

These puzzles are quite difficult and even ADVANCED students will probably need a block outline card, at least in the beginning. Draw a 3" x 5" (7.5 cm x 17.5 cm) rectangle on the card with the marker. This will provide a guide for constructing each puzzle, but will not show the individual puzzle pieces. INTERMEDIATE students, however, may need an outline card for each puzzle, with the individual pieces outlined, as was done in PUZZLES FOR BEGINNERS.

What kids do

Put each puzzle together on the card, then slide it off onto the table, and put another one together on the card. Do all the puzzles this way. Try them without a card when they feel ready.

What kids and teachers can do

Teachers can point this out to kids: if they find corner pieces and fit them in the block outline, the puzzles are easier to put together.

SET I—THICK SPONGE

LEVEL:

Advanced, possibly Intermediate

SKILLS:

Shape perception, spatial orientation

MATERIALS:

3 sponges of 1 color

5" x 7" (12.5 mm x 17.5 mm) white card and broad black marker

Ruler

SPONGES

PUZZLES

SET II - THIN SPONGE

Four small three-piece puzzles, to be put together with or without the help of outline cards.

LEVEL:
Beginning-Advanced

What teachers do

Copy, laminate, and cut out the patterns that follow, following directions given in the introduction to this section. Trace around the patterns on the sponge with pen, fitting two on each sponge, and cut them out. Use a ruler to mark the puzzle pieces on the sponge pieces, and cut the pieces apart. Most children will need outline cards, either to fit the pieces in the outlines, (BEGINNERS), or to see what the finished puzzle looks like (INTERMEDIATE and ADVANCED). Place the laminated pattern pieces on cards, and outline them with the broad marker. Mark the puzzle pieces for BEGINNERS, but not for INTERMEDIATES and ADVANCED.

SKILLS:
Abstraction

MATERIALS:

1 - 7" x 8" (17.5 cm x 20 cm) sponge sheet for every 2 puzzles, any colors

4 - 7" x 7" (17.5 cm x 17.5 cm) white cards and broad marker

What kids do

BEGINNERS: Place the puzzle pieces directly on the outline cards; later they can try to put them together on the table while looking at the cards. INTERMEDIATES and ADVANCED: Put the puzzles together on the cards or on the table beside the cards; later try to put them together without cards.

What kids and teachers can do

Teachers can encourage kids to put the puzzles together without using outline cards after they have become accustomed to them.

SPONGES

OUTLINES

Small abstract shapes are matched to their outlines on a card.

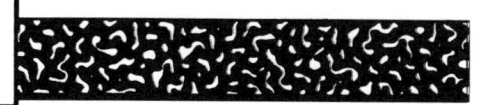

SET II—THIN SPONGE

LEVEL:
Intermediate-Advanced

SKILLS:
Abstraction, visual perception

MATERIALS:
1 - 7" x 8" (17.5 cm x 20 cm) sponge cloth

8" x 10" (20 cm x 25 cm) white card and broad marker

What teachers do

Mark and cut the sponge into 2" (5 cm) squares. Some will be left over. There should be twelve squares. Cut the squares in abstract shapes, making each shape different. Accuracy is not critical. Arrange the cut shapes on the card and lightly trace around them in pencil. Remove the shapes and go over the lines with marker, using a ruler if necessary. Laminate the card.

What kids do

Match the pieces to the outlines on the card.

What else kids can do

ADVANCED students may like to duplicate the pattern of the outline card by placing the sponge shapes on the table beside or below the card, in the same pattern.

SPONGES

SQUARES

Small squares of two colors to be arranged in several ways.

What teachers do

Mark and cut the sponge into 2" (5 cm) squares. Some will be left over. There should be 24 squares. Using the marker, make an 8" x 12" (20 cm x 30 cm) grid with 2" (5 cm) squares on the white card. Laminate the card.

What kids do

Place the squares on the card in ways they like—make a checkerboard, put the colors in rows or other patterns. Put the card aside and make patterns on the table or stack the squares in towers.

What kids and teachers can do

Students really need help to see the possibilities of these simple squares. Teachers can suggest any of the arrangements mentioned in **What kids do.**

SET II—THIN SPONGE

LEVEL:
Intermediate-Advanced

SKILLS:
Design, alternation, organization

MATERIALS:
2 - 7" x 8" (17.5 cm x 20 cm) sponge cloths in 2 colors

10" x 14" (25 cm x 35 cm) white card and broad marker

SPONGES

PATTERNS

Large and small geometric shapes to be sorted or arranged in repeating sequences.

SET II—THIN SPONGE

LEVEL:
Intermediate-Advanced

SKILLS:
Duplication

MATERIALS:
4 sponge sheets in 4 colors (or sponge scraps)

4 - 4" x 10" (10 cm x 25 cm) white card and broad marker; colored markers or crayons to match the colors of the sponge

What teachers do

Copy, laminate, and cut out the patterns that follow. Place them on the sponge and trace around them, making six large and six small sizes of each shape and color, and cut out. Place differing combinations of sponge shapes on the cards and mark around them with pencil. Remove the shapes and color the outlines with markers or crayons to match the sponges. Laminate the cards. Put out one card at a time, change as needed.

What kids do

Duplicate the pattern on a card by making rows beneath it, or by repeating the pattern in a continuous line if space permits.

What else kids can do

Play a "What's missing?" game: Put the shapes in rows on the table. One person may close his eyes while the other removes one of the sponge shapes. The person with closed eyes opens his eyes, and guesses. For example, "You took the small yellow triangle". Removed pieces are not returned to the game.

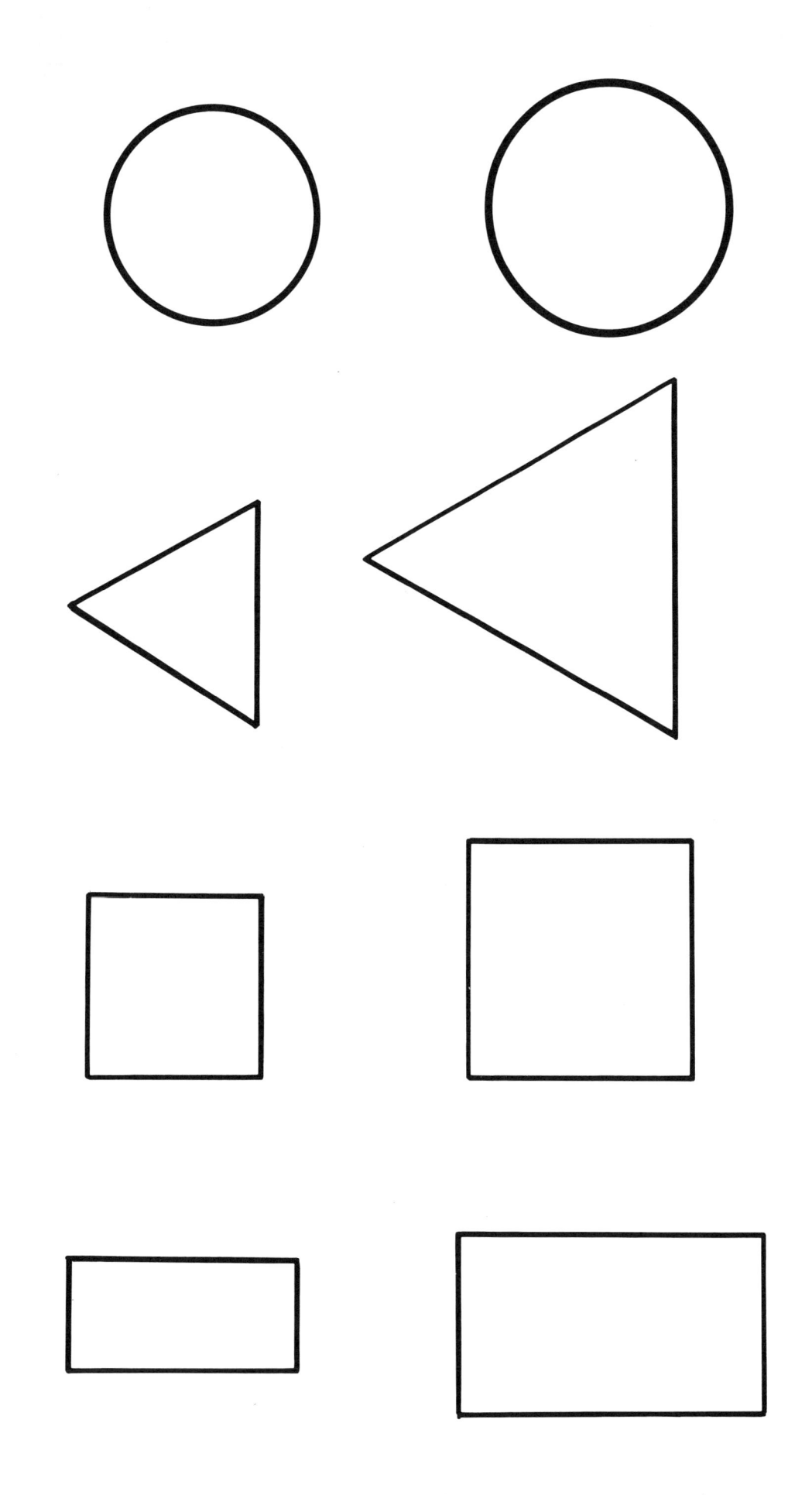

SPONGES

SET II—THIN SPONGE

LEVEL:
Intermediate-Advanced

SKILLS:
Shape recognition, social interaction

MATERIALS:
Sponge scraps of assorted colors

2 - 6" x 9" (15 cm x 22.5 cm) white cards and colored markers

LOTTO

A little cooperative game for three players.

What teachers do

Copy, laminate, and cut out the pattern pieces that follow. Place them on the sponge, using colors randomly. Trace around them with pen, and cut them out. Make two identical sets of sponge pieces. Place them randomly on the cards, making a different arrangement on each card, and trace around them lightly in pencil. Remove the sponge pieces and go over the outlines with markers (or crayons) to match the colors of the sponge pieces. Laminate the cards.

What kids do

Play a game with two friends. Two will be players and one will be caller. The players have the cards and the caller has the sponge pieces. The caller selects the pieces one at a time and holds them for the players to see. The player whose card has an outline of the piece takes it and places it on the outline. The players are partners, so there is no winner. When both cards are filled, the players may exchange cards, or trade places with the caller, and play again if they wish.

What kids and teachers can do

A teacher can be one of the players or the caller and play the game with the kids.

SPONGES

ALPHABET (UPPER CASE)

Upper case letters for arranging alphabetically or matching with ALPHABET (LOWER CASE).

What teachers do

Copy, laminate, and cut out the patterns that follow. Place them on the sponge, crowding together to conserve sponge. Mark around them with pen and cut out. The upper-case alphabet should be on display in the classroom for the children to use as a guide.

What kids do

Put the letters in the activity in alphabetical order—there may be a few letters or the whole alphabet—or match them with ALPHABET (LOWER CASE).

What kids and teachers can do

When an adult works with a child or several children, this time can be used for teaching recognition of letters, vowels, consonants, beginning and ending sounds of words, formation, sequence, etc. The independent activities described in **What kids do** are ADVANCED, but the ones with an adult can be used for children of any age for which they seem appropriate and relevant. Think of the letters as a teaching tool, as well as a learning activity.

SET II—THIN SPONGE

LEVEL:
Intermediate-Advanced

SKILLS:
Letter recognition

MATERIALS:
2 1/2 - 7" x 8" (17.5 cm x 20 cm) sponge sheets in one color

D I M
C H
G L
B
F K
A E J

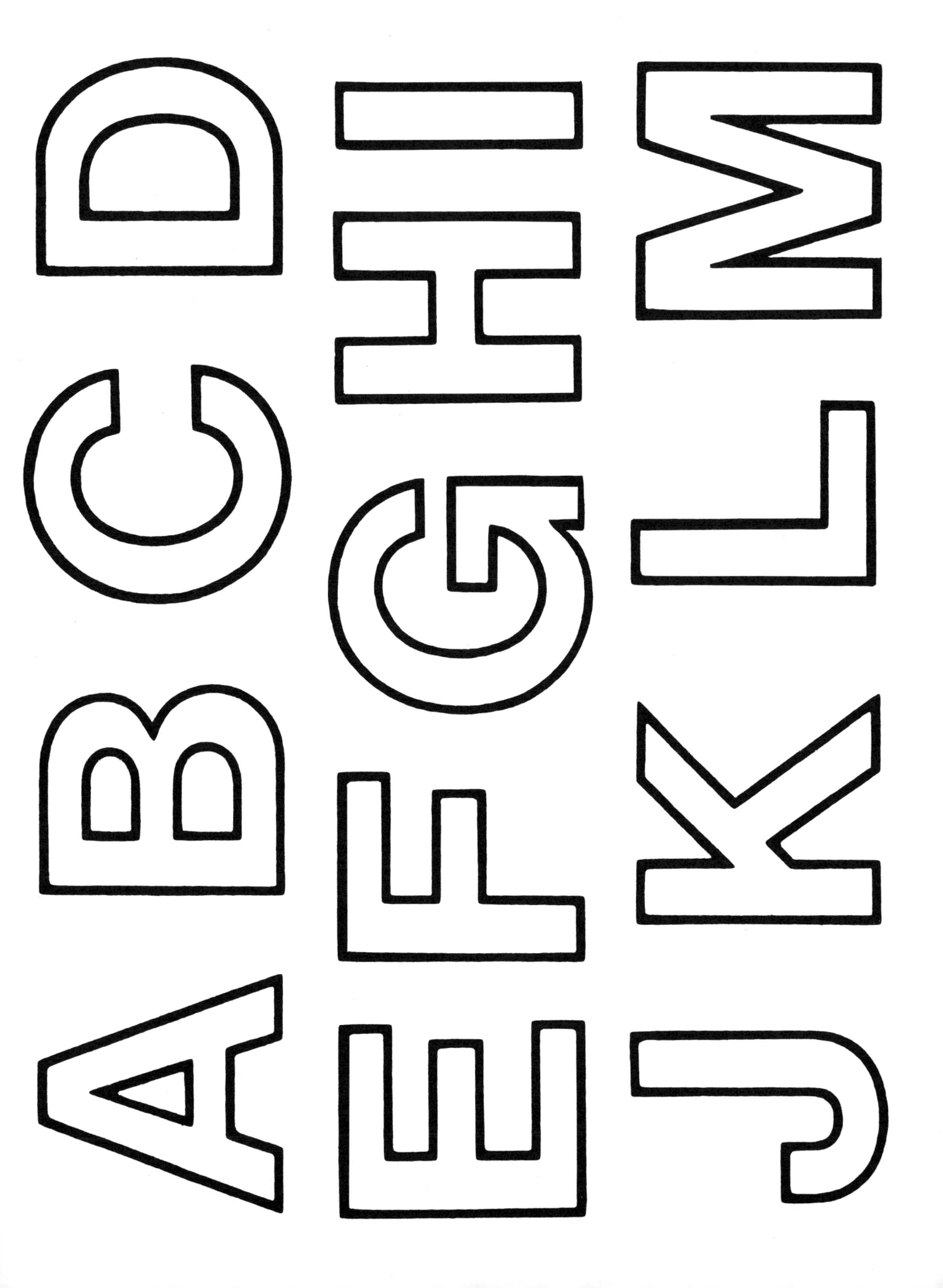

N O P Q
R S T U V
W X Y Z

SPONGES

ALPHABET (LOWER CASE)

Lower case letters for ordering alphabetically or matching with ALPHABET (UPPER CASE).

What teachers do

Copy, laminate, and cut out the patterns that follow. Place them on the sponge, crowding together to conserve sponge. Mark around them with pen and cut out. The lower-case alphabet should be on display in the classroom for the children to use as a guide.

What kids do

Put the letters in the activity in alphabetical order—there may be a few letters or many—or match them with ALPHABET (UPPER CASE).

What kids and teachers can do

When an adult works with a child or several children, this time can be used for teaching recognition of letters, vowels, consonants, beginning and ending sounds of words, formation, sequence, etc. The independent activities described in **What kids do** are ADVANCED, but the ones with an adult can be used for children of any age for which they seem appropriate and relevant. Think of the letters as a teaching tool, as well as a learning activity.

SET II—THIN SPONGE

LEVEL:
Intermediate-Advanced

SKILLS:
Letter recognition

MATERIALS:
2 1/2 - 7" x 8" sponge sheets in one color—a different color than that used for ALPHABET (UPPER CASE)

d h m
c g l
b f k
 j
a e i

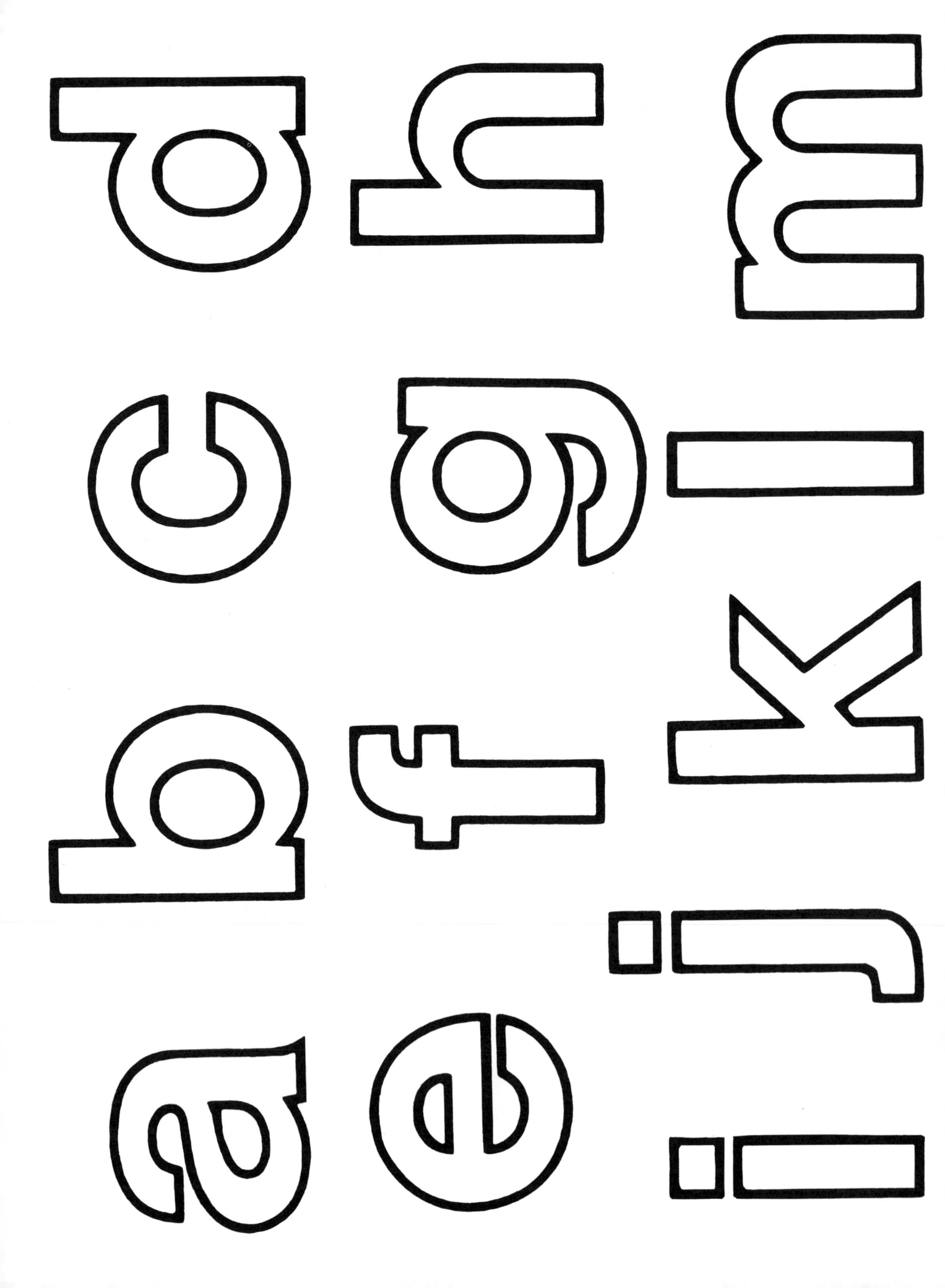

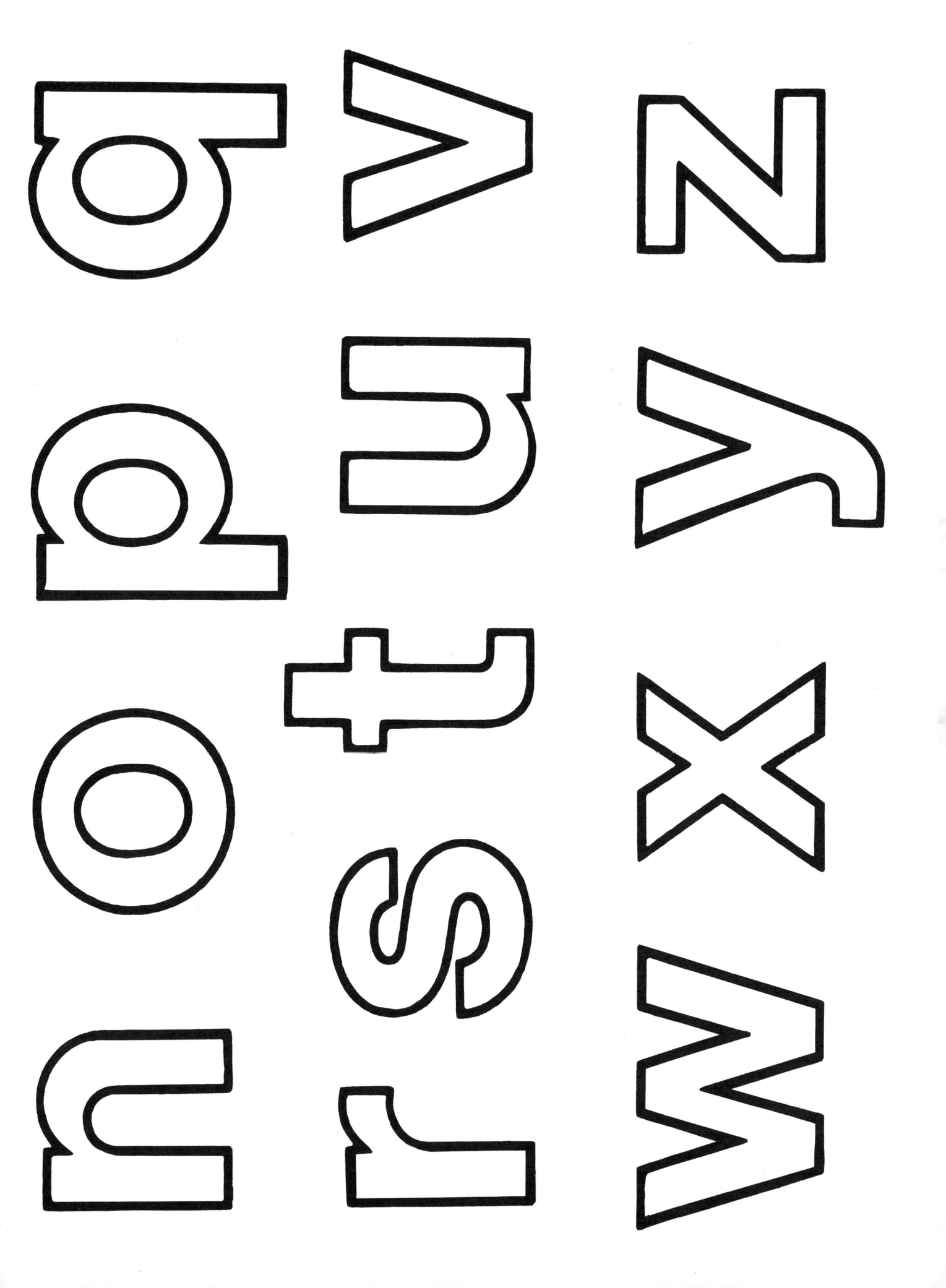

SPONGES

NUMBERS

SET II—THIN SPONGE

LEVEL:
Intermediate-Advanced

SKILLS:
Number recognition

MATERIALS:
1 - 7" x 8" (17.5 cm x 20 cm) sponge sheet for each set of numbers 1 to 10

Individual numbers from one to ten or twenty, to be used several ways.

What teachers do
Copy, laminate, and cut out the patterns that follow. Crowd them together on the sponge, mark around them with pen, and cut out. Extend the set to twenty or more if you want, using more sponge, and the children can use them for matching activities. You will need to provide a sectioned container for storage if you make more than one of each number. A chart showing numbers ordered from one to ten (or twenty) should be on display in the classroom.

What kids do
Order the numbers one to ten or twenty. Order them from ten (or twenty) to one.

What kids and teachers can do
Use the numbers as a teaching tool, as well as a learning activity. Use them in teaching number formation, recognition, sequence, etc. either in teacher-led activities or as independent learning activities.

1 2 3
4 5 6
7 8 9
10

SPONGES

GRAPH

A two-step activity: children place sponge pieces on a grid card matching both color and shape.

What teachers do

Copy, laminate, and cut out the patterns which follow for the sponge shapes. Trace around them on sponge, making one shape in each color, and cut out. On the card, make a 9" x 9" (22.5 cm x 22.5 cm) grid, divided into sixteen squares, each 2 1/4" (about 5 cm). Trace around one of each of the shapes in a vertical column left of the grid. Color a small rectangle or large dot above each of the columns above the grid to match the colors of the sponge pieces. Laminate the card.

What kids do

Put the sponge pieces in the spaces that match their shape and color.

What kids and teachers can do

If a child needs or requests help with this, the two of you can take turns placing the sponge pieces until she is able to do it alone. It's helpful for the teacher to point out that the vertical columns determine the colors and the horizontal rows determine the shapes.

SET II—THIN SPONGE

LEVEL:
Intermediate-Advanced

MATERIALS:
4 - 7" x 8" (17.5 cm x 20 cm) sponge sheets in 4 colors, or sponge scraps

11" x 12" (27.5 cm x 30 cm) white card and marker; colored markers or crayon to match colors of sponges

SPONGES

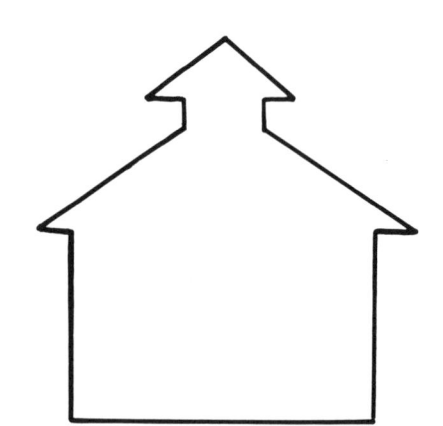

SPONGES

SPONGES

FRACTIONS—CIRCLE

A stacking activity with a whole circle, halves, thirds, and fourths.

What teachers do

Make a paper pattern: cut a 6 1/2" (16.25 cm) diameter circle. Mark around it with a fine point felt tip pen on each of the sponge sheets and cut them out. Leave one sponge circle as it is. Fold the paper circle in half; place it on a sponge circle, mark on the fold line, and cut the sponge circle in half. Make the fourths next; leave thirds to the last. For fourths, fold the paper circle in half as before, then in half again. Place the folded circle pattern on a sponge circle, mark and cut into fourths. Use the paper pattern to experiment to make a pattern for thirds; this is a bit tricky—think of a pie cut into three equal wedges. When you have a cut pattern for a wedge which will make three fairly equally sized wedges, mark around it on the last sponge circle and cut it into thirds.

What kids do

Put the whole circle on the table first, then stack the other pieces on top of it. Put both halves of the circle together, the thirds together, and the fourths together, in any order.

What kids and teachers can talk about

Talk about things one or both of them have divided as these circles are divided—apples, cookies, pizza, etc. How many people could share an apple if it was cut each of the ways?

SET II—THIN SPONGE

LEVEL:
Intermediate-Advanced

SKILLS:
Manual dexterity, reasoning

MATERIALS:
4 - 7" x 8" (17.5 cm x 20 cm) sponge sheets, in 4 colors, or all one color

SPONGES

FRACTIONS—SQUARE

A stacking activity with a whole square, halves, thirds, and fourths.

SET II—THIN SPONGE

LEVEL:
Intermediate-Advanced

SKILLS:
Manual dexterity, reasoning

MATERIALS:
4 - 7" x 8" (17.5 cm x 20 cm) sponge sheets, in 4 colors, or all one color

What teachers do

Make a paper pattern: cut a 6 1/2" (16.25 cm) square. Mark around it with a fine point felt tip pen on each of the sponge sheets and cut them out. Leave one sponge square as it is. Fold the paper pattern in half either horizontally or vertically. Place the folded pattern on a sponge square, mark on the fold line and cut the sponge on the marked line, making halves. Refold the paper pattern in thirds, making each third approximately 2 1/8" (about 5.33 cm). Place the folded pattern on a sponge square and mark in thirds; cut on the marked lines. Refold the paper pattern into fourths: fold in half in one direction, then in half in the other direction. Place the folded pattern on the last sponge square, mark into fourths, and cut on the lines.

What kids do

Put the whole square on the table first, then stack the other pieces on top of it. Put both halves of the square together, the thirds together, and the fourths together, in any order.

What kids and teachers can talk about

Talk about things that might be cut like these squares, such as sandwiches. How many people could share a sandwich cut each of the ways?

SPONGES

FRACTIONS—TRIANGLE

A stacking activity with a whole triangle, halves, thirds, and fourths.

What teachers do

Make a paper pattern: cut a triangle which is 7 1/2" (about 19 cm) on all sides; it should measure approximately 6 1/2" (about 16.25 cm) from the tip of each of the three points to the base opposite each point. Mark around it with a fine point felt tip pen on each of the sponge sheets and cut them out. Leave one sponge triangle as it is. Fold the paper pattern in half, from one tip to the center of the base opposite that tip. Place the folded pattern on one sponge triangle, mark, and cut the sponge on the line, making halves. To make thirds and fourths, use a ruler and the felt tip pen to mark the cutting lines directly on the remaining two sponge triangles. For thirds, make a 4 1/2" (11 cm) line from either of the points to the center of the triangle. From the end of this line, make a connecting line to each of the other two points, dividing the triangle into thirds. To divide the last triangle into fourths, cut a small paper triangle which is 3 3/4" (almost 10 cm) on all sides. Center it inside the remaining sponge triangle so that each of the points of the small paper triangle is at the center of each of the sides of the large sponge triangle. Mark and cut into fourths.

What kids do

Put the whole triangle on the table first, then stack the other pieces on top of it. Put both halves of the triangle together, the thirds together, and the fourths together, in any order.

What kids and teachers can talk about

Talk about the number of pieces of these triangles—talk about triangles and wonder why so few things are shaped triangularly.

SET II—THIN SPONGE

LEVEL:
Intermediate-Advanced

SKILLS:
Manual dexterity, reasoning

MATERIALS:
4 - 7" x 8" (17.5 cm x 20 cm) sponge sheets, in 4 colors, or all one color

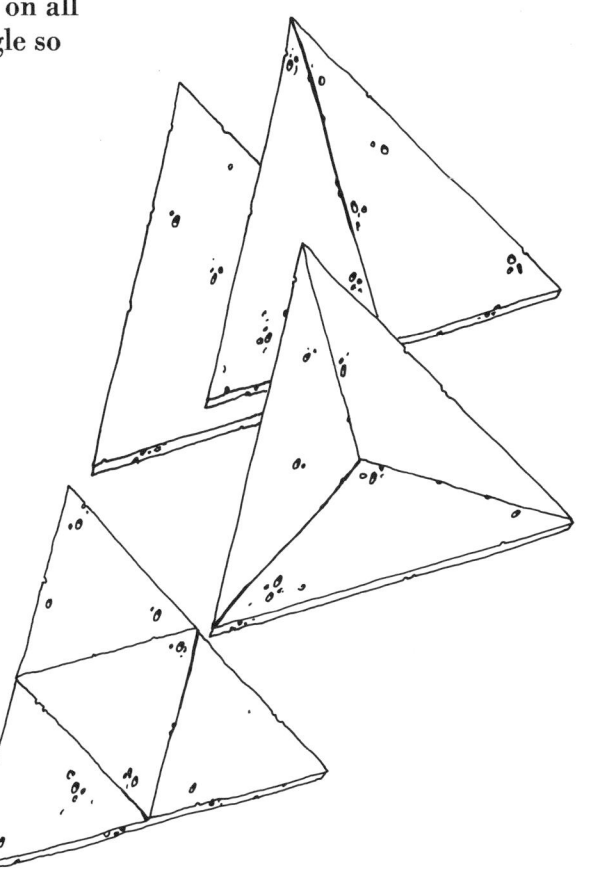

SPONGES

SET II—THIN SPONGE

LEVEL:
Intermediate-Advanced

SKILLS:
Manual dexterity, reasoning

MATERIALS:
4 - 7" x 8" (17.5 cm x 20 cm) sponge sheets, in 4 colors, or all one color

FRACTIONS—RECTANGLE

A stacking activity with a whole rectangle, halves, thirds, and fourths.

What teachers do

Make a paper pattern: cut a rectangle which is 6" x 8" (15 cm x 20 cm). Mark around it with a fine point felt tip pen on each of the sponge sheets and cut them out. Leave one sponge rectangle as it is. Fold the paper pattern in half crosswise; place the folded pattern on a sponge sheet, mark on the fold line and cut the sponge in half. Refold the pattern in thirds crosswise, making each third a little less than 2 3/4" (about 8 cm) wide. Place the folded pattern on a sponge sheet, mark it in thirds, and cut. Refold the pattern in fourths—fold in half in either direction, and then in half again. Place the pattern on the last sponge rectangle, mark in fourths, and cut.

What kids do

Put the whole rectangle on the table first, then stack the other pieces on top of it. Put both halves of the rectangle together, the thirds together, and the fourths together, in any order.

What kids and teachers can talk about

Talk about rectangles and things that are rectangular—doors, etc.

SPONGES

CUTOUTS (ROUND)

Sponge rounds with shape cutouts are matched to cards containing the same shapes.

What teachers do

Trace around a bottle cap, cup, etc. which is about 2 5/8" (about 6.5 cm) diameter, to make ten circles on the sponge cloth, and cut out the circles. Cut paper patterns of the cutout shapes: a square, circle, rectangle, triangle, diamond, semi-circle, octagon, trapeoid, hexagon, ellipse (oval). Make the square 1" (2.5 cm) and the other shapes of compatible size. These patterns may be used to make CUTOUTS (SQUARE) also. Trace around one shape in the estimated center of each card, and color solidly with black marker. Trace around the paper shapes in the estimated center of the sponge circles, using a fine point felt tip pen. Cut out the shapes with small sharp-pointed scissors, such as manicure scissors; discard the cutout shapes.

What kids do

Place each sponge round on the card which has its matching shape.

What kids and teachers can talk about

Talk about the names of these shapes.

SET II—THIN SPONGE

LEVEL:

Intermediate-Advanced

SKILLS:

Shape recognition, matching

MATERIALS:

2 - 7" x 8" (17.5 cm x 20 cm) sponge sheets in the same or different colors, or scraps in assorted colors

10 - 4" (10 cm) square white cards and broad black marker

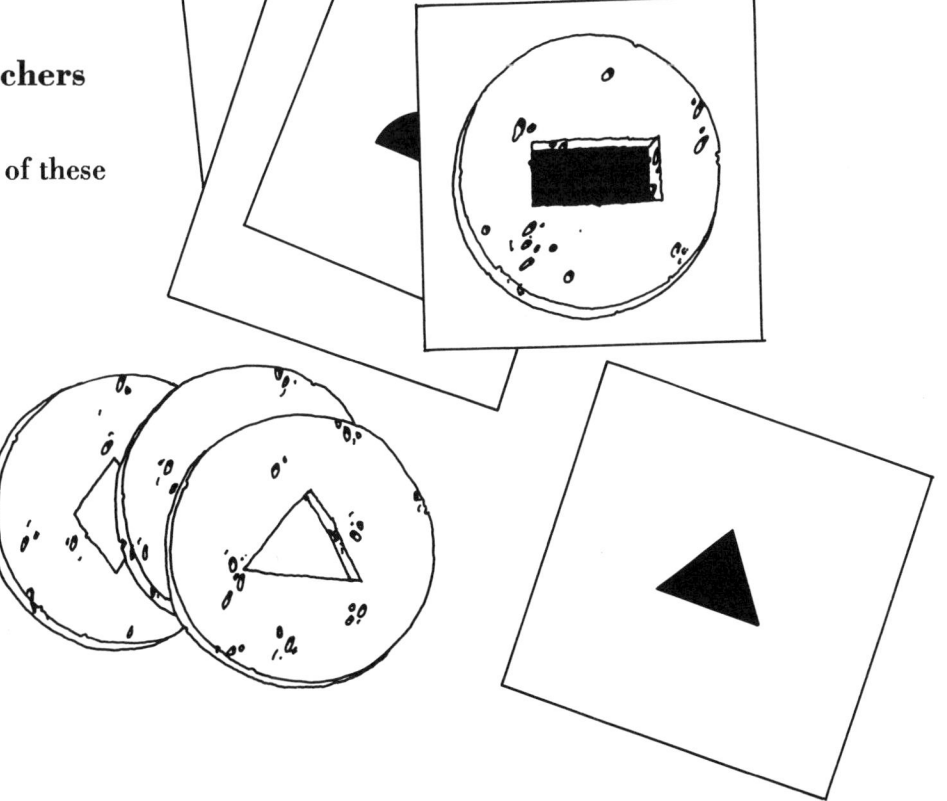

SPONGES

CUTOUTS (SQUARE)

Sponge squares with cutouts are fitted on squares containing matching raised shapes.

SET II—THIN SPONGE

LEVEL:
Intermediate-Advanced

SKILLS:
Shape matching, manual dexterity

MATERIALS:
4 - 7" x 8" (17.5 x 20 cm) sponge sheets, 2 each of 2 colors

Glue—see glue in the introduction to this section

What teachers do

Measure, mark, and cut each sponge sheet in half crosswise (with long sides at the top and bottom, short sides at ends). Cut each half in crosswise fourths—every 2 1/2" (7.5 cm)—to make six 2 1/2" (7.5 cm) squares from each sheet. Only ten squares of each color will be used. Cut paper patterns for the following shapes: square, circle, rectangle, triangle, diamond, semi-circle, octagon, trapezoid, hexagon, ellipse (oval). Make the square 1" (2.5 cm) and the other shapes of compatible size. These shapes may also be used for CUTOUTS (ROUND). Place one paper shape in the estimated center of each sponge square of one color, and trace around it with a fine point file tip pen. Carefully cut out the shapes with small pointed scissors, such as manicure scissors. Dip one side of each sponge cutout shape in glue and position it in the estimated center of each of the squares of the second color. Allow to dry thoroughly.

What kids do

Fit the squares with cutouts on the matching raised shapes of the other squares.

What kids and teachers can talk about

Talk about the names of the shapes. Some kids may need help in learning to press the sponge pieces together.

STICKERS

Grouping

89

STICKERS

What kids do

Categorize and group small squares showing stickers.

What teachers do

You know what an agreeable combination kids and stickers are. Stickers are everywhere kids are. You can buy stickers in supermarkets, gift and toy stores, school supply stores, and party shops, or you can order them from school supply catalogs. The stickers I refer to here are the ones, I believe, that are the most widely available. However, almost any attractive stickers can be used, and the more unique, the better. Each activity can be a true one-of-a-kind. Avoid stickers with printing, such as "award" stickers and those with "busy" designs; bold simple designs are best for young children. Modify your STICKERS activities for BEGINNERS—simple shapes and designs are most suitable for them. Older children will enjoy the challenge of more detailed pictures.

My favorite brand of stickers is Mrs. Grossman's, sold in card shops and other stores and school supply catalogs. Other brands used in the activities are Hallmark, Eureka, and Dennison, all available through school supply catalogs or the sources previously mentioned. Most school supply companies which have catalogs have toll-free phone numbers you can use to request a catalog.

Most packaged stickers contain four or more identical sheets of stickers, with each sheet containing six or more stickers, each different. Some packaged stickers contain a wide assortment, perhaps ten to twenty designs on each of four sheets. Use these to make PAIRING activities as described. Very small stickers ("miniatures") can be used for SORTING and CATEGORIES activities, grouping two or three small stickers on each square, making two or more cards alike. See SORTING and CATEGORIES for examples of this type.

Making stickers activities

Making STICKERS activities is easy. Just use a copier to make copies of the grid page in the STICKERS section on white card stock, affix stickers in the squares and laminate the card by hand or machine. You can also use posterboard and apply self-sticking laminating film or adhesive-backed clear plastic by hand. The grid contains twenty 2" (5 cm) squares. Use as many card pages as

STICKERS

needed for each activity. Cut on the lines to make individual sticker squares.

How kids use stickers activities

STICKERS can be used several ways; you may think of some in addition to the ones I suggest. Children like new ways of using the same stickers, so you can occasionally introduce alternative ways of using them. Here are two of my favorite ways:

■ On a grid card. This is the simplest way. The marked grid spaces define the arrangement of the sticker squares. Just copy the grid page on colored card stock (to distinguish it from the white sticker squares), and laminate it. Some activities may not fill all the spaces on the grid card.

■ On a work surface without any guide. This is a more advanced method, requiring organizational skills, but many children prefer it because it gives them a greater degree of control over the activity. Children must be able to identify the lead squares with this method—the squares which set the pattern for the rest. Children may sort the squares into groups or piles, or into rows as shown. Sorting into rows has an added advantage of allowing children to see completed groupings and compare their similarities and differences. It also makes mistakes obvious.

Children can place squares in either vertical or horizontal rows. Until your students are thoroughly familiar with the squares and the process, you should probably demonstrate either vertically or horizontally—not both. Later they can try the other direction.

Other creative ways teachers have used the sticker squares require extra materials, but you may want to try them:

■ Magnet-backed: small squares of self-stick magnetic tape (from hardware or school supply stores or catalogs) are attached to the backs of the sticker squares and they are sorted on a small metal magnetic board, such as the kind used with magnetic numbers and letters. A non-aluminum cookie sheet can also be used in place of the magnetic board, as can a large metal hot pad (the kind used in cooking).

■ On a hookboard: small cuphooks are put in rows on a piece of plywood and a small hole is punched in the top center of each sticker square. The squares are placed on the hooks in rows.

91

STICKERS

Types of stickers

Each teacher's sticker collection will be individual, and guidelines for making activities are necessarily general in nature. Most stickers can be used in one of these ways:

■ SORTING—assorted pictures, one kind of sticker on each square; students group like ones together.

Examples are:

Farm animals (Dennison, Eureka, Mrs. Grossman's brands)

Seashells (Hallmark brand or others)

Miniatures (Mrs. Grossman's brand or others)

Geoshapes (Mrs. Grossman's brand or others)

Fish (Mrs. Grossman's brand or others)

Butterflies (Dennison, Eureka, Mrs. Grossman's brand)

Bows (Mrs. Grossman's brand)

Pencils/Pens (Mrs. Grossman's brand)

Whimsical animals and characters (many brands)

Birds (Dennison, Eureka, Mrs. Grossman's brand)

Flowers (Eureka, Dennison, Mrs. Grossman's brand)

Smile faces (many brands)

Balloons (Mrs. Grossman's brand)

Dogs (Eureka, Dennison, Mrs. Grossman's brand)

Cats (Eureka, Dennison, Mrs. Grossman's brand)

■ LEFT/RIGHT—an equal number of stickers whose subjects are facing right or left; students sort them into two vertical or horizontal rows or groups.

Examples are:

Animals—several different species (Mrs. Grossman's brand)

Apples (Mrs. Grossman's brand)

■ ORIENTATION—one subject in different postures or positions; students sort them into two rows or groups

Examples are:

Jack-O-Lanterns (Dennison, Eureka, Mrs. Grossman's brand)

Santas (Dennison brand and others)

Frogs (Hallmark brand and others)

STICKERS

Penguins (Mrs. Grossman's brand)

■ LARGE/SMALL—equal number of subjects of each size; students sort them into two rows or groups.

Examples are:

Animals, two sizes of the same species (Mrs. Grossman's brand)

Animals, several species, two sizes of each species (Mrs. Grossman's and other brands)

■ MATCHING (PAIRING)—students pair two alike.

Examples are:

Stickers of many subjects, many brands.

■ COMPONENTS—combinations of stickers on the lead sticker squares, other squares contain components of the lead squares; students find lead squares and their components.

Examples are:

"Accessory" stickers (Mrs. Grossman's brand)—small stickers of sports equipment, tools, toys, hats, clothing, etc.; these can be used with animal stickers, as though the animal is holding or wearing the accessories, or they can be used without animal stickers. Miniatures of other kinds may also be used.

■ CATEGORIES—"families" or "go-togethers"—similar things; can be stickers left over from other activities; students sort in rows or groups. Examples are:

Stickers of many brands, leftover, and odd or mismatched stickers from your own collection. Four to six animals, toys, flowers, dishes, etc. can be grouped together because they are related; four to six related groups make one activity

STICKERS

SORTING ACTIVITIES FOR STICKERS

Sorting sticker squares by color, design, number, or size

What teachers do

Copy the grid page given in this section on the white card. For INTERMEDIATES and ADVANCED: if a set of stickers contains 4-6 different types of stickers, affix one of each type to the squares on the grid card. If a set contains stickers of only two types, affix 8-12 stickers of each type to the squares. For BEGINNERS, use the same procedure, making only 8-12 squares. Laminate the grid page and cut the squares on the lines.

What kids do

Find the sticker squares that are exactly alike and group them either vertically or horizontally, as the teacher has suggested.

What kids and teachers can talk about

Talk about the stickers—the names of the things pictured, their colors, functions, etc.

LEVEL:
Beginning-Advanced

SKILLS:
Distinguishing color and size differences, attention to detail, distinguishing subtle design differences

MATERIALS:
One set of 16 to 24 stickers for each activity for INTERMEDIATE-ADVANCED, 8 to 12 for BEGINNERS; see the examples given in TYPES OF STICKERS in the introduction to the STICKERS section

8 1/2" x 11" (21 cm x 27 cm) white card

STICKERS

LEVEL:
Beginning-Advanced

SKILLS:
Distinguishing subtle differences, awareness of directionality

MATERIALS:
One set of 16 to 24 stickers for each activity for INTERMEDIATE-ADVANCED, 8 to 12 for BEGINNERS; see the examples given in TYPES OF STICKERS in the introduction to the STICKERS section

8 1/2" x 11" (21 cm x 27 cm) white card

LEFT/RIGHT ACTIVITIES FOR STICKERS

Separating sticker squares with subjects facing left or right into two groups

What teachers do

Copy the grid page given in this section on the white card. For INTERMEDIATES and ADVANCED: affix 8-12 stickers of the subject facing in each direction to the squares on the grid card. For BEGINNERS: use 4-6 stickers of the subject facing in each direction. Laminate the grid page and cut the squares on the lines.

What kids do

Find the sticker squares that are exactly alike and group them either vertically or horizontally, as the teacher has suggested.

What kids and teachers can talk about

Talk about left and right, which hand is which, which foot is which.

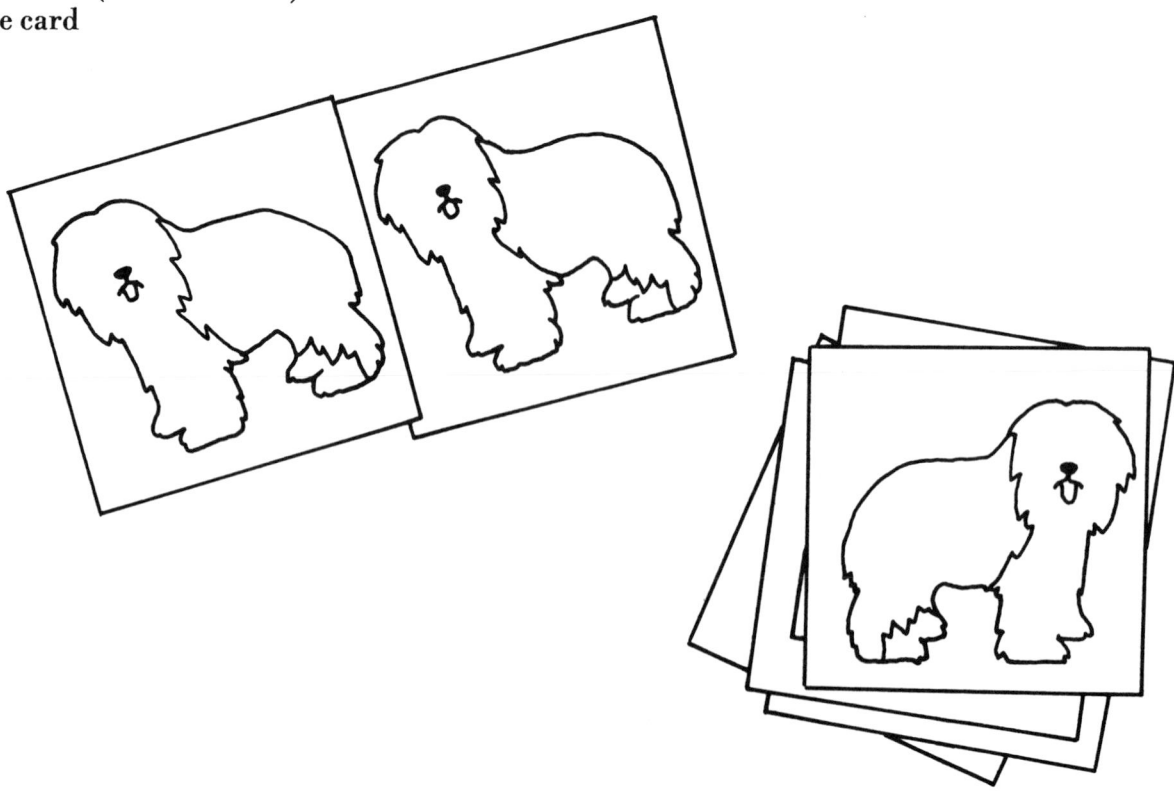

STICKERS

ORIENTATION ACTIVITIES FOR STICKERS

Grouping sticker squares by different orientations of the subject

What teachers do

Copy the grid page given in this section on the white card. For INTERMEDIATES and ADVANCED: affix 4-6 stickers of the subject in each orientation to the squares on the grid card. For BEGINNERS: use 2-4 stickers of the subject in each orientation. Laminate the grid page and cut the squares on the lines.

What kids do

Find the sticker squares that are exactly alike and group them either vertically or horizontally, as the teacher has suggested.

What kids and teachers can talk about

Talk about the stickers—what makes them different, even though the differences are slight.

LEVEL:
Beginning-Advanced

SKILLS:
Distinguishing differences in posture, position, orientation

MATERIALS:
One set of 16 to 24 stickers for each activity for INTERMEDIATE-ADVANCED, 8 to 12 for BEGINNERS; see the examples given in TYPES OF STICKERS in the introduction to the STICKERS section

8 1/2" x 11" (21 cm x 27 cm) white card

STICKERS

PAIRING ACTIVITIES FOR STICKERS

Matching two stickers that are identical

LEVEL:
Beginning-Advanced

SKILLS:
Attention to detail, distinguishing differences in feature and design

MATERIALS:
One set of 16 to 24 stickers for each activity for INTERMEDIATE-ADVANCED, 8 to 12 for BEGINNERS; see the examples given in TYPES OF STICKERS in the introduction to the STICKERS section

8 1/2" x 11" (21 cm x 27 cm) white card

What teachers do
Copy the grid page given in this section on the white card. For INTERMEDIATES and ADVANCED: affix one sticker of each type to the squares on the grid card. For BEGINNERS: make 4 to 6 pairs. Laminate the grid page and cut the squares on the lines.

What kids do
Find the sticker squares that are exactly alike and group them as the teacher has suggested.

What kids and teachers can talk about
Talk about the pictures on the stickers—what they remind you of, what they are, etc.

STICKERS

LARGE/SMALL ACTIVITIES FOR STICKERS

Separating sticker squares with subjects of two sizes into two groups

What teachers do
Copy the grid page given in this section on the white card. For INTERMEDIATES and ADVANCED: affix 8-12 stickers of the subject of each size to the squares on the grid card. For BEGINNERS: use 4-6 stickers of the subject of each size. Laminate the grid page and cut the squares on the lines.

What kids do
Find the stickers that are the same size and group them either vertically or horizontally, as the teacher has suggested.

What kids and teachers can talk about
Talk about large and small, who is large, who is small, what is large, what is small. Talk about larger and smaller, largest and smallest.

LEVEL:
Beginning-Advanced

SKILLS:
Distinguishing size differences

MATERIALS:
One set of 16 to 24 stickers for each activity for INTERMEDIATE-ADVANCED, 8 to 12 for BEGINNERS; see the examples given in TYPES OF STICKERS in the introduction to the STICKERS section

8 1/2" x 11" (21 cm x 27 cm) white card

STICKERS

LEVEL:
Intermediate-Advanced

SKILLS:
Recognizing parts of a whole

MATERIALS:
Approximately 24 "accessory" stickers (Mrs. Grossman's brand) for each activity, or a combination of accessory stickers and animal stickers; see examples given in TYPES OF STICKERS in the introduction to STICKERS section

8 1/2" x 11" (21 cm x 27 cm) white card

COMPONENTS ACTIVITIES FOR STICKERS

Identifying stickers used in combinations

What teachers do

Copy the grid page given in this section on the white card. Affix three different "accessory" or miniature stickers to a square to make a lead square; put stickers identical to the ones on the lead square on each of three suares to make the component squares. Repeat this three times, using different combinations (the same kind of sticker may be used more than once) to make four lead squares and three matching component squares for each lead square. ANIMAL ACCESSORY cards can be made the same way: use an animal sticker with three accessory stickers on each lead square; make the component squares as above. Position the accessory stickers to appear as though the animal is holding or wearing them. Laminate the grid page and cut the squares on the lines.

What kids do

Find three squares with one sticker on each square to match each of the lead squares with more than one sticker, and group them as the teacher has suggested.

What kids and teachers can do

Teachers need to explain and demonstrate these activities thoroughly. Show the importance of finding lead squares first; discuss the accessories, and help the children learn to organize the cards that go together.

STICKERS

CATEGORIES ACTIVITIES WITH STICKERS

Grouping stickers that go together or are related

What teachers do
Copy the grid page given in this section on white card. Affix one sticker to each square. Laminate the grid page and cut the squares on the lines.

What kids do
Group the stickers that belong together in the manner that the teacher has suggested.

What kids and teachers can talk about
Kids may need help, at least initially, to see how the stickers are related. Conversation about the sticker pictures will make their similarities evident.

LEVEL:
Intermediate-Advanced

SKILLS:
Distinguishing differences, making comparisons, drawing conclusions

MATERIALS:
16 to 24 stickers, 4 to 6 groups of related stickers, 4 to 6 in each group; see examples given in TYPES OF STICKERS in the introduction to the STICKERS section

8 1/2" x 11" (21 cm x 27 cm) white card

CUPS

Measuring and Counting

CUPS

What kids do

These INTERMEDIATE-to-ADVANCED activities are opportunities for measuring common substances and counting small toys and trinkets. The fine-motor control they require makes them unsuitable for BEGINNERS.

What teachers do

Collect these:

- Clear plastic disposable cups, 9-ounce (approximately 270 ml) size, which are made by the Solo Company.

- Measuring tablespoon

- Small scoop

- Approximately 1 1/2 cups (350 ml) uncooked rice.

Hint: Have extra on hand for replenishing the supply.

- Unshelled nuts: Brazils, walnuts, and pecans—a few more of each kind than the number required to fill a 9-ounce (270 ml) cup

- Counters—see individual activities

- Plastic numbers 1 to 10, or cards with written numbers

DEMONSTRATIONS

Demonstrating Cups activities for the children before they begin is vital to their success. Show the children these important points before they use them for the first time:

- For MEASURING activities, the children should be able to see the fill levels at their eye level. They may kneel and leave the cups on the table for filling, or they may lift them to eye level.

- Show the children what clean-up consists of—brushing spilled dry substances off the table into the storage containers, and drying spilled water with the sponge or towel. The workspace should be left clean for the next user, with the substances to be measured and counters in their original containers.

ALSO:

- Expect minor spilling.

- Expect kids to take care of the spilling, and be sure they know how to do so.

CUPS

■ Don't tolerate deliberate messiness—remove the activities until students can handle them. Measuring activities may never be right for some groups, or perhaps some activities will, and some won't. You know your group.

■ Check occasionally to see if the measuring substances need replenishing and count the counters to be sure the correct number are there.

MORE TIPS:

■ These simple materials require almost no construction, but you will want to give thought to the selection of counters for the COUNTING activities. Craft, variety, and toy stores abound with toys and trinkets which fascinate children, and are ready-made learning materials in disguise. Tiny vehicles and animals are two possibilities—there are countless more. Mix and mingle them. Discarded game pieces and miniatures of all kinds are also good. Other suggestions are given in the RINGS introduction for small items which would make good counters; use leftover pieces from one activity in other activities.

■ Measurements for MEASURING activities which use a measuring spoon should be as nearly level as the children can achieve—show them how this is done during your demonstration of the activity. The scoop may be heaped.

■ Experimentation (often translated as "playing" or "puttering") is expected, and indeed, encouraged, with the MEASURING substances and COUNTING counters. This serves a two-fold purpose: FIRST, handling the substances and counters familiarizes the children with their properties, enhancing the materials' effectiveness. SECOND, experimentation satisfies children's natural inclination to touch, allowing them to concentrate fully on the intended objectives of the activity afterward. You can encourage them to carefully pour or dip dry substances back and forth between the cups and storage container before starting the activity, and to play with the toys and counters on the work surface briefly before beginning the activity. Of course, they shouldn't add other things to the materials, and they shouldn't move them from the workspace.

Construction for counting activities is limited to marking numbers on some of the cups, so **What teachers do** is omitted from counting.

VARIATIONS FOR MEASURING ACTIVITIES

Suggestions for variations are given with each MEASURING activity, because it would be a shame to limit these activities to the ones described here, when variations are so enriching for the

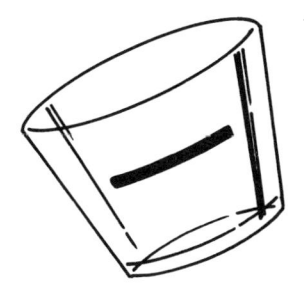

105

CUPS

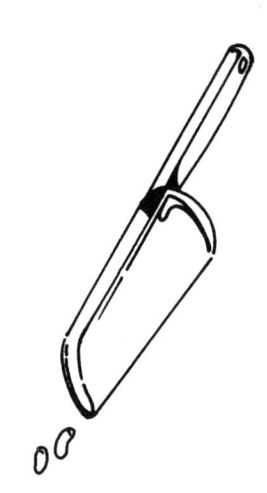

children, and so easily accomplished by the teacher. Children will enjoy, and benefit from, repeating the activities in their original form many times, but simple changes—substitutions of tools and substances—will significantly alter the learning experiences. As an example, measuring rice with a teaspoon is different from measuring with a tablespoon—not only is a different quantity involved, but the physical requirements are different, too—the managing of a small spoon requires more finite movements than managing a large one. Measuring with a small coffee measure offers yet a different challenge.

Of course, measuring rice, which is small-grained, is a different experience from measuring small dried beans, and large dried beans are different from either of these—fewer beans than rice are needed to fill a given space.

Measuring water is vastly different from measuring either rice or beans. Don't be afraid of water! In controlled single-child activities such as these, there are few problems and children will try very hard to live up to your expectation that they will handle the water activities responsibly. Suggestions are given for variations for dipping (spooning) water and for pouring it.

TIPS FOR VARIATIONS

■ A large terry towel placed under water activities will help with clean-up.

■ Teach children the importance of holding the small cup steady with one hand when they pour water from the measuring cup. They sometimes attempt to hold the measuring cup with both hands, which causes spills. They should hold the measuring cup, not the cup to be filled, in the dominant hand.

■ Add a few drops of food color to the water for dipping and pouring to make it more visible (and attractive)—this also minimizes spilling. Remind the children that water used in the activities is not for drinking.

CUPS

DOTS

Putting the number of spoonfuls of rice, beans, or water into cups, as indicated by the number of dots on the cups

What teachers do

Make one large—about 1/2" (1.25 cm)-diameter colored or black dot on cup #1, two dots on cup #2, etc. Use either assorted colors, one color, or black. Cover the dots after they have dried with a coat of clear fingernail polish if they scratch off the cups easily.

What kids do

Place the cups on the table in any order. Put the correct number of level spoonfuls of rice into the cups according to the number of dots shown on them. Do the activity as many times as they like. When finished, pour the rice back into its container, and leave the workspace clean.

What else kids can do

DOTS variations:

- Substitute small dried beans for the rice.
- Substitute colored water for the rice.
- Substitute a measuring teaspoon for the tablespoon.

SET I—MEASURING

LEVEL:
Intermediate-Advanced

SKILLS:
Counting, precision, accuracy

MATERIALS:
5 - 9-ounce (270 ml) plastic cups

Measuring tablespoon

Approximately 1 1/2 cups (350 ml) uncooked rice in a container

Permanent colored marker(s) or black permanent marker

CUPS

GRADUATED FILL LINES

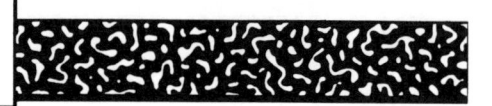

SET I—MEASURING

Spooning rice, beans, or water into cups up to graduated fill lines

What teachers do

LEVEL:
Intermediate-Advanced

Use the marker to make horizontal fill lines at five different and distinct levels on the outside of the cups, making marks about 1 1/2" (3.8 cm) long. Each cup has one mark. Cover the marks after they have dried with a coat of clear fingernail polish if they scratch off the cups easily.

SKILLS:
Accuracy, eye-hand coordination, small motor control

What kids do

Place the cups on the table in any order. Carefully spoon rice into the cups to fill them to the fill lines. Hold the cups up to their eye level to check for accuracy; make corrections if they are needed. Do the activiy as many times as they like. When finished, pour the rice back into its container, and leave the workspace clean.

MATERIALS:

5 - 9-ounce (270 ml) plastic cups

Medium-sized serving or soup spoon

Approximately 1 1/2 cups (350 ml) uncooked rice in a container

Black or colored permanent marker

What else kids can do

GRADUATED FILL LINES variations:

■ Substitute small dried beans for the rice.

■ Substitute colored water for the rice.

■ Substitute a small coffee measure for the spoon.

108

CUPS

NUMBERS

Putting the number of spoonfuls of rice, beans, or water into cups, as indicated by numbers on the cups

What teachers do

Use the marker to make numbers from 1 to 5 on the cups, one number on each cup. Make the numbers bold and easy-to-read, about 5/8" (1.5 cm) tall. When the numbers dry, coat them with clear fingernail polish if they scratch off the cups easily.

What kids do

Place the cups on the table in any order. Put the number of level spoonfuls of rice into the cups according to the numbers shown on them. Do the activity as many times as they like. When finished, pour the rice back into its container, and leave the workspace clean.

What else kids can do

NUMBERS variations:

- Substitute small dried beans for the rice.
- Substitute colored water for the rice.
- Substitute a measuring teaspoon for the tablespoon.

LEVEL:

Intermediate-Advanced

SKILLS:

Counting, small motor control

MATERIALS:

5 - 9-ounce (270 ml) plastic cups

Measuring tablespoon

Approximately 1 1/2 cups (350 ml) uncooked rice in a container

Black or colored permanent marker

CUPS

SAME FILL LINES

SET I—MEASURING

Scooping rice, beans, or water into cups to fill lines of the same level.

LEVEL:
Intermediate-Advanced

What teachers do

Use the marker to make horizontal fill lines at the same level on each of the cups, making the marks about 1 1/2" (3.8 cm) long. Cover the marks after they have dried with a coat of clear fingernail polish if they scratch off the cups easily.

SKILLS:
Accuracy and precision, small motor control

What kids do

Place the cups on the table. Carefully scoop rice into them to the fill lines. Hold the cups up to their eye level to check for accuracy; make corrections if they are needed. Do the activity as many times as they like. When finished, pour the rice back into its container, and leave the workspace clean.

MATERIALS:

5 - 9-ounce (270 ml) plastic cups

Small scoop

Approximately 1 1/2 cups (350 ml) uncooked rice in a container

Black or colored permanent marker

What else kids can do

SAME FILL LINES variations:

■ Use cups with fill lines at a different level from that on these cups.

■ Substitute small dried beans for the rice.

■ Substitute large dried beans, such as limas, for the rice.

■ Omit the scoop and substitute colored water in a 2-cup plastic measuring cup for the rice. Pour into cups to the fill lines.

110

CUPS

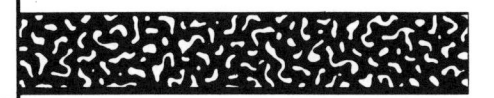

HOW MANY NUTS TO FILL?

Counting the number of different-sized nuts required to fill a cup

What kids do

Count the walnuts as they put them in one of the cups, and put that number or numbered card beside the filled cup. (They may heap the cups as much as they like.) Do the same thing with the Brazil nuts and pecans. They may use the activity as long as they like. When they are finished, put the nuts and numbers back in their containers, and clean the workspace.

What kids and teachers can do

Talk about the names of the nuts; crack some open and see the insides; taste them if they want.

SET II—COUNTING

LEVEL:
Intermediate-Advanced

SKILLS:
Counting

MATERIALS:
3 cups

Unshelled walnuts, Brazils, and pecans, more than enough of each to fill 1 cup, in separate containers

Numbers or numbered cards from 1 to 10 (see introduction to this section) in a container

CUPS

1-10 (TOYS)

SET II—COUNTING

Putting little toys in the cups according to the numbers shown on the cups

LEVEL:
Intermediate-Advanced

What kids do

Place the cups in order. Put the one toy that is like none of the others in the cup marked one, the two toys that are alike in the cup marked two, and so on until all the toys are used. Use the activity for as long as they like. Put the toys back in their container when finished.

SKILLS:
Counting

What else kids can do

Put the toys in rows on the table in order from one to ten, putting the toy that is like no other first, the two toys that are different from all the rest next, and so on.

MATERIALS:

10 cups marked with permanent marker from 1 to 10

55 very small toys and/or trinkets in a container—1 of a kind, 2 of another, 3 of another, etc.—10 different kinds

CUPS

1-10 (FRINGE BALLS)

Putting the numbers of fringe balls in the cups as shown on the cups

What kids do

Place the cups in order. Put one fringe ball in the cup marked one, two in the cup marked two, and so on until all the fringe balls are used. Use the activity for as long as they like. Put the fringe balls back in their container when they are finished.

What else kids can do

Sort the balls by color; sort them by size if more than one size are used. See how many cups are needed to hold all of the balls.

SETS

Putting the same number of golf tees in each cup

NOTE: Before allowing the children to use them, blunt the ends of the golf tees by rubbing them over sand paper or concrete.

What kids do

Place the cups on the table. Put the correct number of golf tees in each cup as is shown on the cup. They will use all the golf tees. Use the activity as long as they like. Put the golf tees back in their container when they are finished.

What else kids can do

Sort the golf tees by color on the table by putting them in groups or rows. Stand them on their large ends on the table in one long row or in one row for each color.

SET II—COUNTING

LEVEL:
Intermediate-Advanced

SKILLS:
Counting

MATERIALS:

10 cups marked from 1 to 10

55 medium-to-large (or mixed sizes) assorted-color fringe balls (pompoms, available at fabric stores) in a container

SET II—COUNTING

LEVEL:
Intermediate-Advanced

SKILLS:
Counting

MATERIALS:

5 cups marked with the same number (a number appropriate for your class)

Colored golf tees, five times the number used on the cups, in a container

CUPS

SET II—COUNTING

LEVEL:
Intermediate-Advanced

SKILLS:
Counting

MATERIALS:
Large colored plastic paper clips, in 5 colors, 1 color per cup, exactly the number needed for the activity

5 or more cups containing varied numbers of clips, 1 color of clip per cup

Numbers or numbered cards from 1 to 10 (see introduction to this section)

LEVEL:
Advanced

SKILLS:
Counting

MATERIALS:
5 or more cups marked with two-digit numbers appropriate for your group

Poker chips or buttons, exactly the number needed for the activity, in a container

HOW MANY CLIPS?

Counting the number of clips in each cup; placing that number in front of the cup

What kids do

Place the cups in any order on the table. Count the clips in the first cup. Find the number or card and place it in front of the cup. Do the same thing with the rest of the cups. Use the activity for as long as they like.

What else kids can do

Sort the clips by color in groups or rows on the table. Put the number beside each group or row which tells how many are in the group or row.

ADVANCED NUMBERS (TWO-DIGIT)

An advanced activity in which chips or buttons are put in cups according to two-digit numbers on the cups

What kids do

Place the cups on the table in any order. Carefully count the number of chips or buttons to match the number written on the first cup and put them in the cup. Do the same with all the cups. Use the activity for as long as they like.

What else kids can do

Sort the chips or buttons in groups or rows on the table. If the activity has chips, try stacking them in one stack or several.

CUPS

MONEY

An advanced activity in which play coins are put in cups according to the prices on the cups

What kids do
Place the cups on the table in any order. Put the coins in each cup to match the numbers written on them.

What else kids can do
Sort the coins by groups or rows on the table. Count the number of coins in each group or row to see which has the most, which has the least.

SET II—COUNTING

LEVEL:
Advanced

SKILLS:
Counting

MATERIALS:
8 cups with prices appropriate for your class written on them

Play coins to match the prices on the cups

POCKETS

Matching

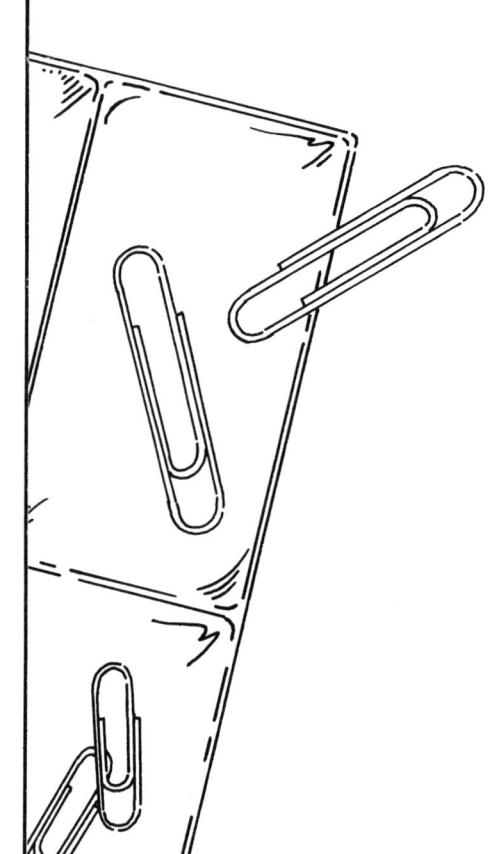

POCKETS

What kids do

Duplicate the contents of clear plastic "pockets," placing items identical in color, number, size, or other characteristics beside the pockets.

What teachers do

Seal small, inexpensive or discarded items in clear plastic business card pockets with tape; provide an identical set of items for matching. Trim away the strip on the plastic pages containing binder holes.

What you need

■ Clear plastic business card file pages (Samsill is a good brand) from a business supply store.

■ Clear plastic tape.

■ Items to fill the pockets—as suggested in each activity; hardware and office supply items, small discards, toys, and sewing notions make good pocket fillers.

These materials can be purchased inexpensively and most require no preparation prior to inserting them in the pockets, so these activities go together very quickly. You will want to have a few extra of most items for replacement of those lost.

To use POCKETS, the children place matching items beside the filled pockets. The pocket page may be turned vertically or horizontally.

In a few activities such as STAMPS, the set of matching items is fragile and should be protected to prevent loss. These activities' instructions specify laminating the matching items or sealing them in pockets and cutting them apart. However, items for matching should be enclosed only when necessary, because the tactile experience is diminished when the children can't actually hold the objects in their hands.

Pocket pages and the matching items can be stored together in large clear plastic self-closing bags (freezer weight) as I suggested in the introduction to the book.

POCKETS

COINS

Matching the number and denomination of play coins to those enclosed in pockets

What teachers do
Seal 1 to 6 coins in the pockets, using combinations appropriate for your students, using fewer for BEGINNERS, more for INTERMEDIATE and ADVANCED. Be sure the duplicating set is identical to the sealed one.

What kids do
Look at the coins in the pockets carefully and place coins that match them beside the pockets. They may also turn the page over and match the coins again, as the coins will look different on the reverse side.

What kids and teachers can talk about
Talk about the coins—their names, value, etc. Can these coins be spent? Look at the same denominations of real coins—do they look alike or different? Why?

LEVEL:
Beginning-Advanced

SKILLS:
Recognizing subtle distinctions, money awareness

MATERIALS:
2 identical sets of realistic play coins, plastic or metal—enough for 10 pockets, 1 to 6 coins per pocket

POCKETS

SEWING TRIMS

Matching sewing trims to the ones enclosed in pockets

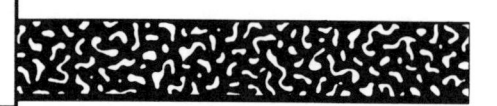

LEVEL:
Beginning-Advanced

SKILLS:
Distinguishing color and pattern differences

MATERIALS:
6" (15 cm) lengths of sewing trims—rick-rack, braid, etc.—in differing colors, sizes and patterns—10 different kinds

What teachers do
Cut the trims in two pieces, 2" (5 cm) and 4" (10 cm) long. Seal the short pieces in the pockets. The long pieces are for matching. If any of the ends of the trims tend to fray, dip the ends 1/4" (6 mm) in white glue.

What kids do
Match the trims to the ones in the pockets by placing them beside the pockets.

What kids and teachers can talk about
Talk about the names of some of these trims, and why people like them on clothes.

POCKETS

RIBBONS

Matching strips of ribbon to those enclosed in pockets

What teachers do

Cut the ribbons in two pieces, 2" (5 cm) and 4" (10 cm) long. Seal the short pieces in the pockets. The long pieces are for duplicating. If any of the ends of the ribbons tend to fray, dip the ends 1/4" (6 mm) in white glue.

What kids do

Match the ribbons to the ones in the pockets by placing them beside the pockets.

What kids and teachers can talk about

How are ribbons used? Are some people in the room wearing ribbons on their clothes or in their hair? Sort the ribbons by color or width.

LEVEL:
Beginning-Advanced

SKILLS:
Making width, color, and pattern comparisons

MATERIALS:
6" (15 cm) lengths of ribbons in varying colors, widths, patterns—10 different kinds

COUNTERS

Matching the number and color of plastic counting discs with those in pockets

What teachers do

Insert 1-6 counters in each pocket and seal with tape. Make an identical set for matching.

What kids do

Place the same number and colors of counters that are in the pockets beside the pockets.

What kids and teachers can do

Count the counters that are in the pockets and those in the matching set. Do both sets have the same number of counters? Sort the counters by color.

LEVEL:
Beginning-Advanced

SKILLS:
Counting, color recognition

MATERIALS:
2 identical sets of multi-colored plastic counting discs (available from school supply stores or catalogs)—enough for 10 pockets

POCKETS

WASHERS

Matching same sized metal washers to those in pockets

LEVEL:
Beginning-Advanced

SKILLS:
Recognizing size distinction, counting

MATERIALS:
2 identical sets of metal washers (available from hardware stores) in assorted sizes—enough for 10 pockets, with 1-6 per pocket

What teachers do
Seal 1 set of washers in the pockets, mixing sizes. Make an identical set to be used for matching.

What kids do
Place the same number and size washers beside those which are in each pocket.

What else kids can do
Sort the washers by size; stack them two ways: stacks of each size and stacks of graduated sizes.

MAGNETS

Matching small novelty magnets to like magnets enclosed in pockets

LEVEL:
Beginning-Advanced

SKILLS:
Recognizing similarities and differences

MATERIALS:
2 identical sets of small novelty magnets—enough for one or more magnets in each of 10 pockets

What teachers do
Seal one or more magnets in the pockets. Make an identical set for matching.

What kids do
Look at the magnets in the pockets carefully. Put magnets that look exactly like the ones in the pockets beside the pockets.

What kids and teachers can do
Talk about the names of things depicted by the magnets. Experiment with the magnets—what will they stick to besides other magnets?

POCKETS

RINGS

Matching rings identical in color, size, and material with those in pockets

What teachers do
Seal 1-6 rings in each pocket, mixing types, sizes, and colors. Make an identical set for matching.

What kids do
Look carefully at the rings in each pocket. Put the same number and kind of rings beside the pockets.

What else kids can do
Sort the rings by type.

LEVEL:
Beginning-Advanced

SKILLS:
Recognizing size differences and color distinction

MATERIALS:
2 identical sets of plastic and metal rings of different colors and sizes (find them in fabric and hardware stores—as curtain rings and hose washers)—enough for 10 pockets

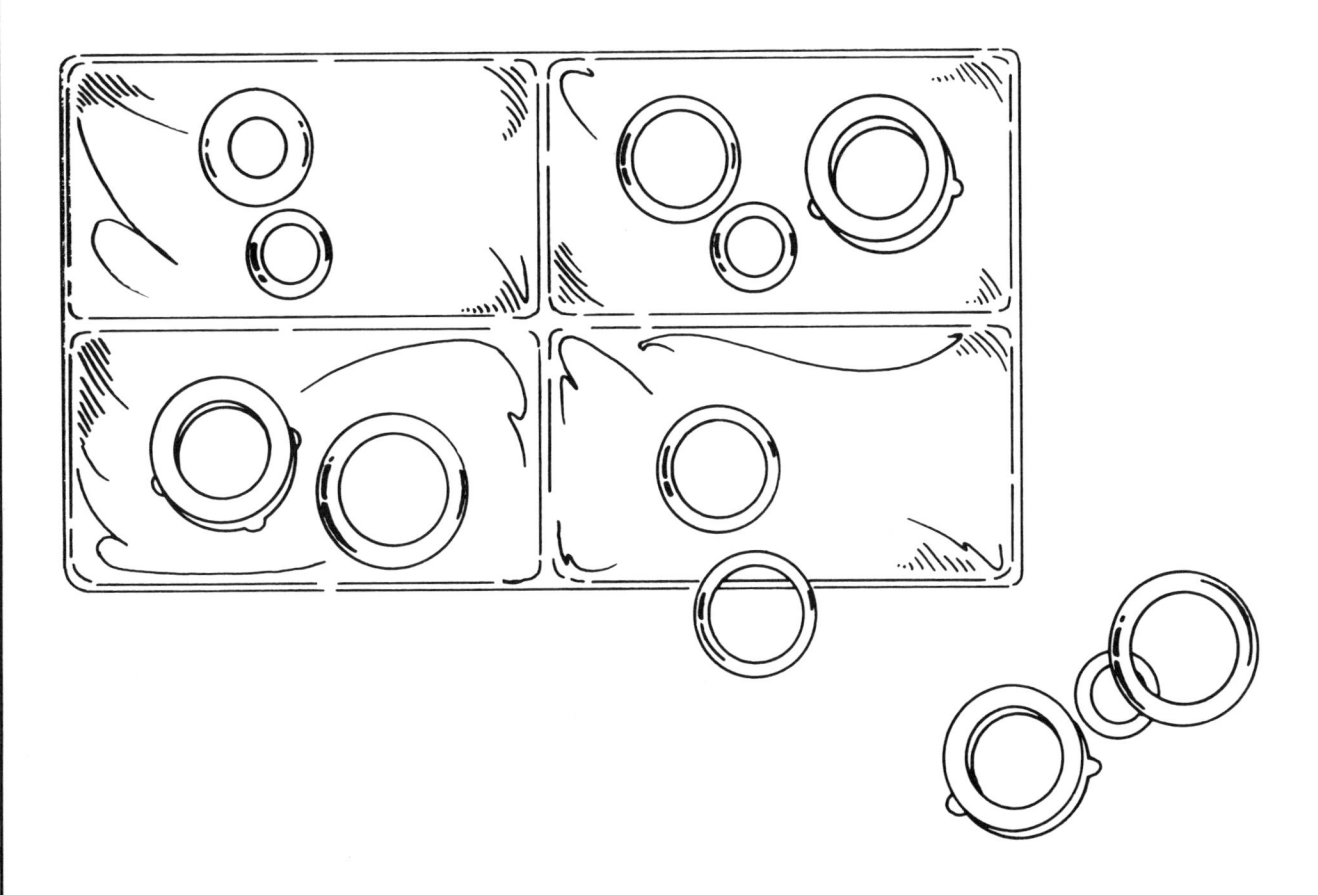

POCKETS

CLIPS (PLASTIC)

Matching the number and color of plastic paper clips with those in pockets

LEVEL:
Beginning-Advanced

SKILLS:
Counting, recognizing color distinction

MATERIALS:
2 identical sets of large plastic paper clips of one type (available in office supply stores) in assorted colors—enough for 10 pockets

What teachers do
Seal 1-6 clips in each pocket. Make a set identical in number and color to be used for matching.

What kids do
Look at the clips in the pockets. Put the same number and color clips beside each pocket.

What else kids can do
Sort the clips by color.

CLIPS (ASSORTED)

Matching paper clips of differing shapes, colors, and materials with those in pockets

LEVEL:
Beginning-Advanced

SKILLS:
Counting, recognizing color distinction

MATERIALS:
2 identical sets of assorted paper clips, metal and plastic, in different shapes and sizes (available in office supply stores)--enough for 10 pockets

What teachers do
The more these clips differ, the more challenging the activity. Put one or more clips in each pocket and seal with tape. Make an identical set for matching.

What kids do
Look at the pockets carefully. Match the clips in the pockets by placing those that look exactly like them beside each pocket.

What else kids can do
Sort the clips several ways: by shape, by color, by material.

POCKETS

ERASERS

Matching small novelty erasers to like erasers in pockets

What teachers do

Seal one or more erasers in the pockets, in differing combinations. Make an identical set for matching.

What kids do

Look at the erasers carefully and place erasers that match the ones in each pocket beside that pocket.

What else kids can do

Sort the erasers by shape.

LEVEL:
Beginning-Advanced

SKILLS:
Developing shape distinction

MATERIALS:
2 identical sets of small novelty erasers (school supplies)—enough for one or more in each of 10 pockets

POCKETS

POKER CHIPS

Matching the number and color of poker chips to those enclosed in pockets

LEVEL:
Beginning-Advanced

SKILLS:
Counting, color matching

MATERIALS:
2 identical sets of multi-colored poker chips—enough for 1 to 4 chips in each of 10 pockets

What teachers do
Insert one or more chips in each pocket, mixing colors, and seal. Make an identical set for matching.

What kids do
Look at the pocket page carefully. Place the same number and color of chips that are in the pockets beside the pockets.

What else kids can do
Sort the chips by color; stack them in towers.

POCKETS

FELT SHAPES

Matching felt shapes to like shapes enclosed in pockets

What teachers do

Mark and cut 2" (5 cm) squares from both colors of felt. Stack the squares of one color with those of the second color and cut freehand shapes from the squares without patterns, cutting two shapes, one of each color, at the same time. Seal one set in the pockets; the other set is for matching.

What kids do

Match the felt shapes to those in the pockets.

What else kids can do

Place the felt shapes on top of the ones in the pockets, matching them carefully.

LEVEL:
Beginning-Advanced

SKILLS:
Shape identification

MATERIALS:
Felt scraps or two 9" x 12" (22 cm x 30 cm) felt rectangles in two colors—available from a fabric store

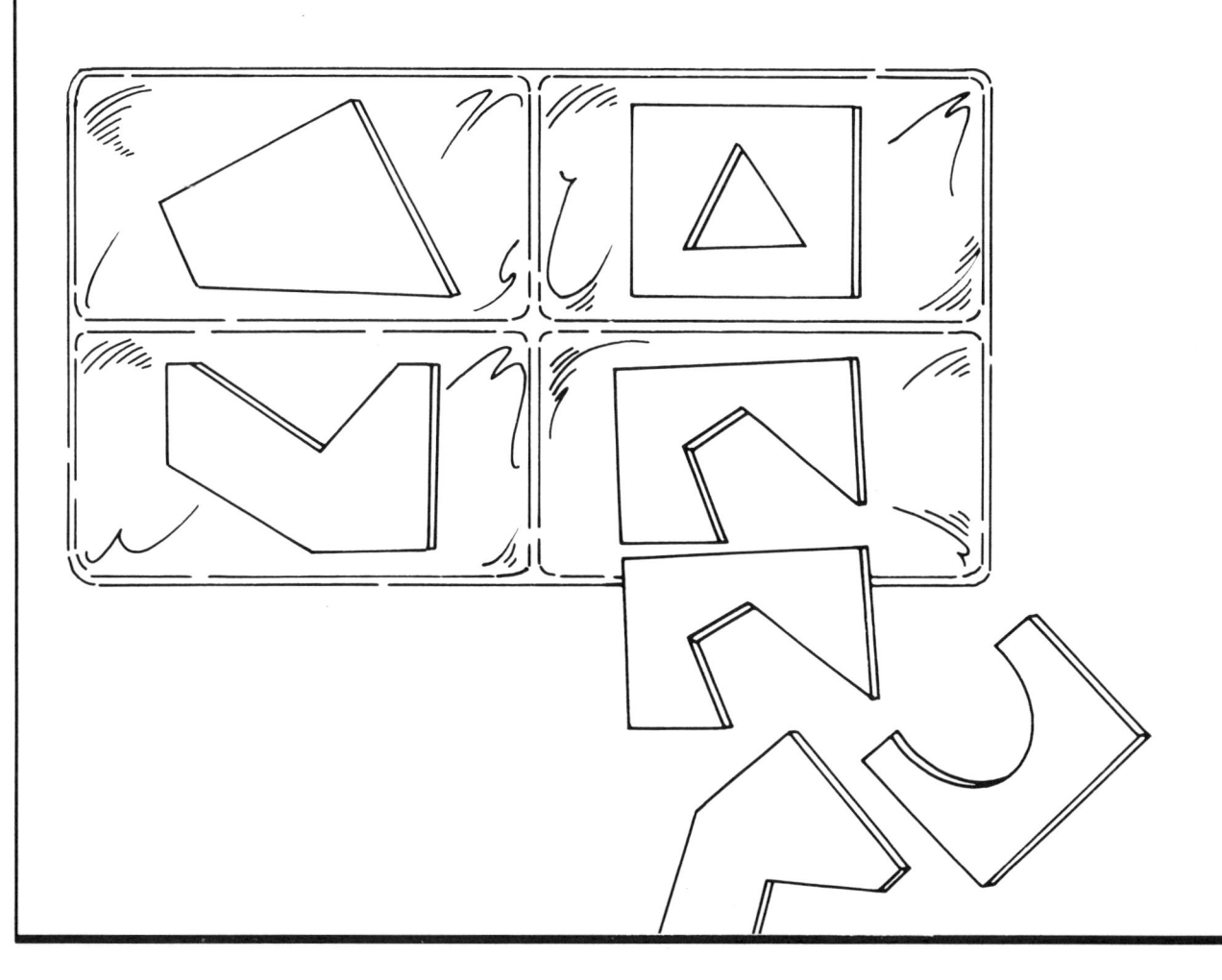

POCKETS

PAPER MONEY

Matching the denomination of play paper money to that enclosed in pockets

LEVEL:
Intermediate-Advanced

SKILLS:
Recognizing subtle distinctions, money awareness

MATERIALS:
2 identical sets of 10 play paper money bills—more than one of each denomination may be used

What teachers do
Fold 1 set of the money into fourths, making sure the denomination shows, and seal them individually in the pockets with tape. You can use more than one of each denomination. Do not fold the money in the matching set.

What kids do
Match the money to the money in the pockets by putting it beside the pockets.

What kids and teachers can talk about
Talk about this money. Can it be spent? Look at real paper money. Does the play money look real? Why do you think it was not made to look exactly like real money?

PEGS

Matching the number and color of wooden or plastic pegs with those in pockets.

LEVEL:
Intermediate-Advanced

SKILLS:
Recognizing numbers and colors

MATERIALS:
2 identical sets of colored wooden or plastic pegs (school supply stores or catalogs)—enough for 10 pockets, 1 to 6 pegs per pocket

What teachers do
Insert 1-6 pegs in each pocket and seal with tape. Make a set which is identical in number and color for matching.

What kids do
Count the pegs in each pocket and place the same number and colors from their matching set of pegs beside the ones in the pockets.

What else kids can do
Sort the pegs of the matching set by color; count the pegs of each set.

POCKETS

BUTTONS

Matching buttons to those enclosed in pockets

What teachers do

Seal one set of buttons in the pockets in combinations suitable for your class, using three to five buttons in each pocket, mixing sizes, shapes, and colors. Be sure the matching set is identical to the sealed one.

What kids do

Place the loose buttons beside those pockets which they match exactly.

What else kids can do

Sort the matching set of buttons by size, without regard to color. Sort them by color, without regard to size. Find other ways to sort them; for example, by the number of holes, whether they are made of metal, wood, or other material.

LEVEL:
Intermediate-Advanced

SKILLS:
Recognition of shape, color, and size, number distinction

MATERIALS:
2 identical sets of buttons in differing sizes, shapes, and colors—enough for 10 pockets, using 3-5 per pocket

LACE

Matching strips of lace to the ones enclosed in pockets

What teachers do

Cut the lace strips in two pieces, 2" (5 cm) and 4" (10 cm) long. Seal the short pieces in the pockets. The long pieces are for matching.

What kids do

Look at the lace pieces carefully—some will look almost, but not quite, alike. Put the ones that match the ones in the pocket, beside, beneath, or on top of the pockets.

What kids and teachers can do

Talk about lace and where you have seen lace before.

LEVEL:
Intermediate-Advanced

SKILLS:
Pattern recognition

MATERIALS:
6" (15 cm) lengths of lace, colored or white, in various patterns and widths—10 different kinds

POCKETS

TEXTURES

Matching textured material samples to like samples in pockets

LEVEL:
Intermediate—Advanced

SKILLS:
Distinguishing texture differences

MATERIALS:
2" (5 cm) squares of various materials—sandpaper, felt, burlap, cloth, cardboard, paper, hardware cloth (screening), plastic, metal, wood, etc.—2 matching sets, 10 different materials

What teachers do
Seal half the texture squares in the pockets.

What kids do
Place the material squares beside the pockets they match.

What kids and teachers can talk about
Talk about these materials, what they are used for and where you have seen ones like them before.

POCKETS

FABRIC TEXTURES

Matching samples of textured fabrics to those in pockets

What teachers do

Apply iron-on interfacing to limp fabrics of the matching set if desired and dip edges of any which tend to fray in white glue. Seal the other set in the pockets.

What kids do

Match the pieces of material to the ones in the pockets by placing them beside the pockets.

What kids and teachers can talk about

Talk about these materials and where you may have seen some like them before.

LEVEL:
Intermediate-Advanced

SKILLS:
Distinguishing texture differences tactually and visually

MATERIALS:
2" (5 cm) squares of various fabrics in one color (to avoid matching by color)—corduroy, velvet, satin, synthetic fur, synthetic leather, burlap, broadcloth, felt, nylon, netting, etc.—2 identical sets—10 different kinds Iron-on interfacing, optional

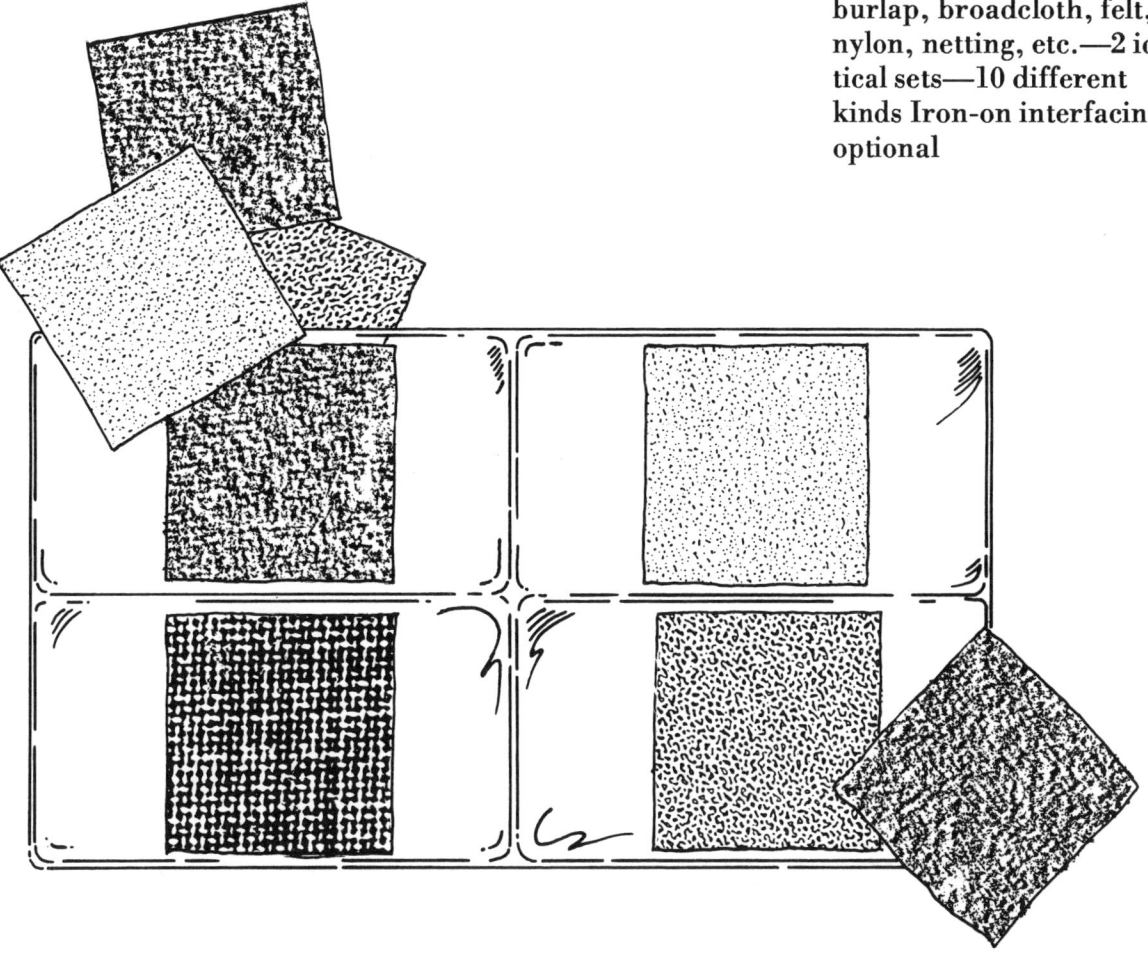

POCKETS

BEANS

Matching different varieties of dried beans with those in pockets

SAFETY NOTE: This activity is not safe for children who might put the beans in their mouths.

LEVEL:
Intermediate-Advanced

SKILLS:
Counting, number recognition

MATERIALS:
2 identical sets of large dried beans such as limas, kidney beans, pink, or pinto beans

What teachers do

Insert 1-6 beans, combining different types, in each pocket and seal with tape. Make sure to have the same number and variety for the matching set.

What kids do

Look at the beans in each pocket and put the same number of each kind of bean beside the ones in the pockets.

What kids and teachers can talk about

Talk about how these beans are prepared as food, and the changes that happen when they are cooked.

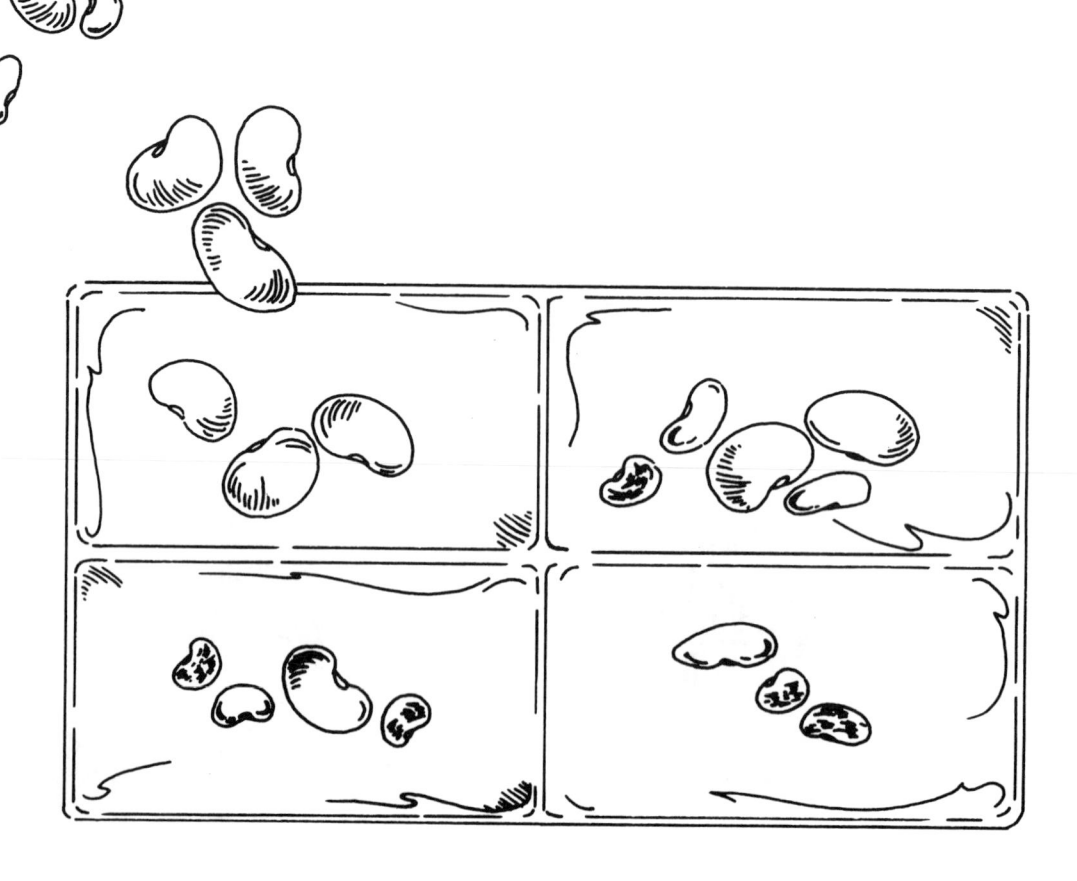

POCKETS

RUBBER BANDS

Matching rubber bands which are alike in size or color to those in pockets

What teachers do

Make two or three different sets of these if you like; one set of same-size, assorted-color bands, a second set of different-sized and different-colored bands. Or make only one set using either combination. Seal the bands in the pockets and make an identical matching set.

What kids do

Put rubber bands that look exactly like the ones in the pockets beside the pockets.

What else kids can do

Sort the rubber bands two ways: by size, by color.

LEVEL:
Intermediate-Advanced

SKILLS:
Recognizing sizes and colors

MATERIALS:
2 identical sets of rubber bands that differ either in color, size, or both—enough for 10 pockets, 1 to 4 per pocket

FLAGS

Matching tiny flags of different kinds to those enclosed in pockets

What teachers do

Insert one flag in each pocket, breaking the ends off the toothpicks if necessary. To protect the duplicating set, laminate them with clear plastic adhesive or seal them inside individual pockets—cut apart carefully on the seams.

What kids do

Look at the flags in the pockets carefully, and place flags that look like them beside each pocket.

What kids and teachers can do

Talk about these flags and, perhaps, look at pictures of flags in books.

LEVEL:
Intermediate-Advanced

SKILLS:
Attention to detail

MATERIALS:
2 identical sets of tiny flags on toothpicks available from party and crafts stores, 10 different kinds

POCKETS

CLIPS (METAL)

Matching the number and size of metal paper clips to those in pockets

LEVEL:
Intermediate-Advanced

SKILLS:
Distinguishing size differences

MATERIALS:
2 identical sets of 2 or more sizes of metal paper clips (not colored)—enough for 10 pockets

What teachers do
Seal 1-6 clips in each pocket, mixing sizes. Make an identical set for matching.

What kids do
Look at the clips in the pockets. Put the same number and size of clips beside each pocket.

What else kids can do
Sort the clips by size. Count the clips of each size.

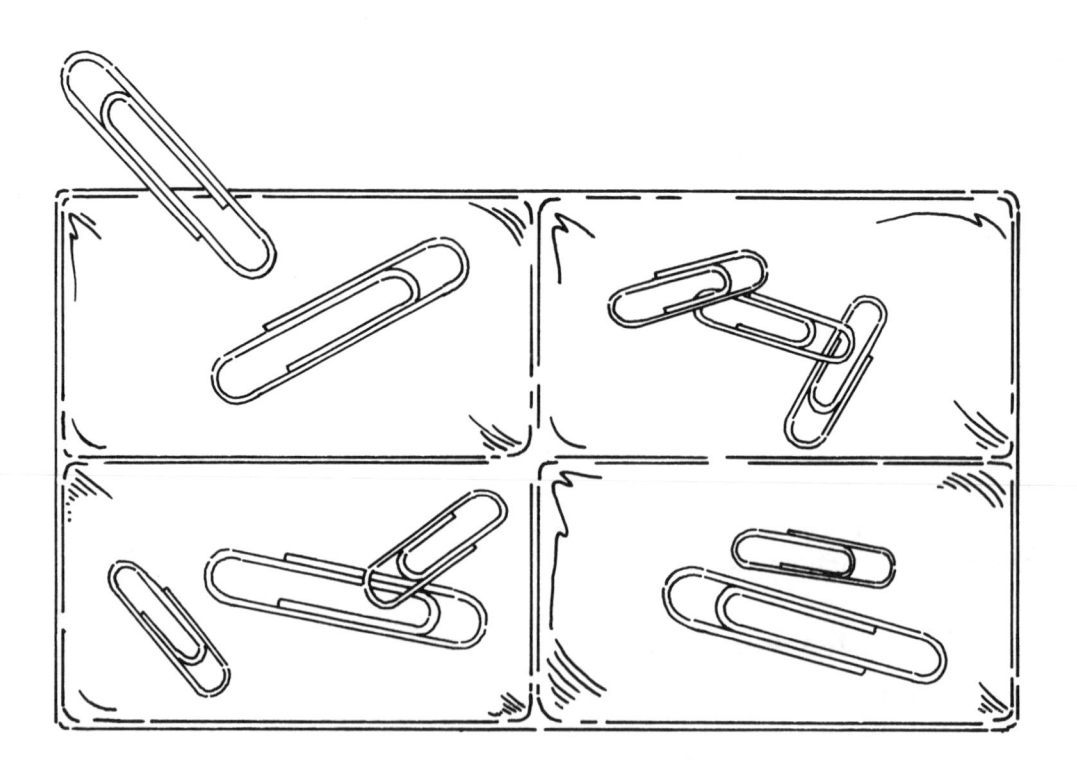

134

POCKETS

FLOWERS/LEAVES

Matching artificial flowers and/or leaves with like ones in pockets

What teachers do

Seal combinations of the flowers and/or leaves in the pockets and make an identical set for matching.

What kids do

Place flowers and leaves that exactly match the ones in the pocket beside each pocket.

What else kids can do

Sort the flowers and leaves by placing like ones together.

LEVEL:
Intermediate-Advanced

SKILLS:
Recognizing differences

MATERIALS:
2 identical sets of very small artificial flower blossoms and/or leaves of different kinds (from crafts and variety stores)—enough for 10 pockets

COLOR SHADES

Matching squares of light and dark shades of paper or felt

What teachers do

Laminate the matching set of samples if they are paper. Seal either the light or dark set in the pockets.

What kids do

Match the light and dark colors by placing the squares beside those in the pockets.

What kids and teachers can talk about

Talk about how dark colors can be made light by adding white to them.

LEVEL:
Intermediate-Advanced

SKILLS:
Light/dark distinction

MATERIALS:
2 sets of 2" squares of colored paper or felt—one set light colors, one set dark colors. For example: blue/light blue, purple/lavender, gold/yellow, brown/tan, black/charcoal, turquoise/aqua, red-orange/orange, dark green/light green, light grey/white, red/pink

POCKETS

STAMPS

Matching postage stamps of various designs to those in pockets

LEVEL:
Intermediate-Advanced

SKILLS:
Developing visual perception

MATERIALS:
2 identical sets of 10 different postage stamps

What teachers do
Seal one set of stamps in the pockets and use one set for matching. Laminate the matching set for protection, leaving a wide border of film around the edges. An alternative to laminating is to seal them with tape inside pockets and cut the sections apart on the seams.

What kids do
Match the stamps to the ones in the pockets by placing them beside each pocket.

What kids and teachers can talk about
Kids may have noticed their parents putting stamps on letters—talk about why the stamps are necessary to send mail.

CARDS

Matching small children's playing cards to those in pockets

LEVEL:
Intermediate-Advanced

SKILLS:
Developing visual perception

MATERIALS:
2 identical sets of 10 different cards from children's games such as "Old Maid" (small size)

What teachers do
Seal one set of cards in the pockets and use one set for matching. Laminating the matching cards will increase their life.

What kids do
Place the cards next to the identical cards in the pockets.

What kids and teachers can do
Talk about the games played games with cards like these. Play those games.

POCKETS

SPICES

Matching packets of different spices with spices in pockets

What teachers do

Cut apart the sections of one clear plastic business card file page on the seams. Put approximately one teaspoonful of each spice in the cut-apart sections, and one in each pocket of an intact business card file page. Seal all sections securely with tape.

What kids do

Place the packets of spices beside the pockets which contain the same spice.

What kids and teachers can talk about

Talk about the names of these spices, and their aromas, if some can be smelled through the plastic.

LEVEL:
Intermediate-Advanced

SKILLS:
Visual discrimination, critical judgment

MATERIALS:
Approximately 2 teaspoonfuls of each of 10 different spices and/or dried herbs such as cinnamon, nutmeg, cloves (whole or powdered), ginger, dry mustard, oregano, basil, paprika, parsley, celery seeds, poppy seeds, anise seeds, caraway seeds, dillweed—don't use pepper of any kind

POCKETS

LEVEL:
Intermediate-Advanced

SKILLS:
Counting, attention to detail

MATERIALS:
Large spangles (sequins) and/or small-to-medium beads (found in handicraft and fabric stores)

SPANGLES/BEADS

Matching spangles and/or beads identical in number, color, and design to those enclosed in pockets

What teachers do

You can make one activity using spangles and one using beads, or you can combine them in one activity. Because of the small size of beads and spangles, the matching set needs to be enclosed to prevent loss. After sealing one or more beads and/or spangles in the pockets, seal an identical set in pockets and cut the sections apart carefully on the seams.

What kids do

Look carefully at the spangles and beads in the pockets. Find the separate pockets which have the same number and color of beads and/or spangles and place them beside the ones in the pockets.

What kids and teachers can talk about

Kids may have seen spangles or sequins used on clothing; most have seen beads as jewelry or clothing; talk about their experiences.

POCKETS

DOMINOES

Matching dominoes with paper copies of the same dominoes in pockets

What teachers do

Use markers to make paper "dominoes" to match the real ones; seal the paper set in the pockets. If you have two sets of dominoes, use real dominoes in the pockets instead of paper copies.

What kids do

Place the dominoes beside the ones in the pockets which they match. Look carefully at the dots and count them if necessary.

What else kids can do

See what else dominoes will do—stack them, topple them, or connect by matching dots.

LEVEL:
Advanced-possibly Intermediate

SKILLS:
Counting, attention to detail

MATERIALS:
10 dominoes, each different

GADGETS

Tinkering

GADGETS

What kids do

Use kitchen tools and utensils with baker's clay, sand, and water. They may make objects with the clay to keep, or simply enjoy it tactually as they do playdough—kneading, rolling, and modeling it. You may be pleasantly surprised to find that when these activities are used as single-child activities, messiness is not a problem. These simple physical activities emphasize tactual expression and enjoyment—areas too often overlooked as valid learning experiences. They can be used when other activities are being used, but should never be used as rewards—they are of themselves important for growth, even though kids may think they are just for fun. Isn't it fortunate that "fun" can also be "learning"?

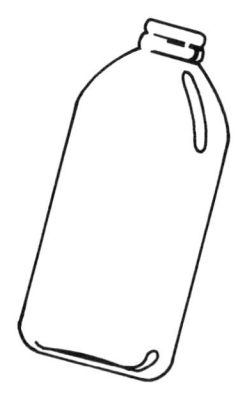

What teachers do

Supply kids with baker's clay, (recipe follows) and sand and water in containers the right size for individual use. Collect simple tools to be used with them.

GADGETS AND BAKER'S CLAY

What kids do

Use everyday tools with baker's clay. They may use the clay for experimentation only, or make objects which can be allowed to dry and harden. The white baker's clay takes color from water-based markers beautifully when it is dry, but it's important to be aware that each clay session need not end with an object to keep. The experience itself is perfectly valid, and if children feel satisfied after a period of experimentation, then the activity should be considered complete. If they do make objects to harden, they need to be allowed to dry (usually a day or two, depending on weather and climate conditions) before being decorated with markers, and, in the case of pendants and beads, stringing on yarn. They may then be taken home in plastic sandwich bags—the bags are needed for protection; these unfired objects are naturally fragile, and the children may be understandably upset if they are broken very soon after being finished. Clay pieces can be baked slowly in a conventional oven or microwave to speed the drying process if necessary. Emphasize the need to keep items fairly small and/or thin to facilitate drying. Turning the objects over after the first day's drying period will help. It's important to remember that these clay activities can be repeated many times without a loss of interest—children will enjoy doing them again and again. They can take clay pieces home, or if they want, add them to an on-going class mosaic. Just glue them close together on a piece of plywood, hardboard (Masonite), or heavy cardboard using white household glue (not school glue) generously. Lay the board flat while pieces are drying; when dry, it can be displayed upright.

Several suggestions are given for what the children may make with the clay, but of course, their ideas are even better and they should be encouraged to follow their own creative leads. Some may need help in seeing possibilities, especially in the beginning. For this reason, you will want to have several "practice sessions" using the clay to acquaint the children with the possibilities it offers. Suggestions for these follow. With the two bead-making activities, ROUND BEADS and FLAT BEADS, use a copier to copy the drawings given with the activities' directions, laminate them, and put them with the BEAD activities when they are used.

All GADGETS AND BAKER'S CLAY activities are for ADVANCED students—those 5 years and older. Younger children

GADGETS

will enjoy kneading, manipulating, and modeling baker's clay as they would playdough, but they are not ready for the activities suggested here. GADGETS AND SAND AND WATER may be used by BEGINNERS, INTERMEDIATES and ADVANCED.

What teachers do

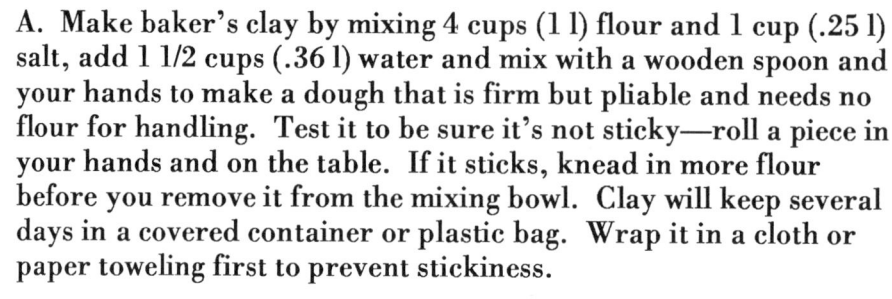

A. Make baker's clay by mixing 4 cups (1 l) flour and 1 cup (.25 l) salt, add 1 1/2 cups (.36 l) water and mix with a wooden spoon and your hands to make a dough that is firm but pliable and needs no flour for handling. Test it to be sure it's not sticky—roll a piece in your hands and on the table. If it sticks, knead in more flour before you remove it from the mixing bowl. Clay will keep several days in a covered container or plastic bag. Wrap it in a cloth or paper toweling first to prevent stickiness.

B. Collect these:

■ A rolling pin of some kind—either an adult one, a child's toy one, or an 8" to 10" (20 cm to 25 cm) length of broom handle, or fat wooden dowel (you will need more than one roller during practice sessions with the children as described; one roller is adequate for the activity when used individually).

■ A dull knife, preferably a metal table knife, and a pastry cutting wheel

■ A wide metal spatula for lifting the rolled clay pieces onto drying trays

■ Objects for stamping designs—empty thread spools of different kinds and sizes, a heavyweight plastic fork, a small spoon, a large metal nut, a washer, a bolt, a large paper clip, metal shank buttons with raised designs, a wooden or plastic peg, and anything else that will make an interesting pattern. For variety, rotate 3 or 4 of these at a time with the activities.

■ Plastic drinking straws for making holes in pendants and beads

■ Cutters—round ones in 2 sizes: A small one the size of a quarter or so, such as a plastic medicine bottle, and a larger one about 2" (5 cm) in diameter, such as a cap from an aerosol spray can. Make a hole in the bottom of each for air to escape.

■ Several drying trays—small plastic serving trays, styrofoam meat trays, or baking sheets for transporting and drying clay pieces

■ Plastic sandwich bags for taking hardened clay pieces home

■ Yarn lengths approximately 24" (60 cm) long for stringing beads or pendants

GADGETS

■ Water-based colored markers to be used for decorating dried clay pieces

■ Name cards—cards with the children's first names (and last-name initials in case of duplicate first names). When clay pieces are drying, the children put their name cards with clay pieces for identification. They also use the name cards as a guide when making their names with clay in the NAMES activity.

■ Letter and number cards (rotate 3-5 of these with the activities). Make small cards, each containing one upper or lower case letter or one single digit number. These are used as guides with the activities for making clay letters and numbers.

■ Laminated cards—use a copier to duplicate the illustrations for ROUND BEADS and FLAT BEADS, cut them out, and glue them to cards. Laminate if possible. Place the appropriate card with the activity, as a suggestion for the children to use. For the other clay activities, the tools with the activities suggest what to make with the clay.

■ Have several clay-handling sessions with small groups of children (up to five or so) before they use it individually. They need to learn thoroughly the techniques for rolling the clay and making balls and ropes. Teacher-pupil sessions will acquaint both of you with baker's clay and its special properties. Sit down with the children, and give everybody, including yourself, a piece of clay the size of a tennis ball.

Session One—Experiment with the clay—poke, punch, roll, and twist it for a while. At this point, the object is to explore the material rather than to make things.

Session Two—Share the rollers and learn to roll out the clay to approximately 1/4" (6 mm) thickness. Children need quite a lot of practice learning to roll the clay evenly.

Session Three—Using stamping tools—Again roll out pieces of clay, then experiment with the stamping tools. Help the children to learn to apply the amount of pressure that is needed to make impressions in the clay without making holes in it. Try the fork two ways—make holes with the ends of the tines and "tracks" with the tines broadside. Make crescents with the edge of the spoon bowl upside down. Try all of the tools.

Session Four—Rolled balls—Teach the children to pinch pieces of clay to make very small balls, about 1" (2.5 cm) in diameter, by rolling the clay on the table and in their hands. See what happens when you use the stamping tools to flatten the balls slightly. Make more balls and make experimental beads by pushing a drinking

GADGETS

straw through the center of the balls, being careful not to squeeze too hard and ruin the shape of the balls, or to squeeze the holes closed.

Session Five—Using cutters—Roll the clay thin and make large and small circles with the cutters. Try cutting a small circle out of a large one, making a doughnut shape. Use the drinking straw to cut holes in circles to decorate them; make a hole near the outside edge of a large circle, no closer than 1/2" (12.5 mm) to the edge. These can become pendants. To make flat beads, make holes in the center of small circles. These experiments in cutting the clay are for learning—don't keep them.

Session Six—Using the knife—Roll out the clay and practice cutting with the knife and pastry wheel. After adequate experimentation, try cutting squares of different sizes, from small to as large as can be cut from the rolled clay. Make the sides as even in length as possible. Also, try rectangles and triangles. Repeat this session if the children need more practice. Practice lifting the cut shapes with the spatula (or hands) onto drying trays. Show them how, if they later make pendants with the shapes, they will make holes with the straw for the yarn, and let everyone try it. Don't save these pieces.

Session Seven—Making ropes—Teach the children to roll egg-sized pieces of clay into ropes on the table with their hands, to about 3/8" (9.5 mm) thickness. Make trial-run letters and numbers ON THE DRYING TRAYS. Pinch off the clay to shorten it as needed. Don't save these.

Teach the children to put all leftover scraps back with the rest of the clay. You can put a large amount in a container, and they can use the amount they need. Notice that rolled and stamped pieces are lifted from the table to the drying tray with the spatula, and rope pieces, such as letters and numbers, are made directly on trays, because they can't be moved without changing the shapes. Don't forget to designate a drying place where the children put the trays holding wet clay pieces. Stress the importance of putting their name cards with pieces to identify them. Plan to allow the children to wash their hands after using clay; it tends to dry slightly on their hands, which feels uncomfortable.

GADGETS

CUTTERS

Cutting circles out of rolled clay; perhaps making them into pendants

What kids do

Roll the clay thin. Cut circles with the cutters. Make holes in them with the straw for decoration, if they like, or make a pendant or pendants for themselves or someone else. Lift them carefully with the spatula onto the drying tray, place their name cards on the trays, and take them to the drying place. After the pieces have hardened, decorate them with markers if they want.

GADGETS AND BAKERS CLAY

LEVEL:
Advanced

SKILLS:
Manual dexterity

MATERIALS:

Baker's clay

Roller

Round cutters—one about the size of a quarter, one about 2" (5 cm) in diameter (see introduction to this section)

Spatula

Plastic drinking straw

147

GADGETS

GADGETS AND BAKER'S CLAY

LEVEL:
Advanced

SKILLS:
Manual dexterity

MATERIALS:
Baker's clay (no roller or tools of any kind)

CLAY/HANDS

Experimenting with clay by kneading and modeling it.

What kids do

See what the clay will do. Find out how it differs from playdough. Experiment with the clay or make small things with it. If they make things to keep, put them on a drying tray with their name cards near the pieces, and put the drying tray in the drying place. Clean their work space. When the clay pieces are hard, decorate them with markers if they want.

GADGETS AND BAKER'S CLAY

LEVEL:
Advanced

SKILLS:
Tactile experience of letter formation

MATERIALS:
Baker's clay

3-5 letter cards for the children to use as guides - see the introduction to the GADGETS section

Stamping tools

LETTERS

Making letters of the alphabet with clay ropes

What kids do

Roll pieces of clay into ropes. Make clay-rope letters ON THE TRAY like the ones on the cards. Make as many of each letter as they like. Decorate them with the stamping tools if they like. Put their name cards on the trays, and put the trays in the drying place. When the letters have hardened, they may want to decorate them with markers before taking them home.

GADGETS

STAMPING TOOLS

Using discards as tools to make impressions in balls of clay

What kids do

Make small balls with the clay. Flatten them making plump "buttons" with the stamping tools. Put them on the drying tray, with their name cards, and take them to the drying place. When the clay pieces are hard, they may want to decorate them with markers.

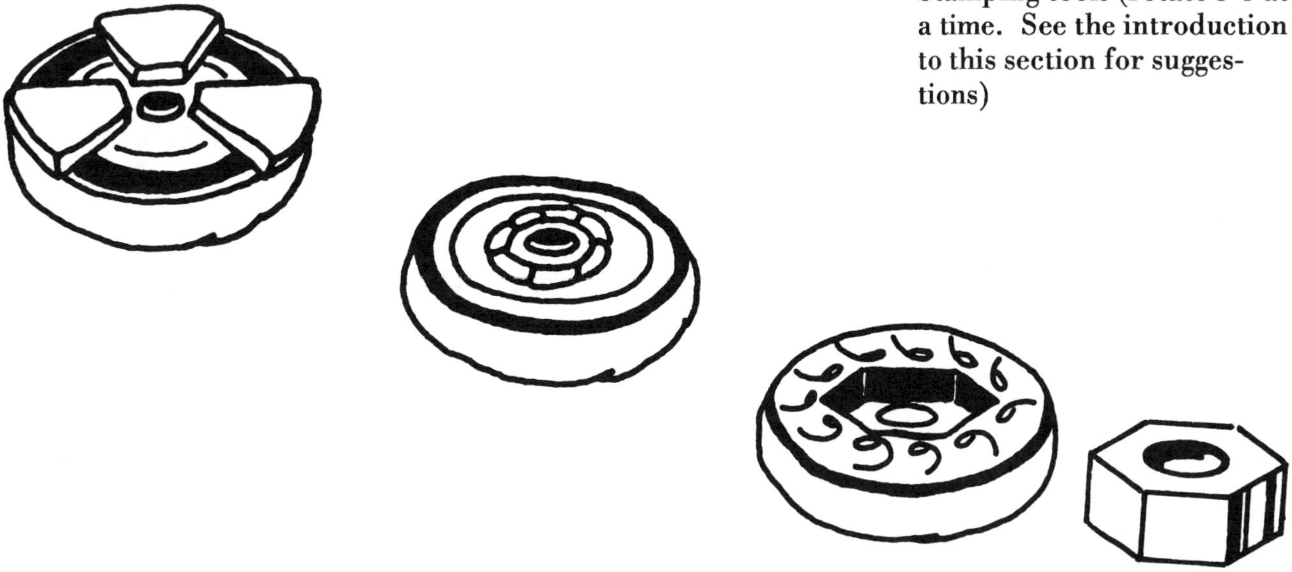

GADGETS AND BAKER'S CLAY

LEVEL:
Advanced

SKILLS:
Manual dexterity

MATERIALS:
Baker's clay

Stamping tools (rotate 3-5 at a time. See the introduction to this section for suggestions)

GADGETS

GADGETS AND BAKER'S CLAY

LEVEL:
Advanced

SKILLS:
Manual dexterity

MATERIALS:
Baker's clay

Roller

Metal table knife

Stamping tools (see introduction to this section)—rotate 3-5 at a time

MATERIALS:
Bakers clay

Stamping tools (see introduction to this section)

Roller

Pastry cutting wheel

STAMPING TOOLS/KNIFE

Cutting clay shapes with a table knife; making them into pendants as an option

What kids do

Roll the clay thin. Use the knife to cut shapes such as squares, rectangles, triangles, or other shapes. Decorate them with the stamping tools, or make them into pendants. Lift them carefully onto the drying trays, place their name cards on the trays, and take them to the drying place. When the clay pieces are hard, they may want to decorate them with markers.

STAMPING TOOLS/PASTRY WHEEL

Cutting shapes with a pastry wheel; making them into pendants as an option

What kids do

Roll the clay thin. Use the wheel to cut shapes such as squares, triangles, rectangles, or other shapes. Decorate them with the stamping tools or make them into pendants. Lift them carefully onto the drying trays, place their name cards on the trays, and take them to the drying place. When the clay pieces are hard, they may want to decorate them with markers.

GADGETS

FLAT BEADS

Making flat beads from circles cut out of rolled clay

What kids do

Roll the clay thin and cut out as many small circles as they want. Use the straw to make a hole in the middle of each circle. Put the circles on trays with their name cards, and put the trays in the drying place. Clean the work space. When the beads have completely dried, they may want to decorate them with markers before stringing them on yarn.

GADGETS AND BAKER'S CLAY

LEVEL:
Advanced

SKILLS:
Manual dexterity

MATERIALS:
Baker's clay

Small cutter approximately 1" (2.5 cm) in diameter

Plastic drinking straw

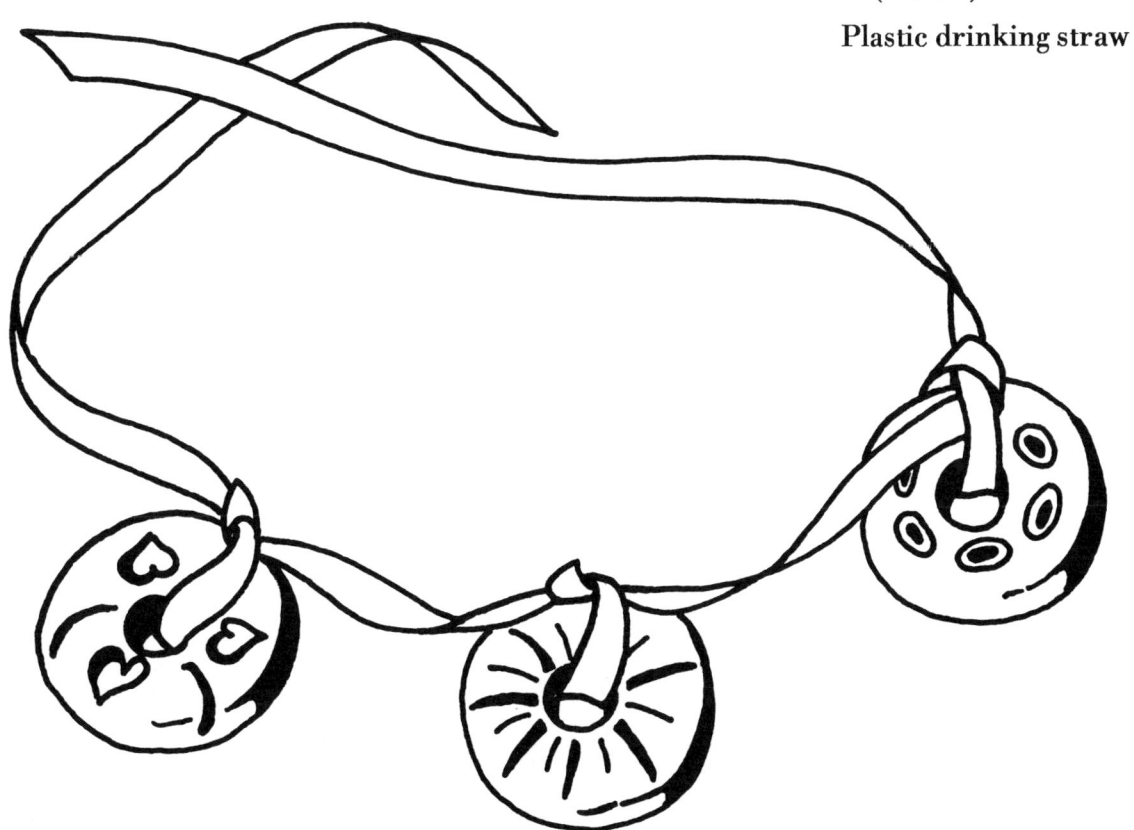

GADGETS

GADGETS AND BAKER'S CLAY

LEVEL:
Advanced

SKILLS:
Manual dexterity

MATERIALS:
Baker's clay
Plastic drinking straw

ROUND BEADS

Making beads from rolled balls of clay

What kids do

Roll very small clay balls with their hands. Push the straw carefully through the middle of each ball to make a hole. Lift the balls onto the drying tray, being careful not to close any of the holes. Put their name cards on the tray, and take the trays to the drying place. When the beads have completely hardened, they may want to decorate them with markers before stringing them on yarn.

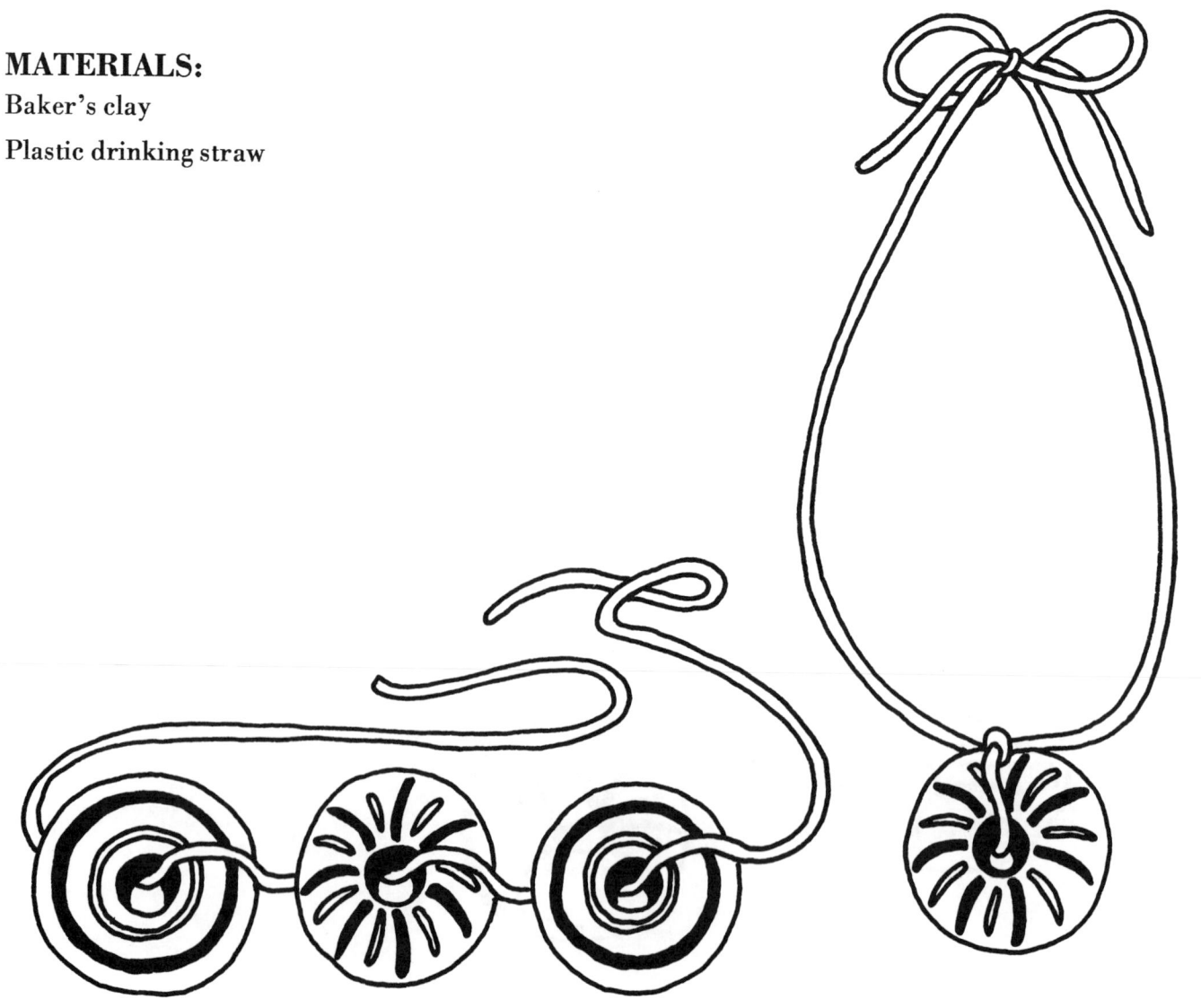

GADGETS

NAMES

Spelling first names with letters made from clay ropes

What kids do

Roll pieces of clay into ropes. Find their name cards, and make clay-rope letters to spell their names or initials ON THE TRAY. Decorate the letters with the stamping tools if they like. Put the tray in the drying place, and clean their work space. When the letters have hardened, they may want to decorate them with markers before taking them home.

GADGETS AND BAKER'S CLAY

LEVEL:
Advanced

SKILLS:
Tactile experience of letter formation

MATERIALS:
Baker's clay

Name cards (initials for very long names)—a name card for each child using first names only, or first names and the first letter of last names in case of duplicate first names. Use block-style printing, making first letters upper case and the remaining letters lower case.

Stamping tools

153

GADGETS

NUMBERS

Making numbers one to ten with clay ropes

What kids do

Roll pieces of clay into ropes. Make clay-rope numbers ON THE TRAY like the ones on the cards. Make as many of each number as they like. Decorate them with the stamping tools if they want. Put their name cards on the trays, and put the trays in the drying place. When the numbers have hardened, they may want to decorate them with markers before taking them home.

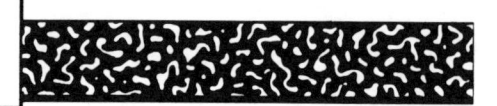

GADGETS AND BAKER'S CLAY

LEVEL:
Advanced

SKILLS:
Tactile experience of number formation

MATERIALS:
Baker's clay

3-5 number cards for the children to use as guides - see the introduction to the GADGETS section

Stamping tools

GADGETS

GADGETS AND SAND AND WATER

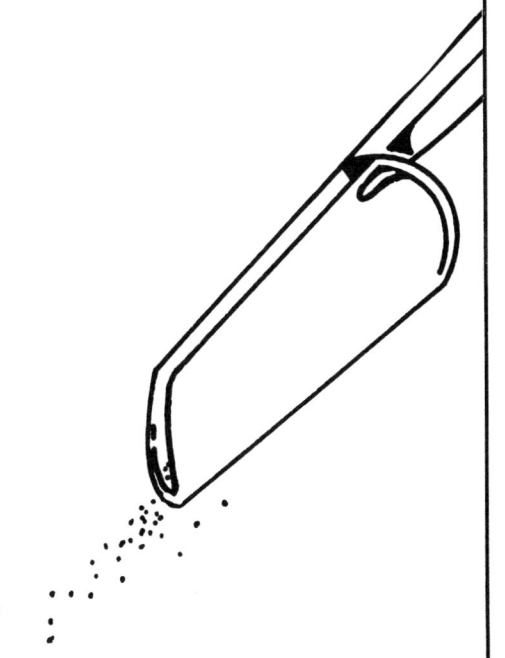

What kids do
Use kitchen utensils for pouring, sifting, and measuring activities with sand and water.

What teachers do
Collect these:

■ Containers for sand and water—the same kind can be used for both. Large, plastic, oversized dishpans or totes are ideal; they should hold 3-8 gallons (11.5-30.5 liters).

■ Fine clean sand to fill the sand container approximately 1/3 full. A craft or hobby store is a good source for sand. Play-box or "sharp" sand is too coarse for this activity. Fine, flowing sand is needed.

■ A large-mesh strainer for SAND, a small strainer for WATER

■ Dried beans—1 or more kinds—for SAND

■ 2 funnels—a small one and a medium one

■ 3 to 5 small-mouthed plastic bottles, preferably clear, such as vinegar and cooking oil bottles, for SAND, 3 to 5 for WATER

■ A small and medium-sized scoop for SAND

■ One set of dry-ingredient plastic measuring cups for SAND

■ 2 sets of measuring spoons for SAND

■ Large slotted spoon for WATER

■ 8-10 corks of assorted sizes or same size for WATER

■ 8-10 ping-pong balls and plastic containers, such as margarine tubs

■ Sponge pieces—see FLOATING THINGS activity

■ Small figures—people, vehicles, buildings, trees, etc. for SAND/VILLAGE

■ Gelatin molds, muffin tin, plastic ice-cube tray, plastic cartons, etc. for SAND/MOLDS

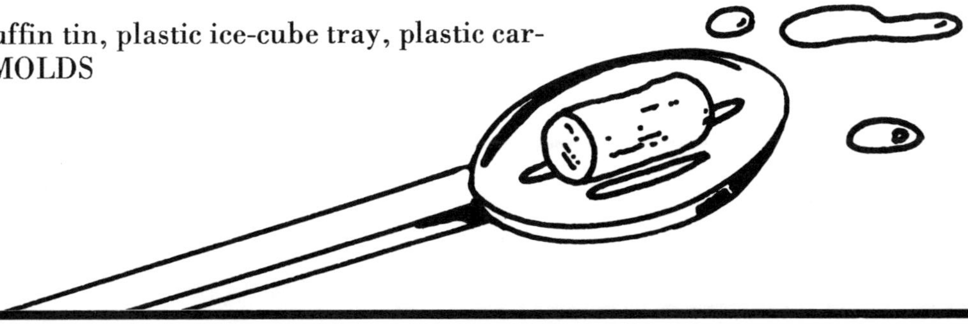

155

GADGETS

- 12" to 24" (30 cm to 60 cm) lengths of clear plastic tubing (available from a hardware store or home center)—one large diameter, one small diameter

- A funnel that fits in each piece of tubing

- A meat baster (in houseware stores), a rubber-bulb syringe (in auto supply stores), and a plastic pump bottle (in houseware stores)

- Plastic squeeze bottle, spray bottle, and sprinkler bottle (in houseware stores)

If you will not be putting the sand away, you may want to have a cover for it to denote times when it may not be used. Some plastic containers come with lids, or you may use a piece of plywood or pegboard. Water should be emptied after use. Fill the sand and water tubs approximately 1/3 full of sand or water to minimize spilling and splashing. A large bath towel placed under the water tub will catch spills. Remind children to push up long sleeves and, perhaps, wear a plastic art smock while using the water activities. If you have a large class, you may want to have more than one container of sand and water, but only one child should use each one at a time, and of course, nothing but sand and water equipment should be used with them. These activities are such favorites with children, they will want to do them alone.

GADGETS

MEASURING CUPS AND SPOONS

Measuring sand with measuring cups and spoons

What kids do
Use the spoons and cups to dip, pour, and measure the sand for as long as they like.

GADGETS AND SAND

LEVEL:
Beginning

SKILLS:
Experimentation with measurement

MATERIALS:
Sand in a 3- to 8-gallon plastic tub

1 set of dry-ingredient measuring cups

1 set of measuring spoons

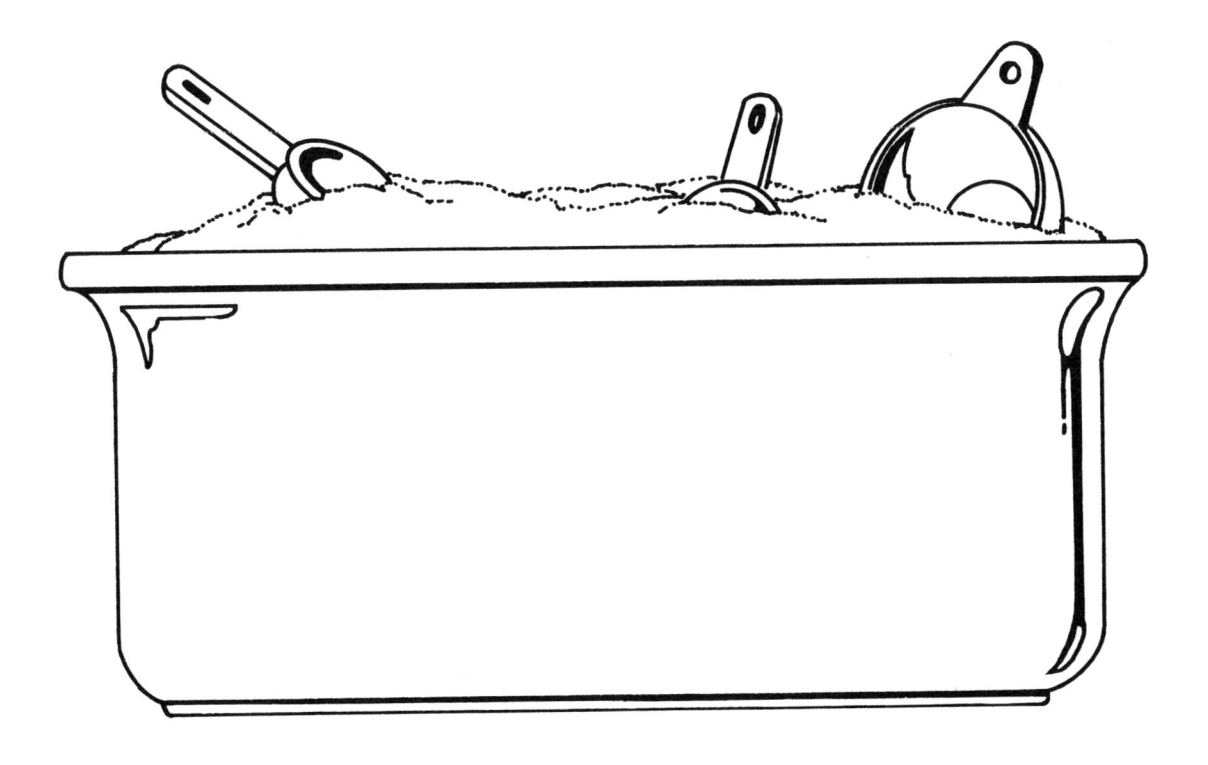

GADGETS

STRAINER/BEANS

Using a strainer to separate dried beans from sand

GADGETS AND SAND

LEVEL:
Beginning-Advanced

SKILLS:
Eye-hand coordination, manual dexterity

MATERIALS:

Sand in a 3- to 8-gallon plastic tub

Large-mesh strainer

Dried beans—1 or more kinds (or rotate kinds)—in a plastic container

What kids do

Mix the beans throughout the sand with their hands. Sift the sand to separate the beans, and put the beans in the container. Put them back in the sand and sift it again if they want. Use the activity as long as they like. They should separate the beans from the sand and put the beans back in the container when they finish the activity.

GADGETS

FUNNELS/BOTTLES

Using funnels and scoops to fill bottles with sand

What kids do

Put the funnel in one bottle at a time. Using a scoop, fill it with sand. Empty and fill the bottles as many times as they like.

GADGETS AND SAND

LEVEL:
Beginning-Advanced

SKILLS:
Eye-hand coordination, manual dexterity

MATERIALS:
Sand in a 3- to 8-gallon plastic tub

1 medium-sized funnel, 1 small funnel

3 to 5 plastic bottles of different sizes

1 small and 1 medium-sized scoop

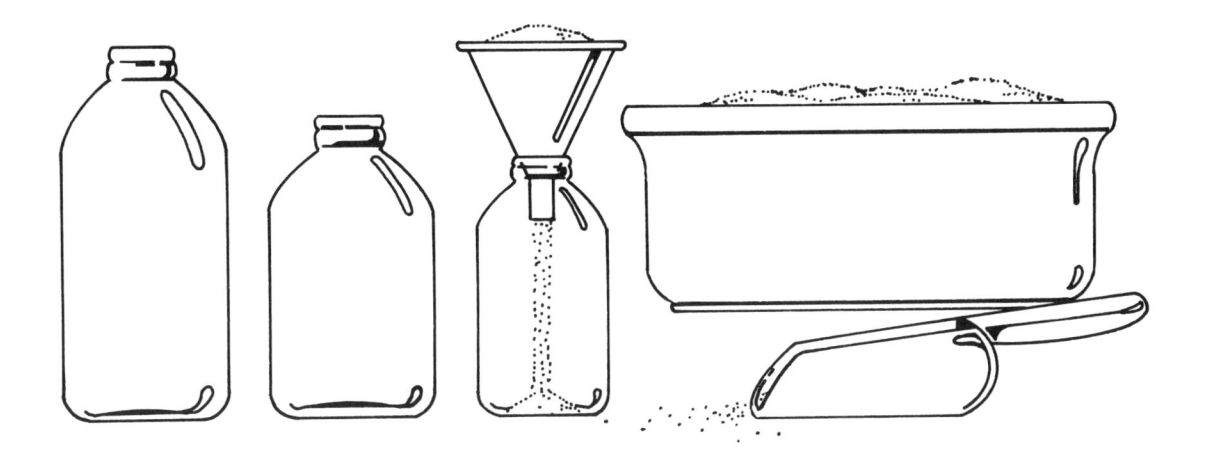

GADGETS

GADGETS AND SAND

LEVEL:
Beginning-Advanced

SKILLS:
Manual dexterity

MATERIALS:
Sand, in a 3- to 8-gallon plastic tub, dampened with enough water to hold a shape

5 or more containers to use as molds—plastic cups, gelatin molds, muffin tins, plastic ice-cube trays, plastic cartons, etc

LEVEL:
Beginning-Advanced

SKILLS:
Fantasy, manual dexterity

MATERIALS:
Sand in a 3- to 8-gallon plastic tub dampened with water

Small toy people, vehicles, buildings, trees, etc..

MOLDS

Making molded shapes with damp sand

What kids do
Make sand shapes with the molds, by packing the molds tightly with sand and upending them in the sand to unmold them.

VILLAGE

Making a village with people and vehicles in sand

What kids do
Build a little village in the sand.

GADGETS

FLOATING THINGS

Removing floating objects from water with a slotted spoon and strainer

What kids do

Dip the objects one at a time from the water with the strainer or spoon. Put them back in the water and repeat if they like.

GADGETS AND WATER

LEVEL:

Beginning-Advanced

SKILLS:

Manual dexterity, experimentation with flotation

MATERIALS:

Water in a 3- to 8-gallon plastic tub

Small tea strainer

Slotted spoon

Corks—8 to 10 of assorted sizes or same size

Ping-pong balls—8 to 10

Scraps of sponge—8 to 10 pieces of various sizes and shapes

GADGETS

FUNNELS AND BOTTLES

Using funnels to fill bottles with water

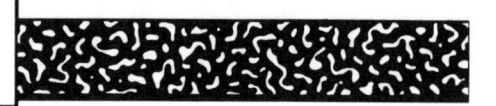

GADGETS AND WATER

What kids do

Put a funnel in the bottles one at a time and fill them with water from the pitcher. Empty and fill them as many times as they like.

LEVEL:
Beginning-Advanced

SKILLS:
Eye-hand coordination, manual dexterity

MATERIALS:

Water in a 3- to 8-gallon plastic tub

1 small and 1 medium-sized plastic pitcher (or a 1-cup and a 2-cup liquid measuring cup)

1 small and 1 medium-sized funnel

3-5 plastic bottles of different sizes

GADGETS

FUNNELS AND TUBES

Pouring water through tubes with funnels in them

Note: If the funnels are difficult for children to fit into the tubing, glue them in permanently with epoxy or other plastic-and vinyl-bonding glue.

What kids do

Fit the funnels in one end of each of the pieces of tubing. Place the other end of the tubing into the tub of water. Use the cups to pour water into the funnels and watch it flow through the tubing and back into the tub.

GADGETS AND WATER

LEVEL:
Beginning-Advanced

SKILLS:
Eye-hand coordination, experimentation with gravity

MATERIALS:

Water in a 3- to 8-gallon plastic tub

12" to 24" (30 to 60 cm) length of clear plastic tubing, medium-to large diameter (hardware store or home center)

12" to 24" (30 to 60 cm) length of clear plastic tubing, small diameter (hardware store or home center)

2 funnels to fit snugly into the lengths of tubing

1-cup and 2-cup plastic liquid measuring cups

GADGETS

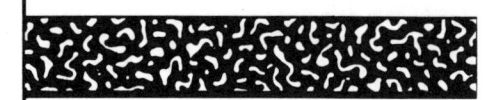

GADGETS AND WATER

LEVEL:
Beginning-Advanced

SKILLS:
Experimentation with squeeze, spray, and sprinkler bottles

MATERIALS:

Water in a 3- to 8-gallon plastic tub

Clear plastic squeeze bottle, medium size, or 1 medium-sized and 1 small bottle

Sprinkler top and plastic bottle to fit it (sprinklers are used to dampen clothing for ironing—available in housewares departments of supermarkets)

Plastic spray bottle, preferably with trigger-type sprayer

3 plastic cups or containers of differing sizes

SQUEEZE, SPRAY, AND SPRINKLE

Using squeeze, spray, and sprinkler bottles with water

Note: This activity may be used indoors or outdoors. Save the spray bottle for outdoor use only, using only the sprinkler and squeeze bottles indoors.

What kids do

Experiment with the bottles by squeezing and sprinkling water into the tub and plastic containers. Outdoors, spray water into the tub, on the ground or plants, but never on people.

GADGETS

SIPHON AND SUCTION

Using a baster, syringe, and pump with water

What kids do

Learn to draw water into the baster or syringe by compressing the bulb, and to empty it by releasing the bulb, catching the water in one of the plastic containers if they wish. Fill the pump bottle with water, replace the pump cap and pump water into the containers or the tub of water.

GADGETS AND WATER

LEVEL:
Intermediate-Advanced

SKILLS:
Experimentation with siphoning, pumping, and suctioning

MATERIALS:

Water in a 3- to 8-gallon plastic tub

Meat baster (housewares department of supermarket)

Rubber-bulb syringe (auto supplies department of supermarket or auto supply store)

Plastic pump bottle (used with ketchup; housewares department of supermarket)

3 plastic cups or containers of differing sizes

TRANSPARENCIES

Superimposing

TRANSPARENCIES

What kids do

Match outlines on transparent overlays to pictures on cards. TRANSPARENCIES are of three types:

■ DIFFERENT-SHAPE: assorted pictures which are clearly distinguishable from each other (these are the simplest to match)

■ DIFFERENT-SIZE: graduated-size drawings of one subject, requiring care in matching sizes (moderately difficult)

■ RELATED-SHAPE: related subjects of similar shapes, requiring close attention to detail (most difficult of the three).

The matching process involves identifying and matching pictures and their outlines and, then, positioning the transparency over the picture so that the outlines match exactly. Because overlays are clear, children must first determine which side of the outline will match the picture. Then they should place the overlay carefully over the picture. They should be encouraged to hold overlays and pictures in their hands when matching them, rather than casually placing overlays on top of pictures spread on the table. By holding them in their hands, and by turning them so they align exactly, children can experience the satisfaction of seeing the lines suddenly converge, confirming their choices. The circular shapes preclude alignment by matching corners, as would be possible if they were square or rectangular. When working with the overlays of graduated sizes, the children should arrange them from large to small or small to large. The fine muscle control and critical judgment required for these activities make them unsuitable for BEGINNERS.

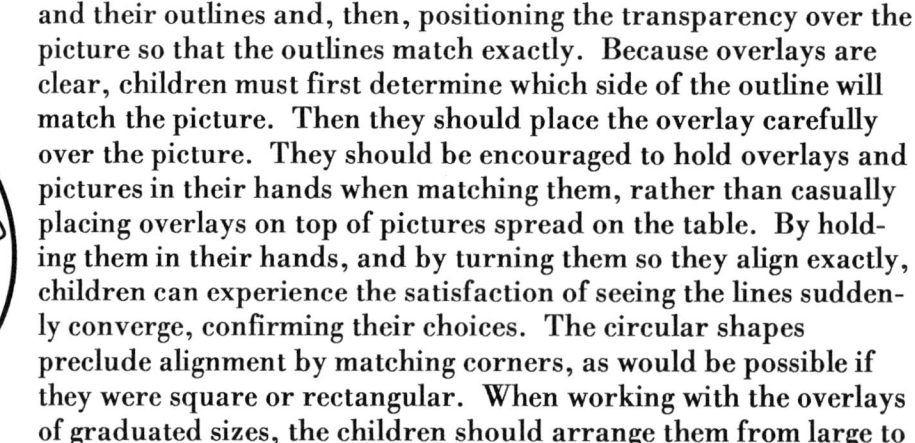

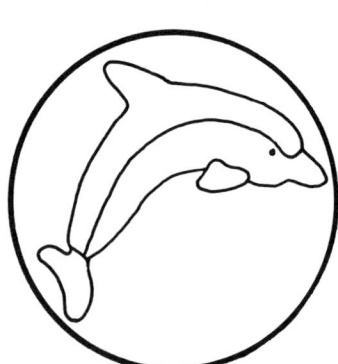

What teachers do

Copy, color, mark, and cut. COPY: Copy the picture pages which follow (with a copier) on white card stock which can be purchased at office supply stores or printing shops. COLOR: Color pictures with markers and laminate them or cover them with clear contact paper. Use water-based markers for coloring the pictures, such as the ones children use; permanent markers will bleed through the card, and permanency is not a concern since the pictures will be laminated. Crayola brand cone-tipped (not fine-line) markers work beautifully, and cover the areas quickly when turned slightly on the side. Pictures need not be colored realistically in every case. Colored card stock—which does not need to be colored—can also be used for duplicating the pictures. This

TRANSPARENCIES

method is quicker though not quite as attractive and interesting as the colored pictures on white card. MARK: Outline the pictures on overhead projector transparencies with black marker. CUT: Cut out transparencies and pictures.

Overlays are made with the clear sheets that are used with overhead projectors. These are sold in office supply or teacher supply stores. The black pen used for the overlay outlines can also be bought in office supply or teacher supply stores. Several brands of markers will work, but if you use an overhead transparency pen, be sure it is permanent, not washable—read the description on the pen to tell which kind it is. Sanford Sharpie fine point permanent marker is also good, and is available wherever office and school supplies are sold.

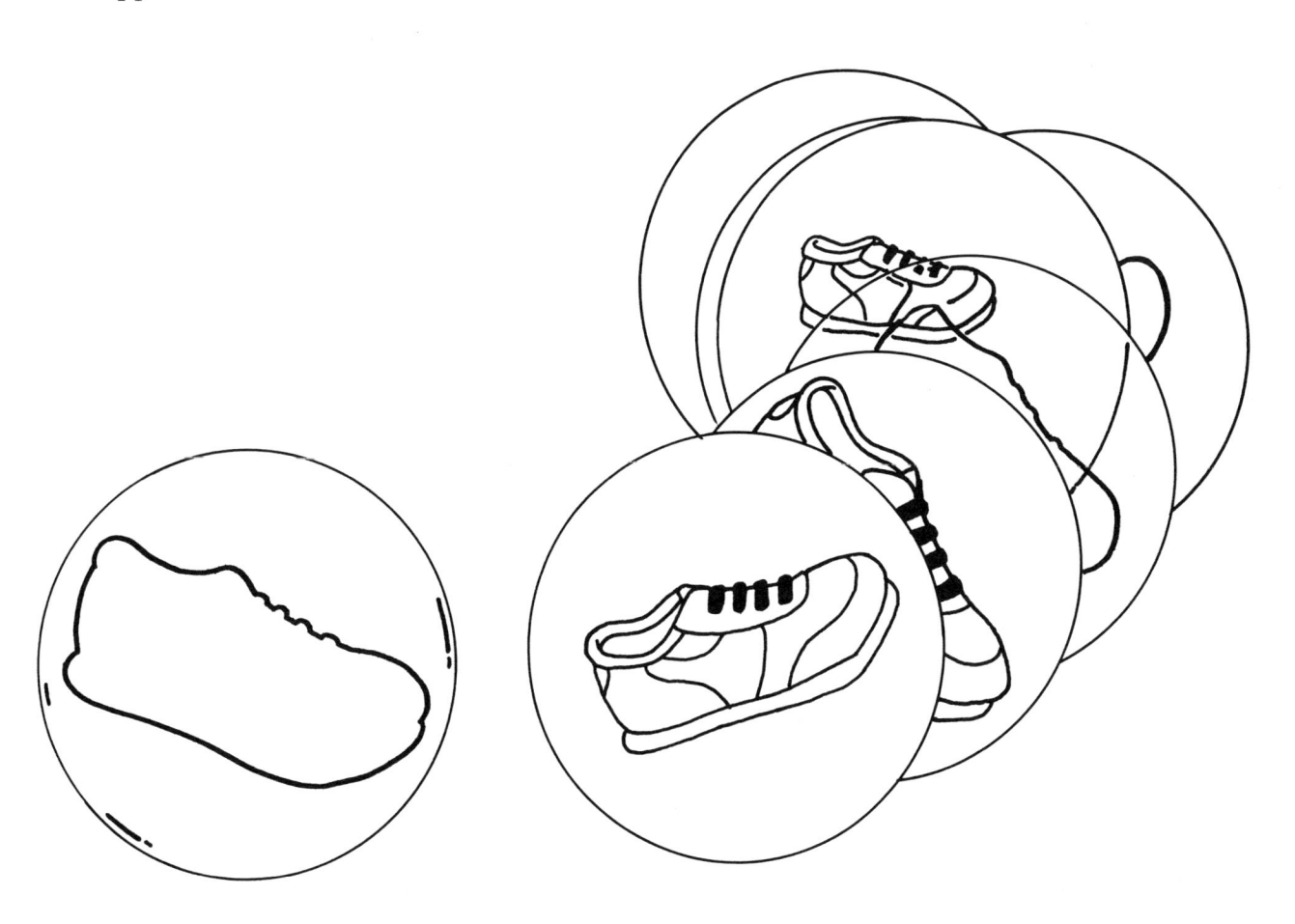

169

TRANSPARENCIES

LEVEL:
Intermediate-Advanced

SKILLS:
Shape discrimination, attention to detail, fine motor control

MATERIALS:
1 - 8 1/2" x 11" (21 cm x 27 cm) overhead transparency sheet

1 - 8 1/2" x 11" (21 cm x 27 cm) white card

Overhead projector pen, fine point, permanent black

Water-base colored markers, broad-tip

TRANSPARENCIES

Clear overlays with outlines are matched with colored pictures of distinctly different shapes, related shapes, or graduated sizes.

What teachers do

Copy the picture page for the desired activity with a copier on card stock. Color the pictures as desired with colored markers and laminate the card. Paper clip the transparency sheet over the card of colored pictures. Outline the pictures, but not the frames around them, with the permanent black pen. Leaving them clipped together, cut out each outline and colored picture on the circular frame around the picture.

What kids do

Spread the pictures and outlines on the work surface. Find a matching outline for each picture and place it over the picture, making the lines match exactly. They may separate them and match them again if they want. Arrange overlays of graduated sizes from small to large or large to small.

What kids and teachers can talk about

TRANSPARENCIES are rich with conversation potential. Teachers and kids can talk about the names of the things pictured, their colors, and their functions.

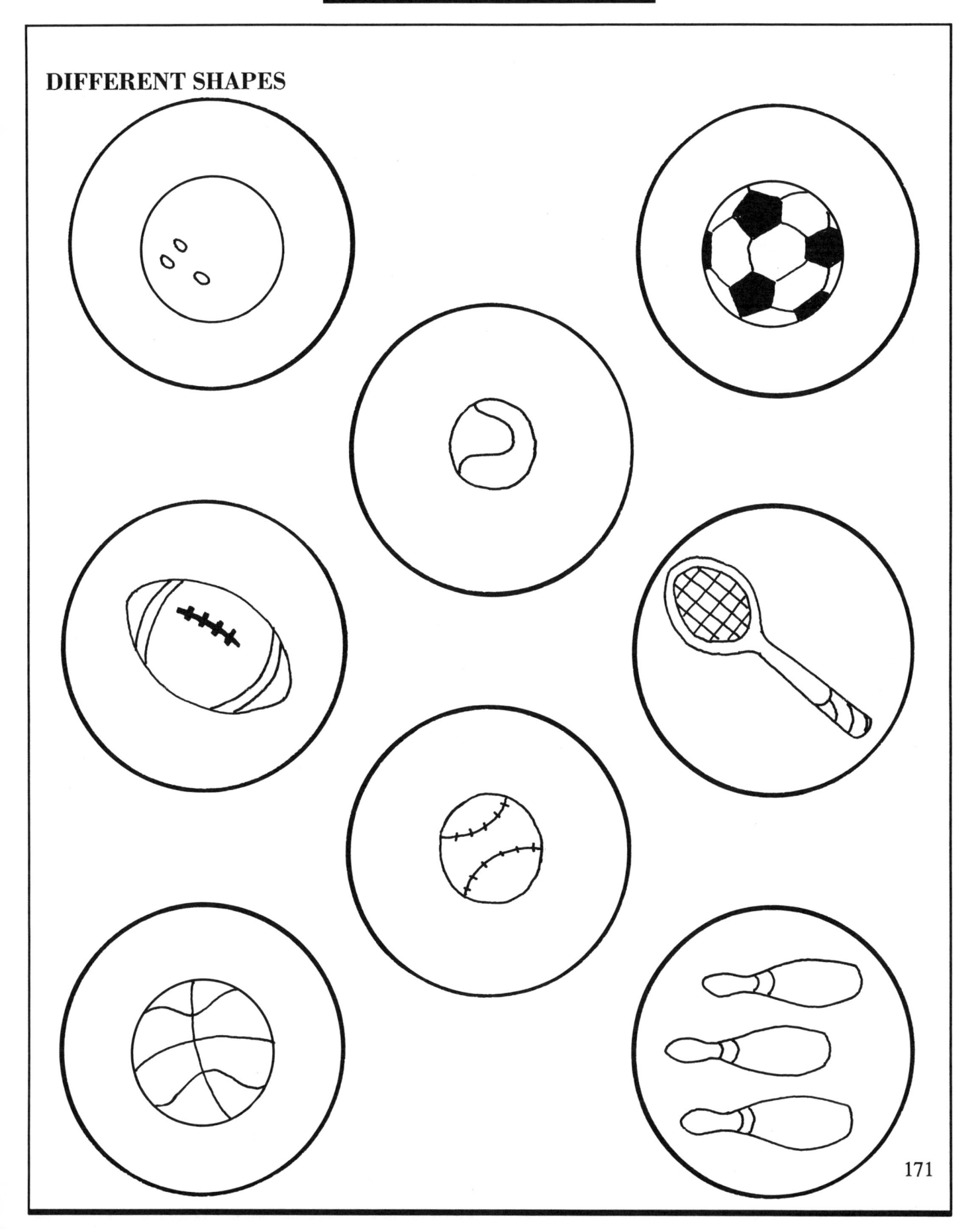

TRANSPARENCIES

DIFFERENT SHAPES

171

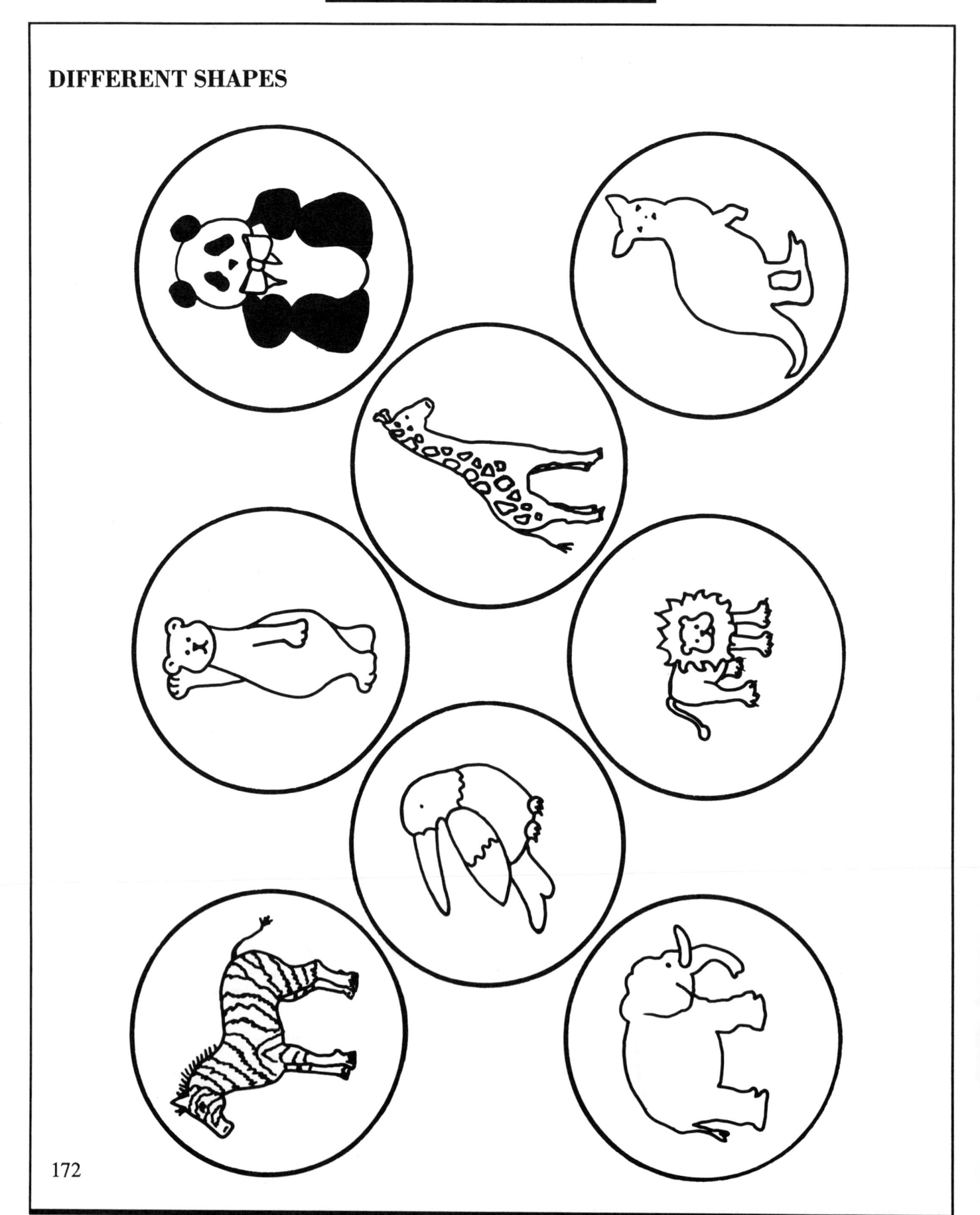

TRANSPARENCIES

DIFFERENT SHAPES

172

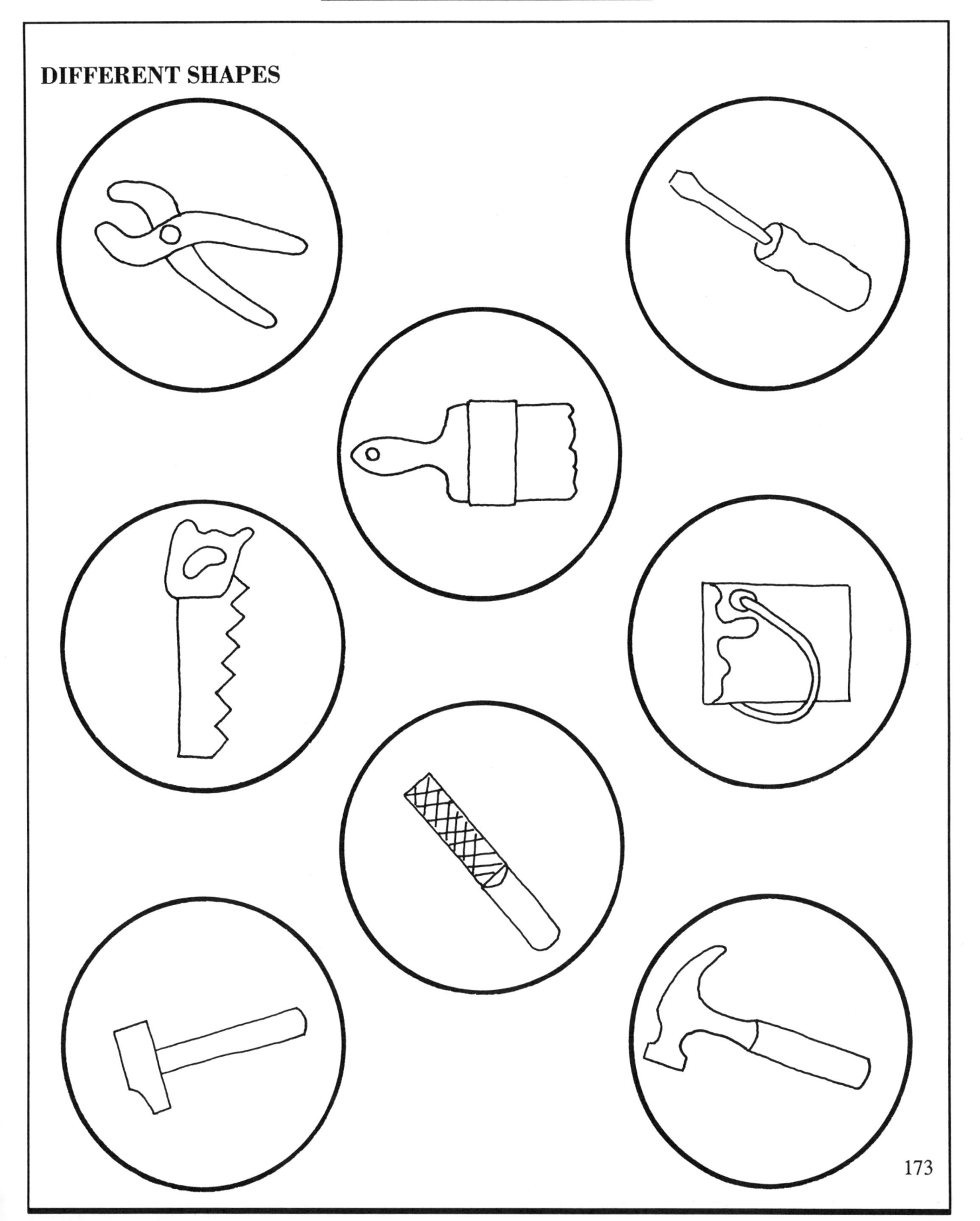

TRANSPARENCIES

DIFFERENT SHAPES

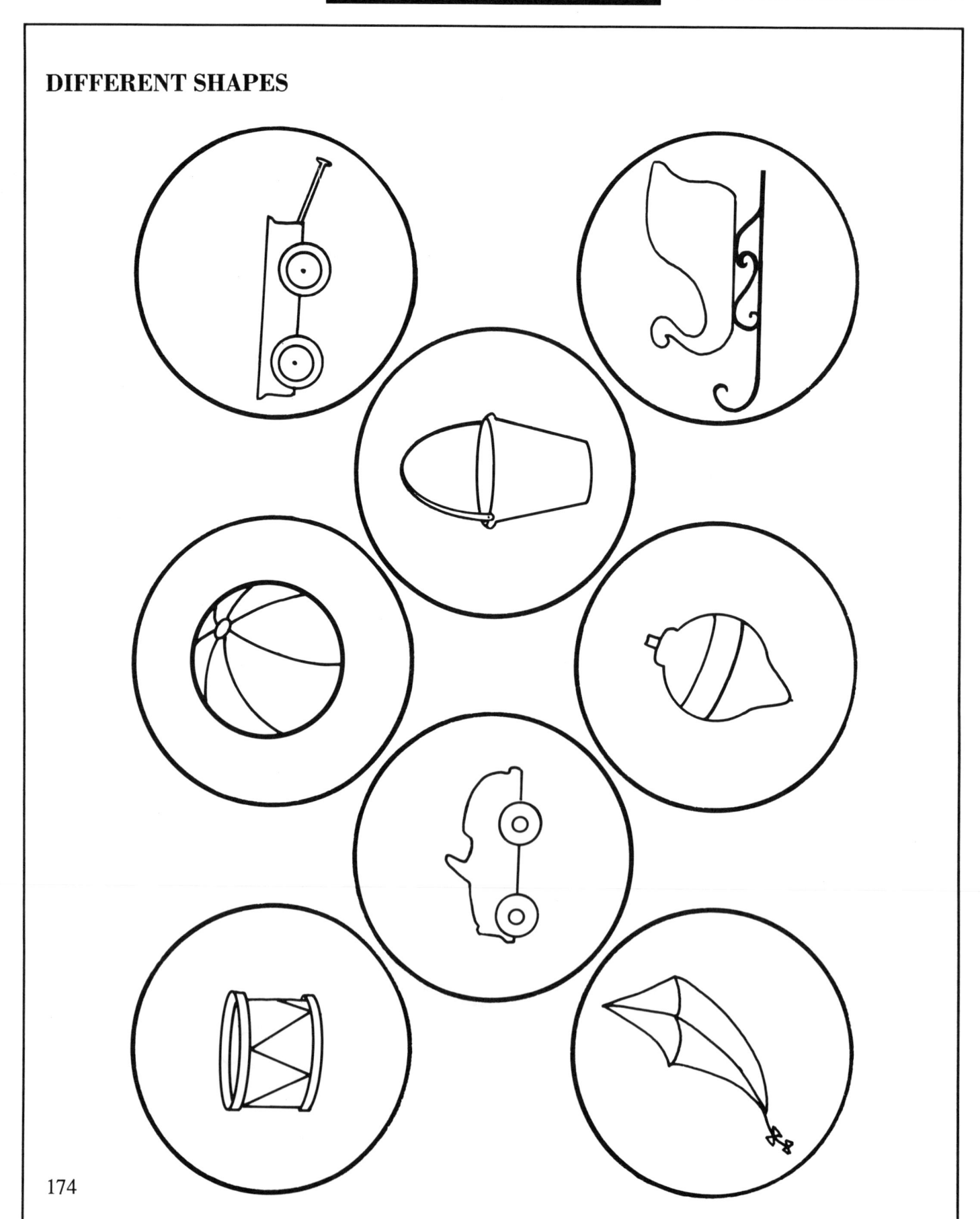

TRANSPARENCIES

DIFFERENT SHAPES

174

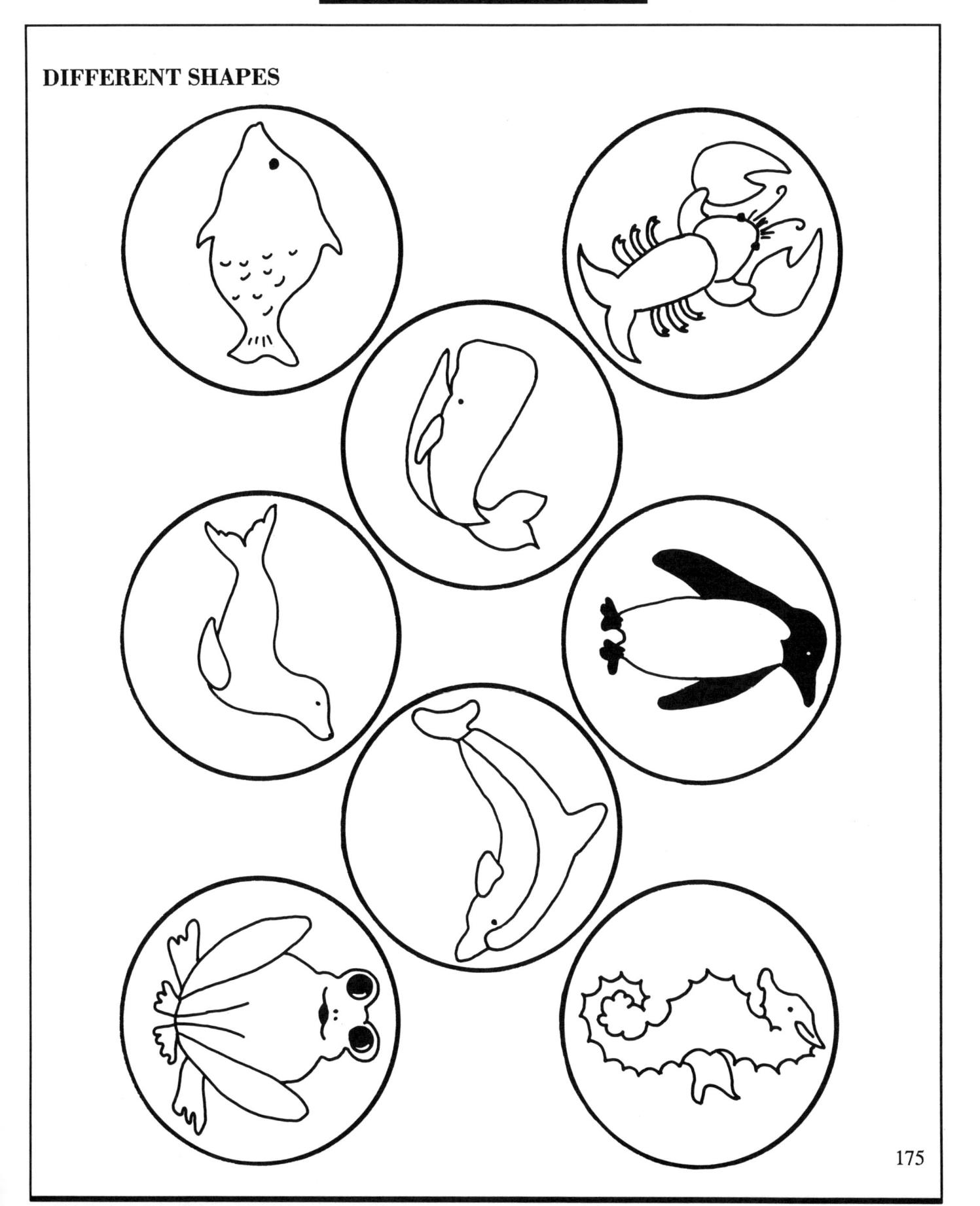

TRANSPARENCIES

DIFFERENT SHAPES

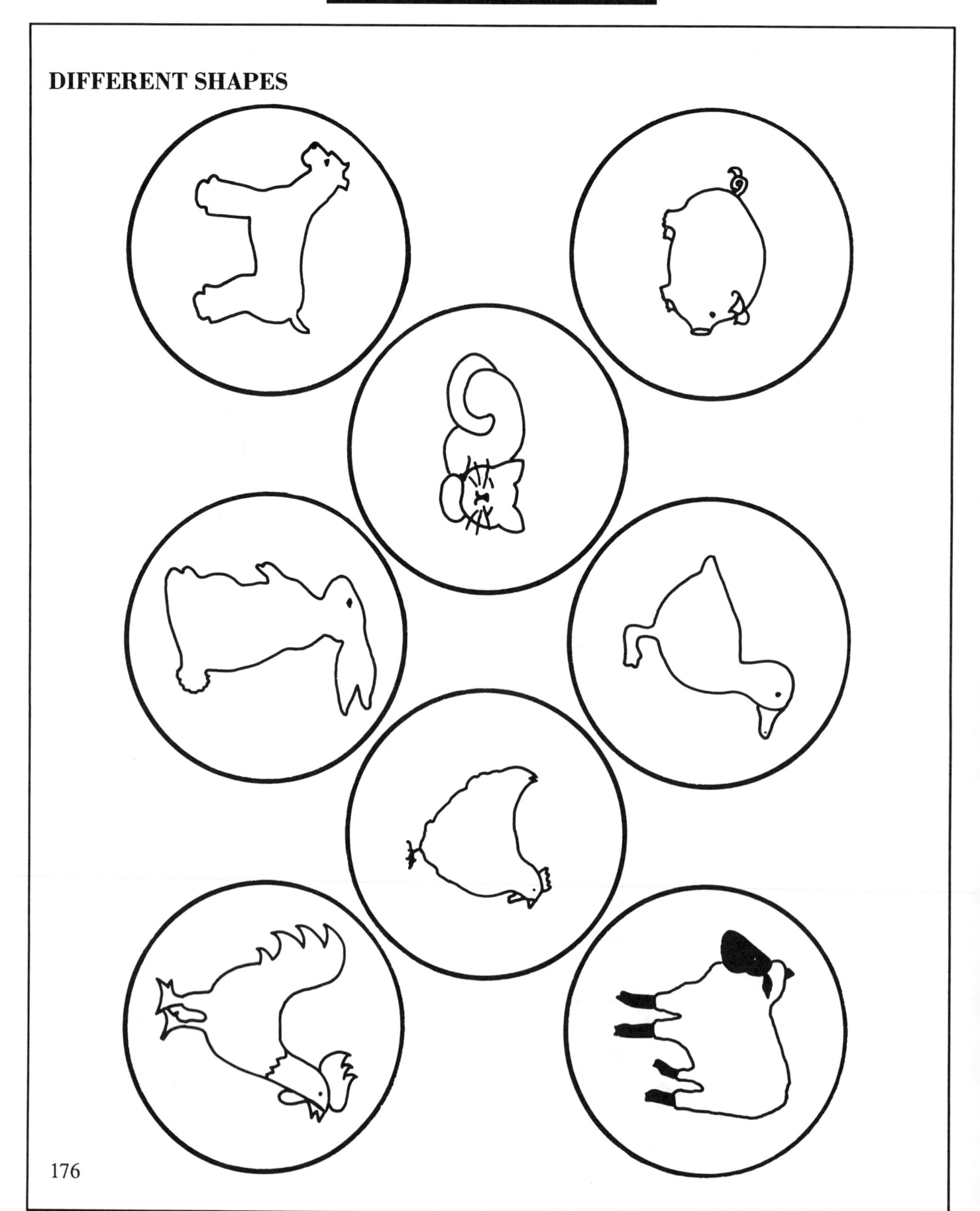

TRANSPARENCIES

DIFFERENT SHAPES

176

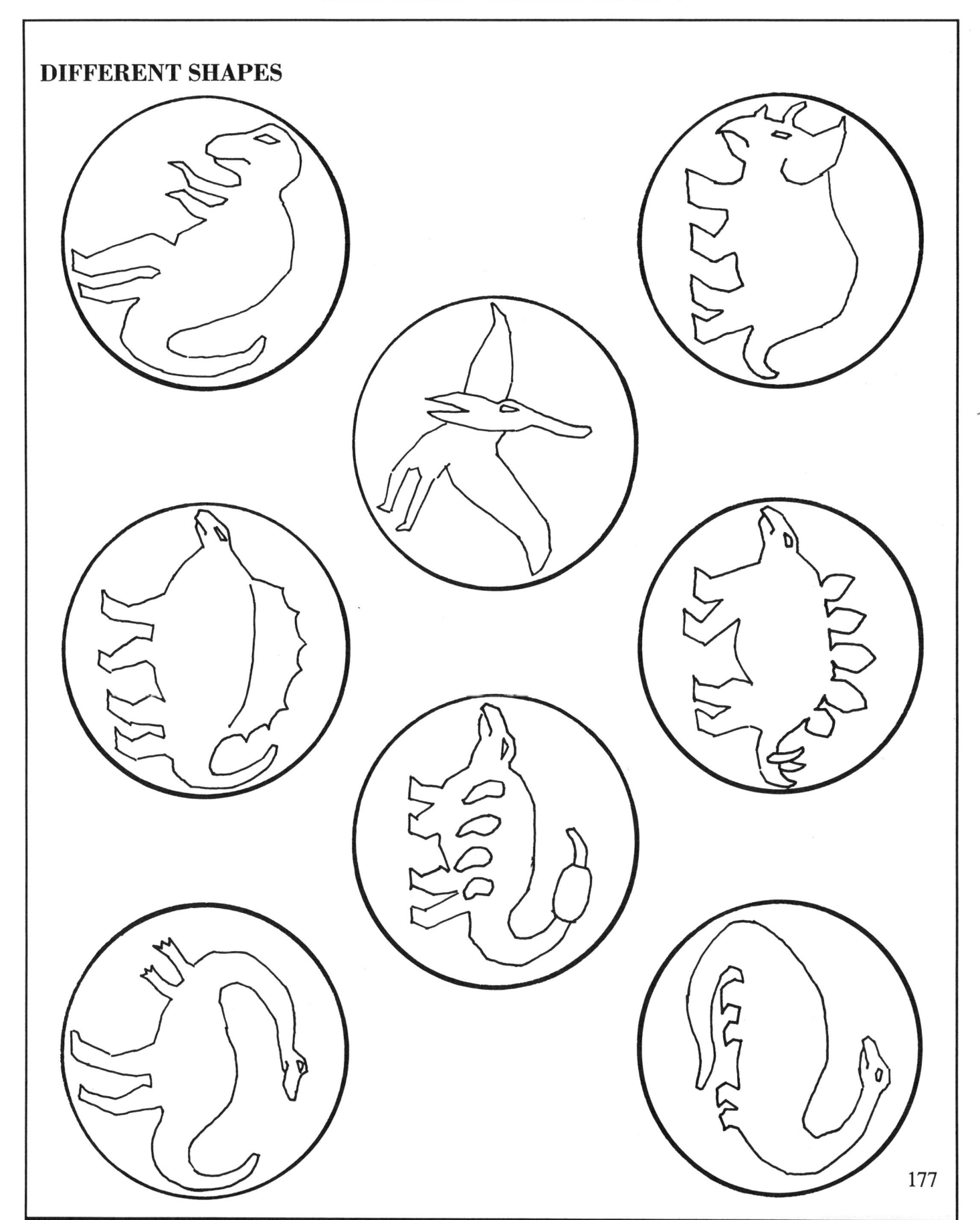

TRANSPARENCIES

DIFFERENT SHAPES

177

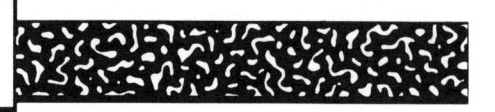

TRANSPARENCIES

DIFFERENT SHAPES

178

TRANSPARENCIES

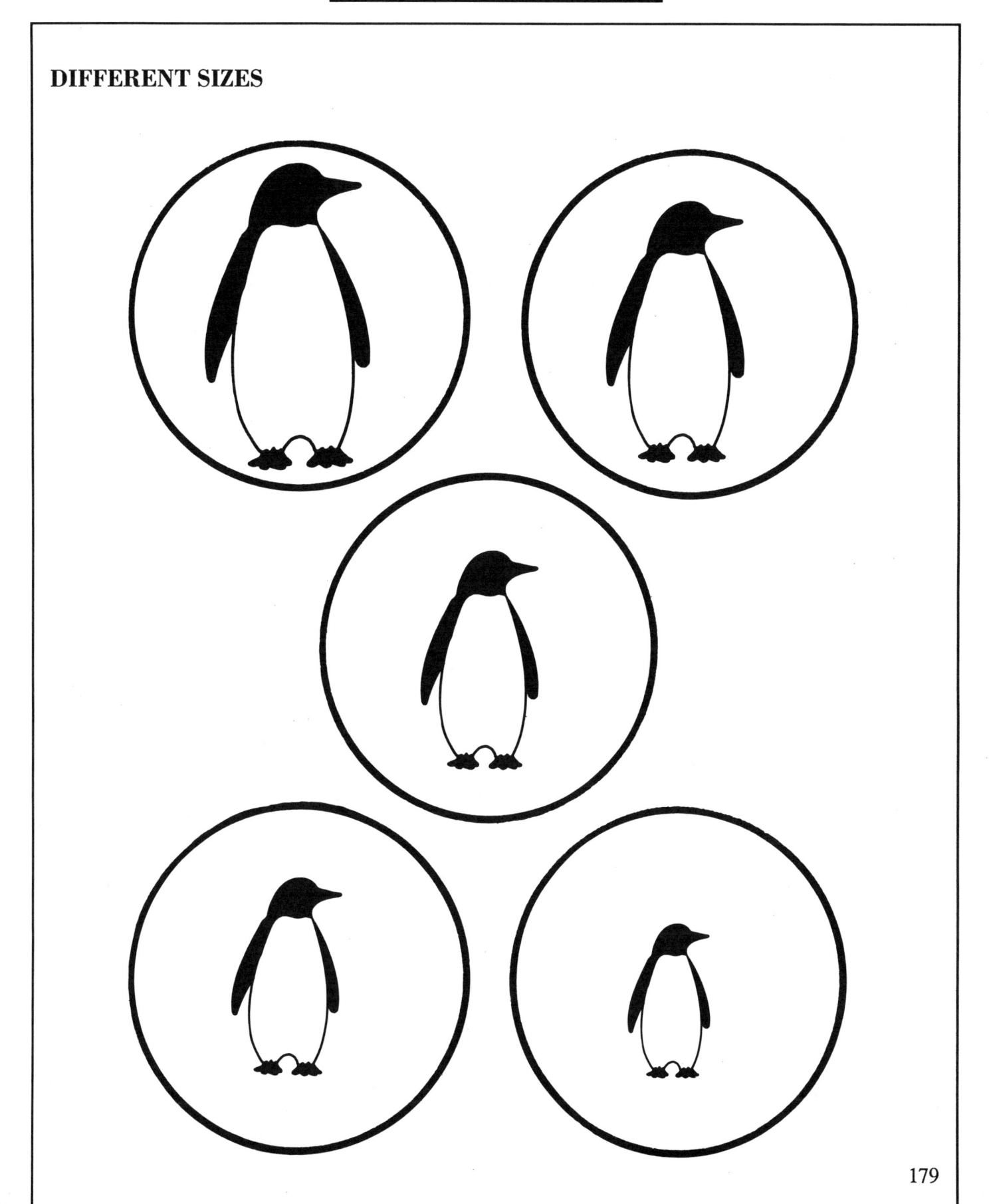

DIFFERENT SIZES

TRANSPARENCIES

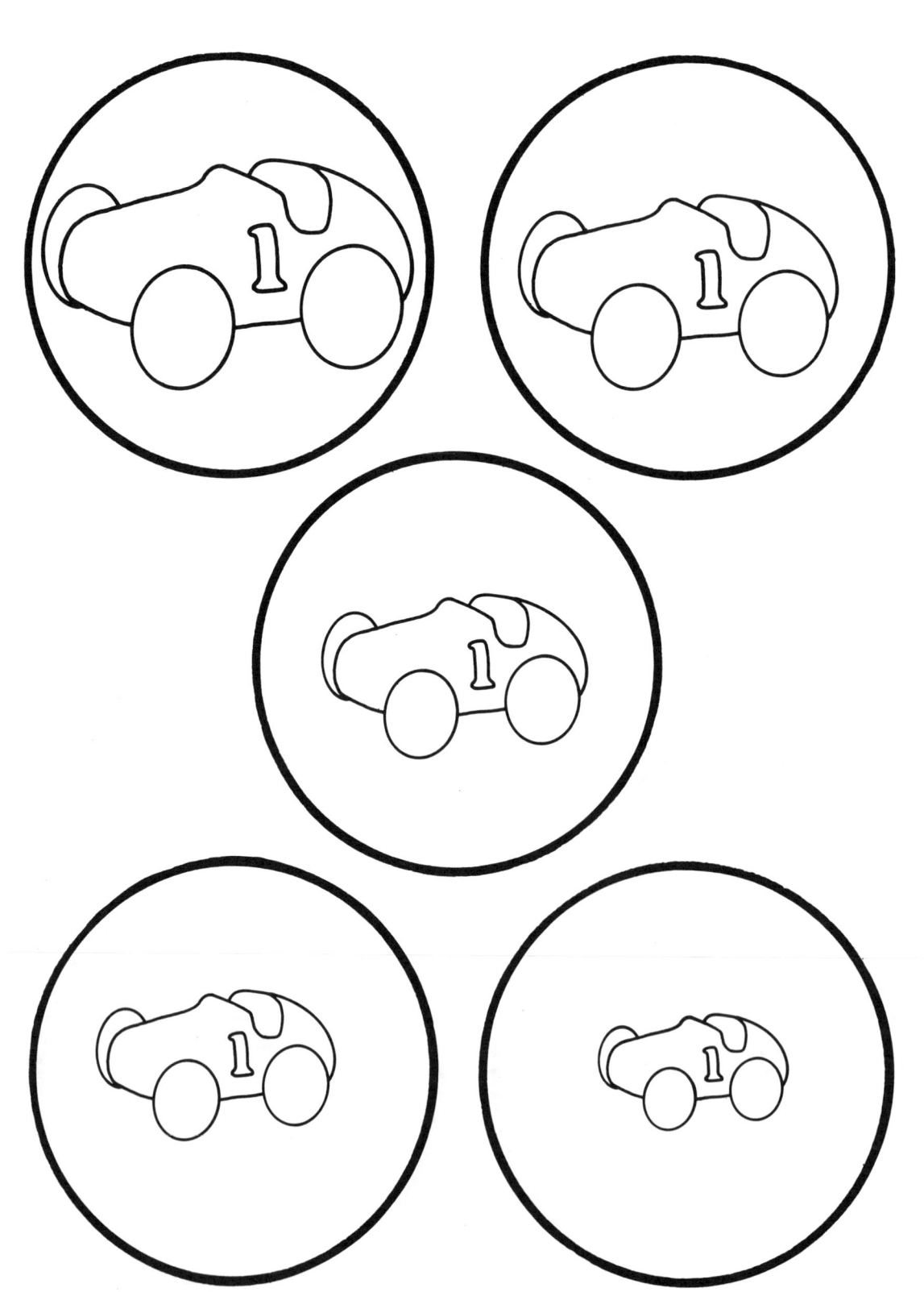

DIFFERENT SIZES

180

TRANSPARENCIES

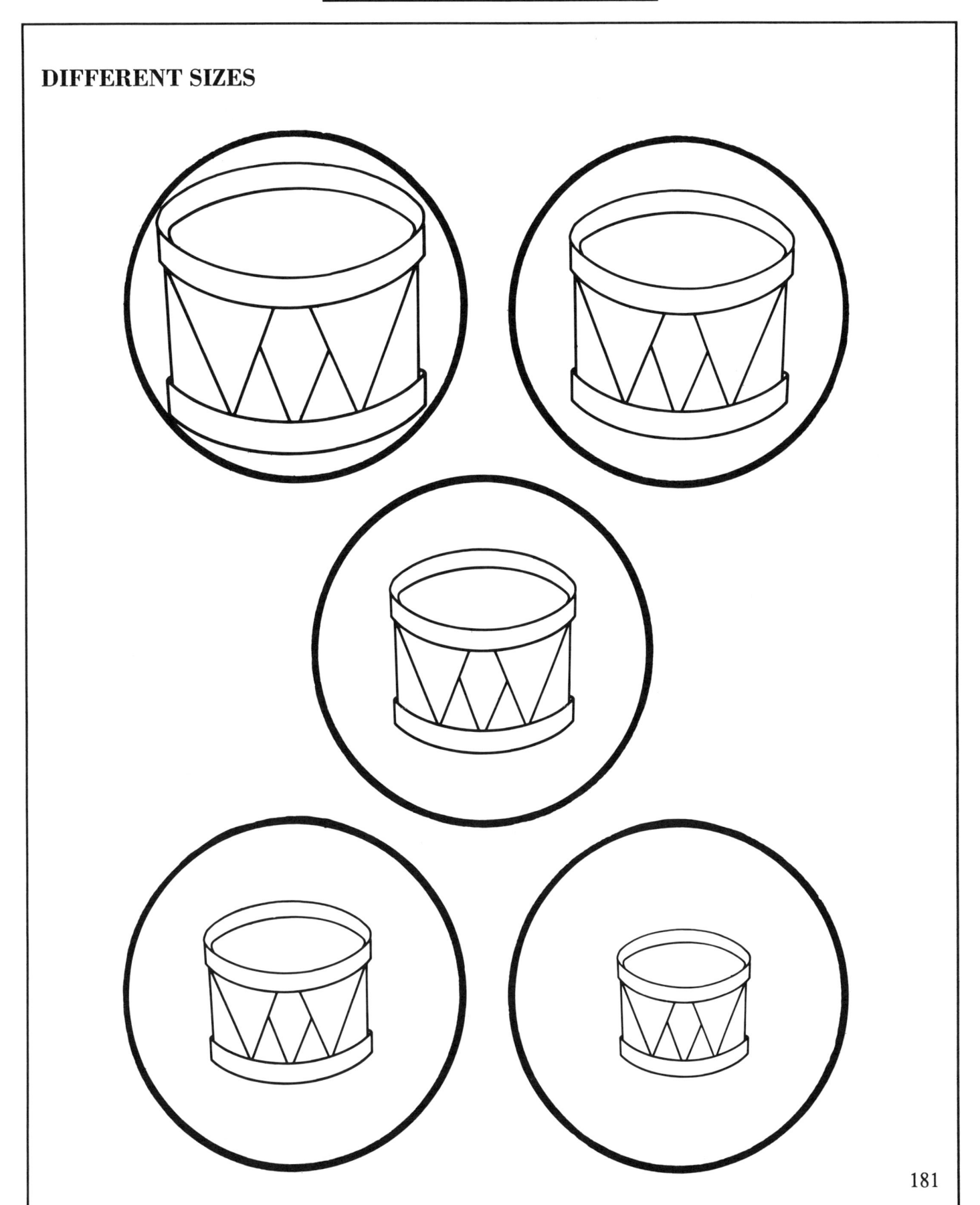

DIFFERENT SIZES

TRANSPARENCIES

DIFFERENT SIZES

TRANSPARENCIES

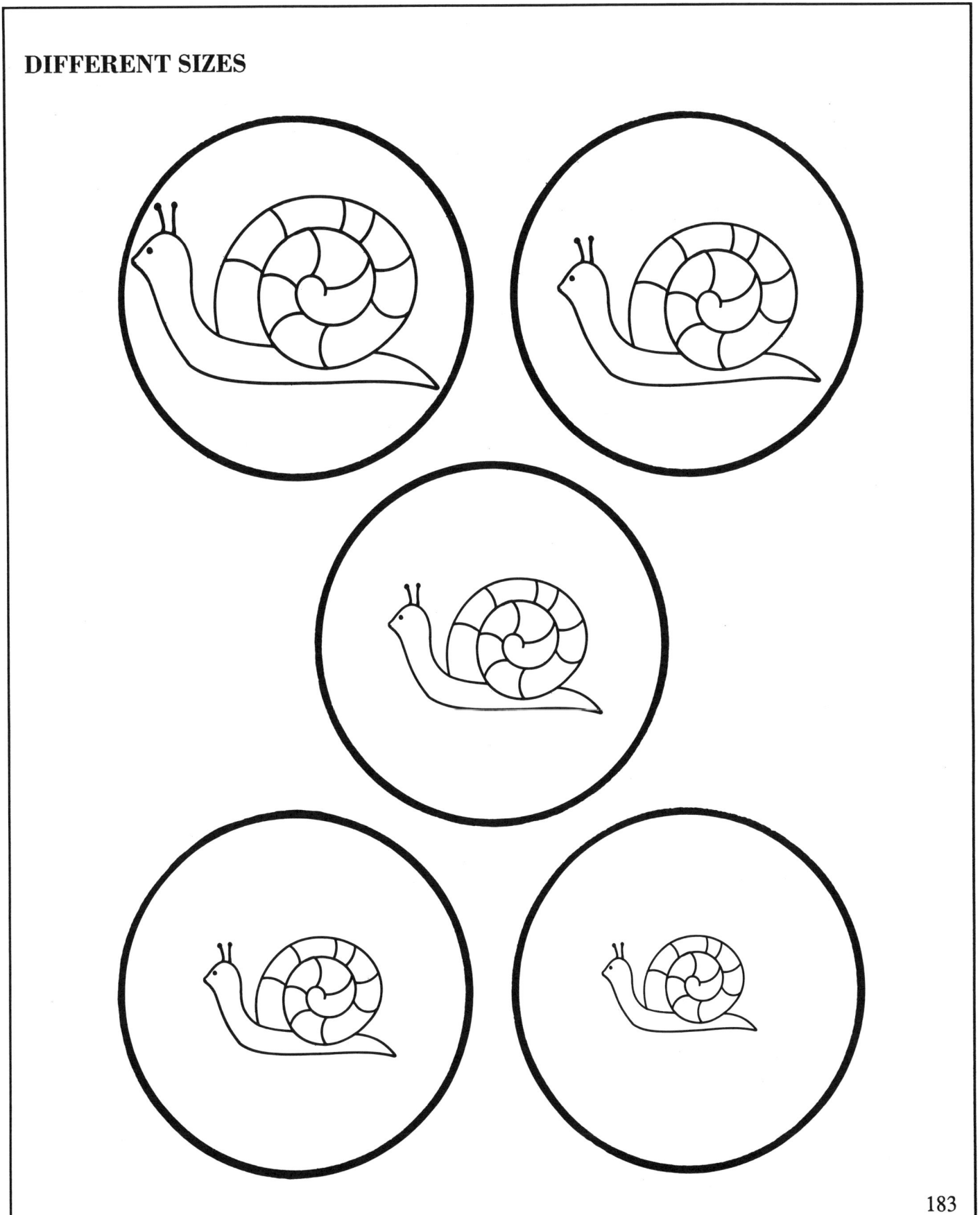

DIFFERENT SIZES

183

TRANSPARENCIES

DIFFERENT SIZES

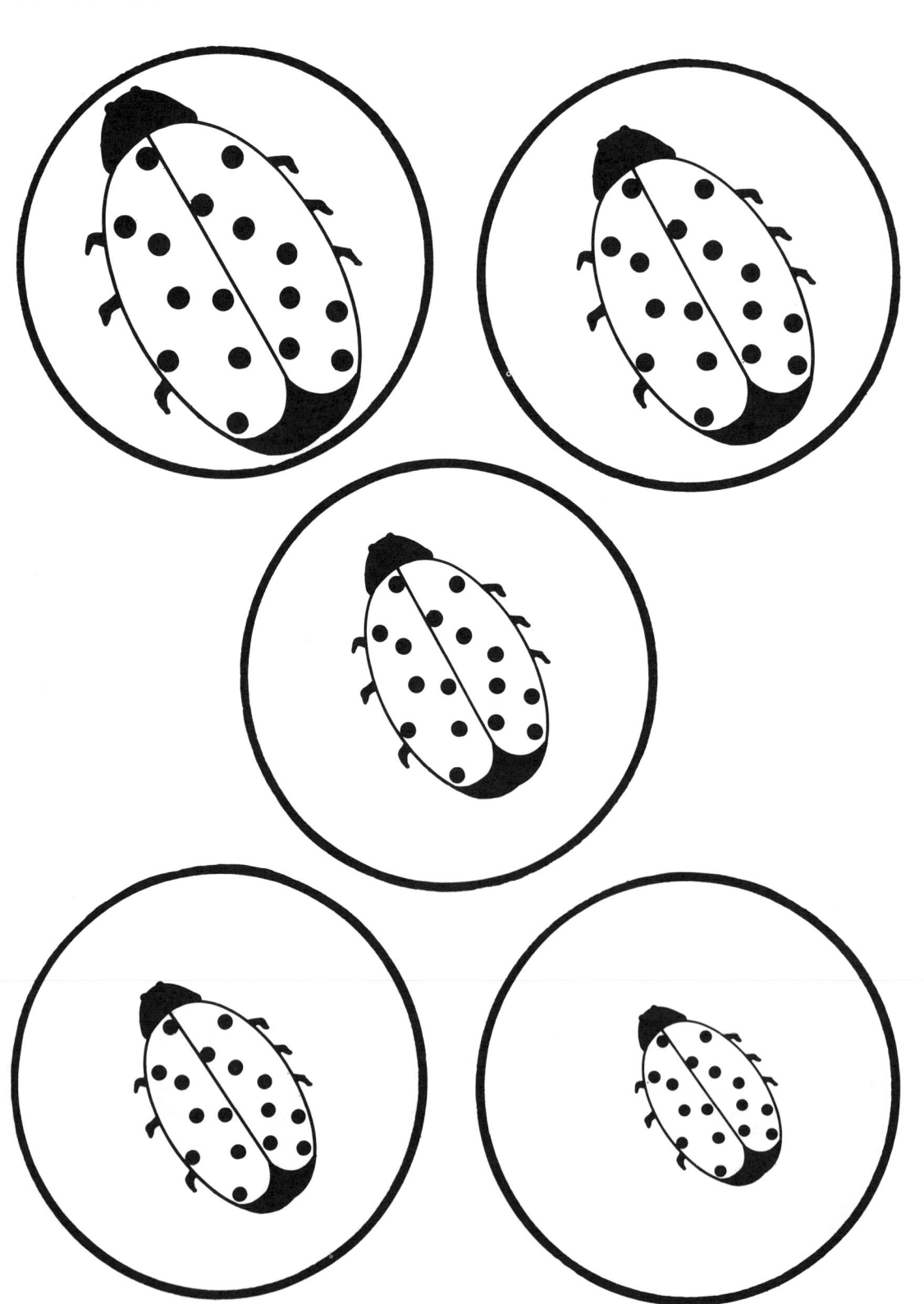

TRANSPARENCIES

DIFFERENT SIZES

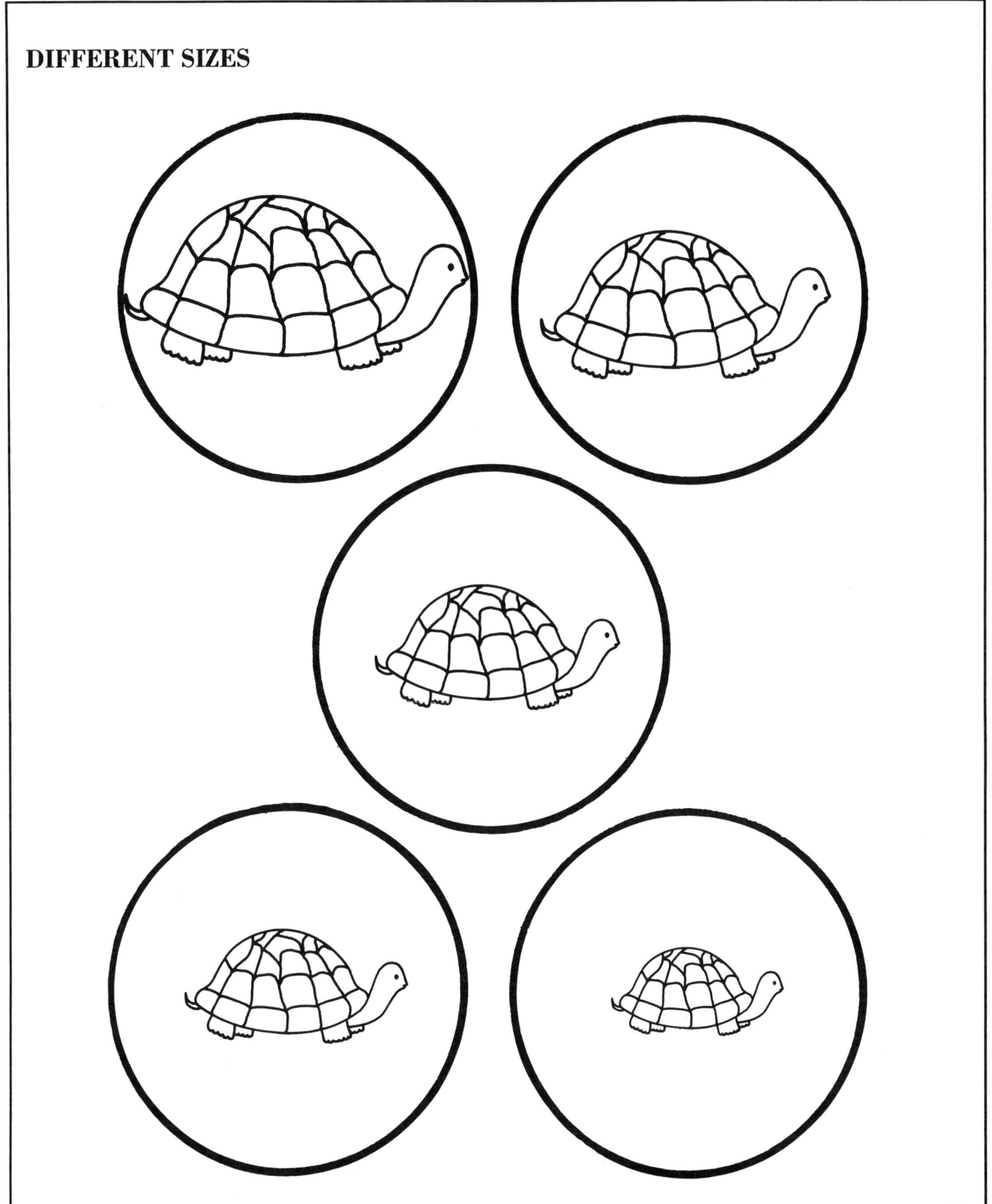

185

TRANSPARENCIES

DIFFERENT SIZES

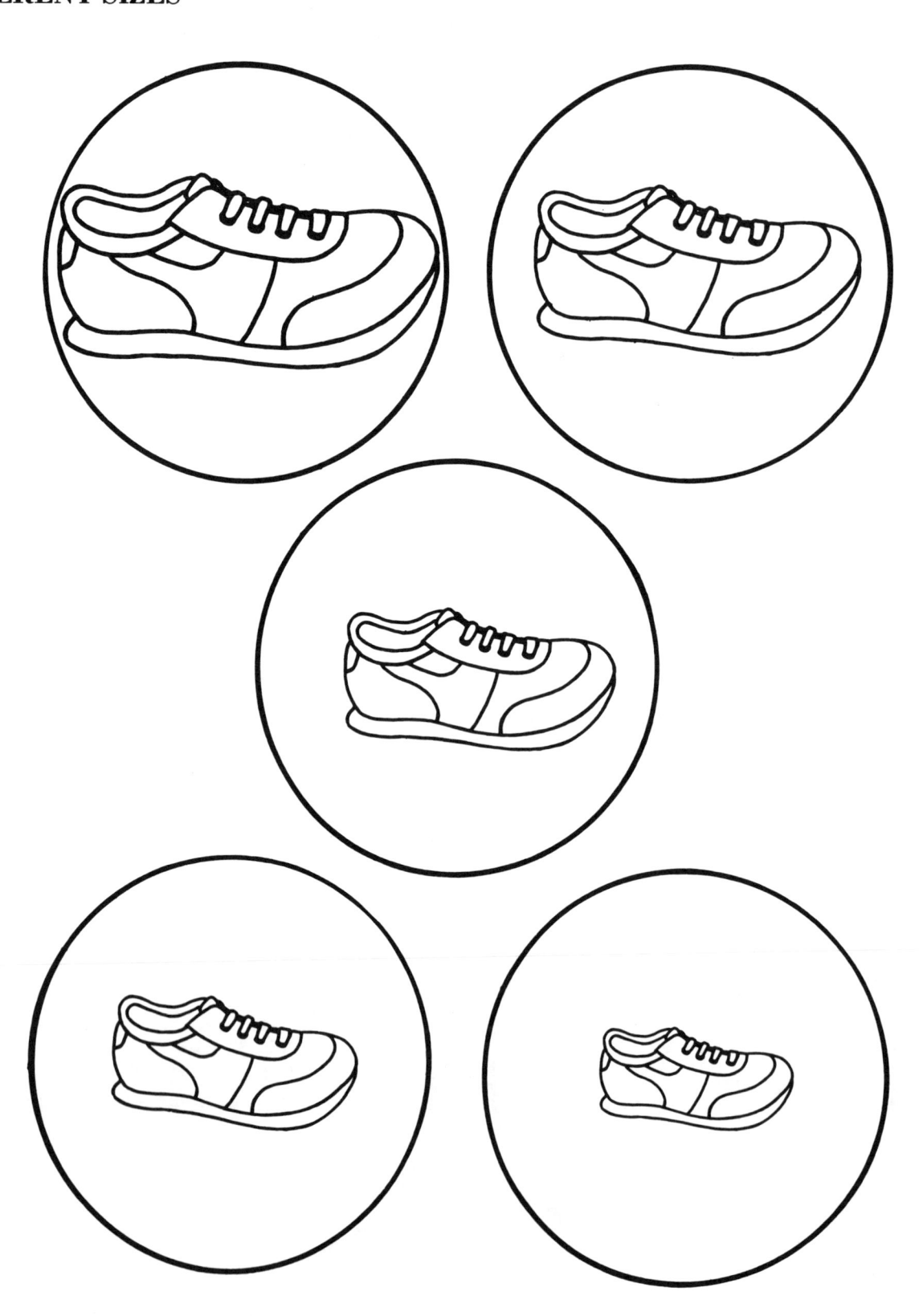

186

TRANSPARENCIES

RELATED SHAPES

187

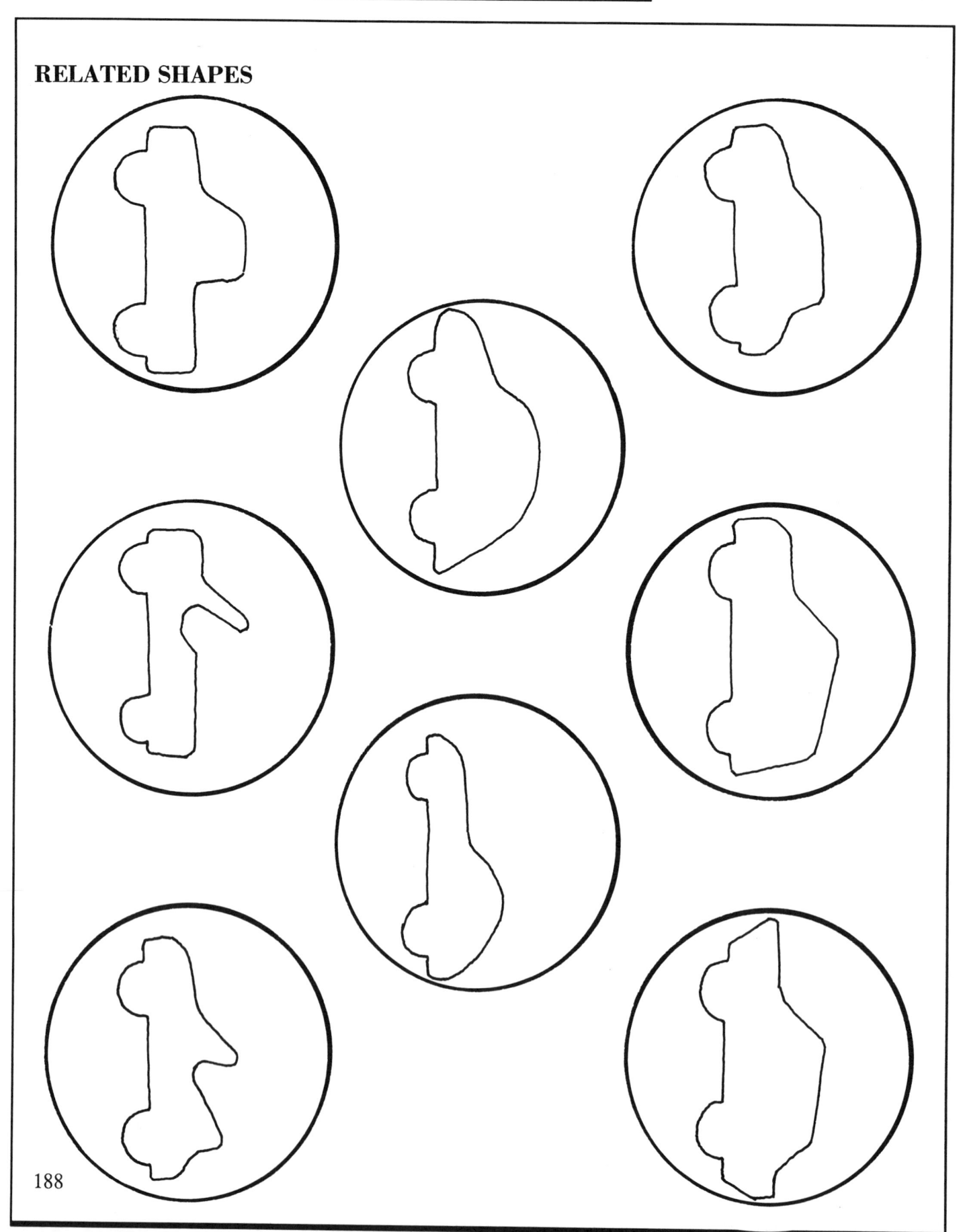

TRANSPARENCIES

RELATED SHAPES

188

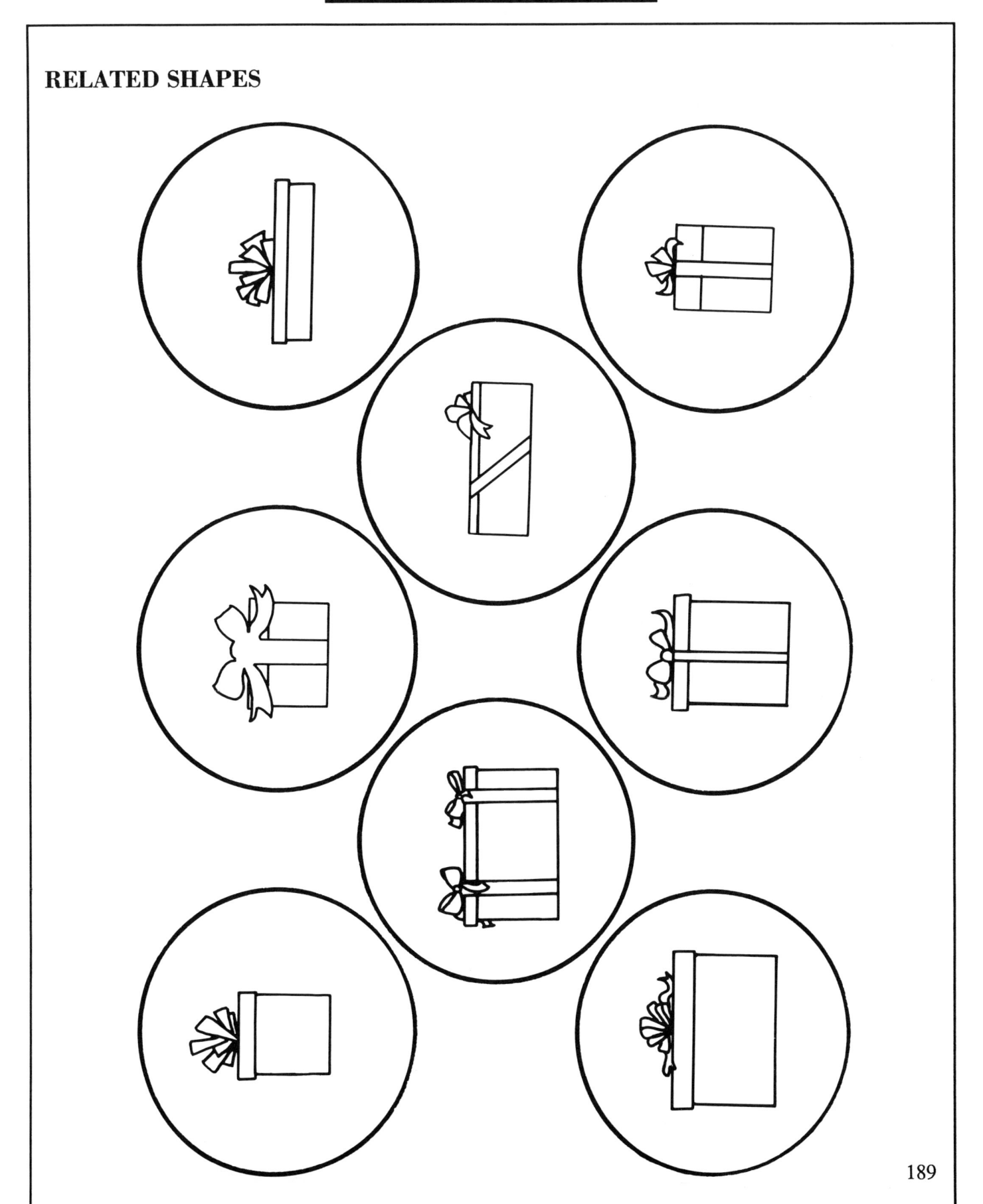

TRANSPARENCIES

RELATED SHAPES

189

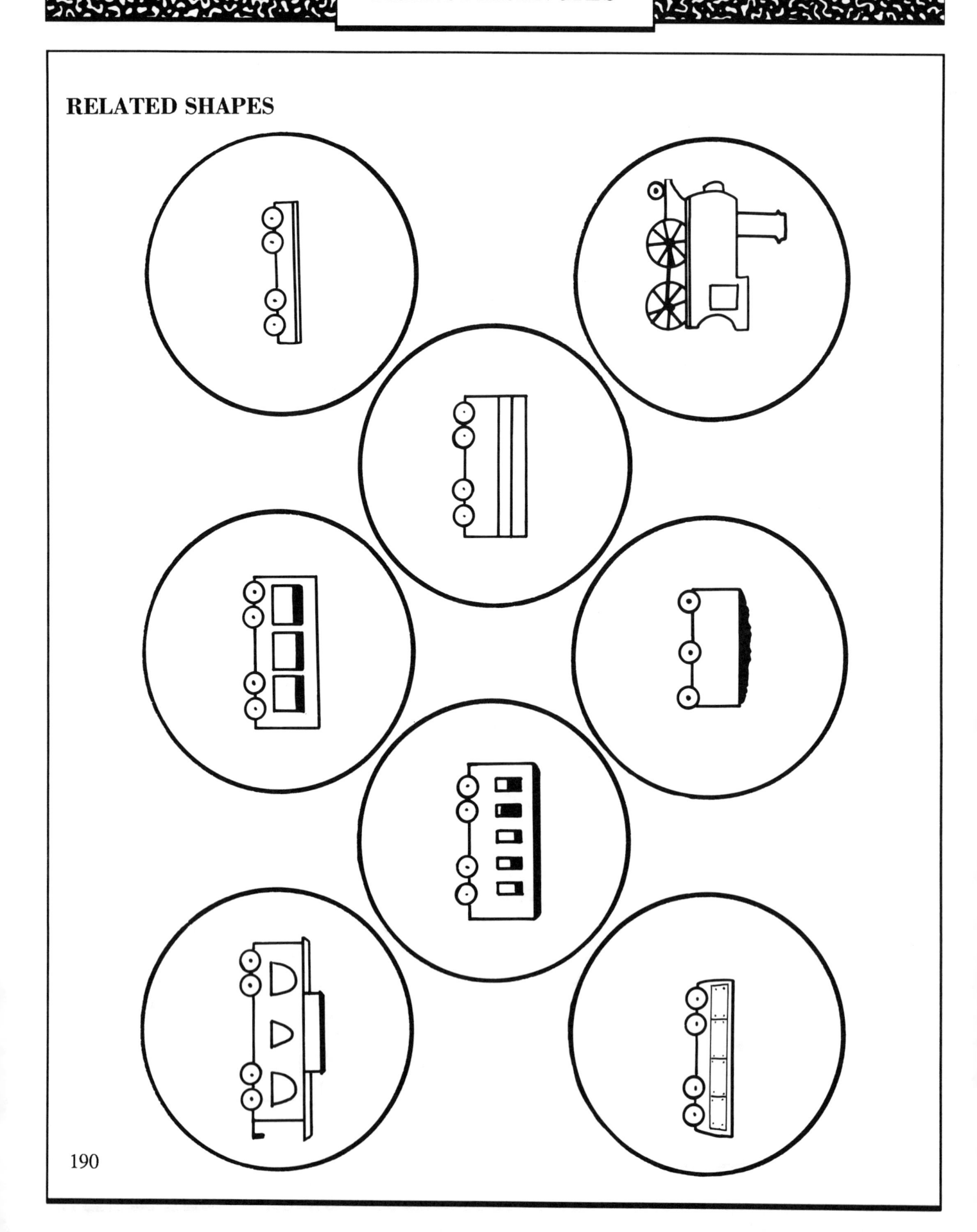

TRANSPARENCIES

RELATED SHAPES

190

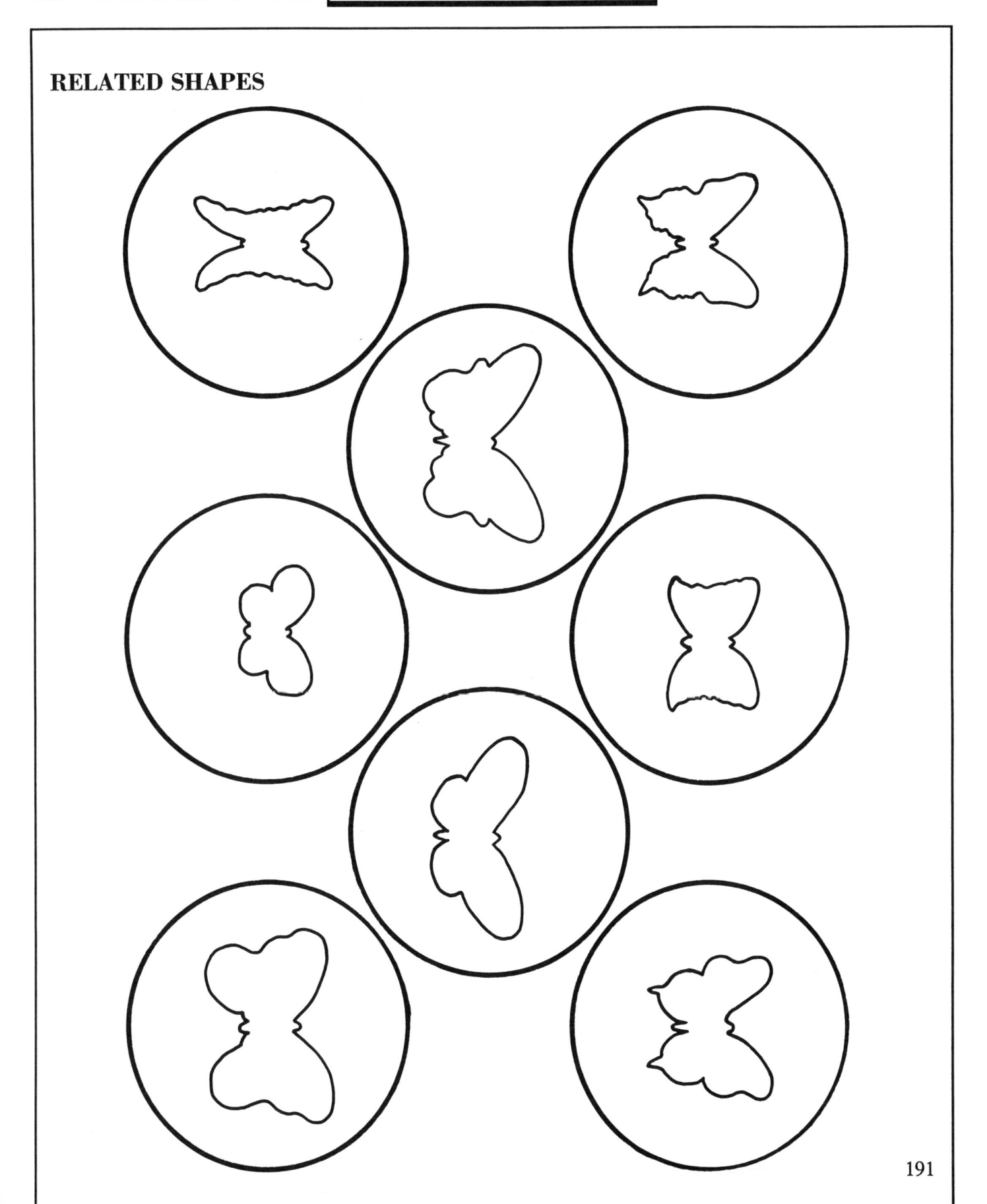

TRANSPARENCIES

RELATED SHAPES

191

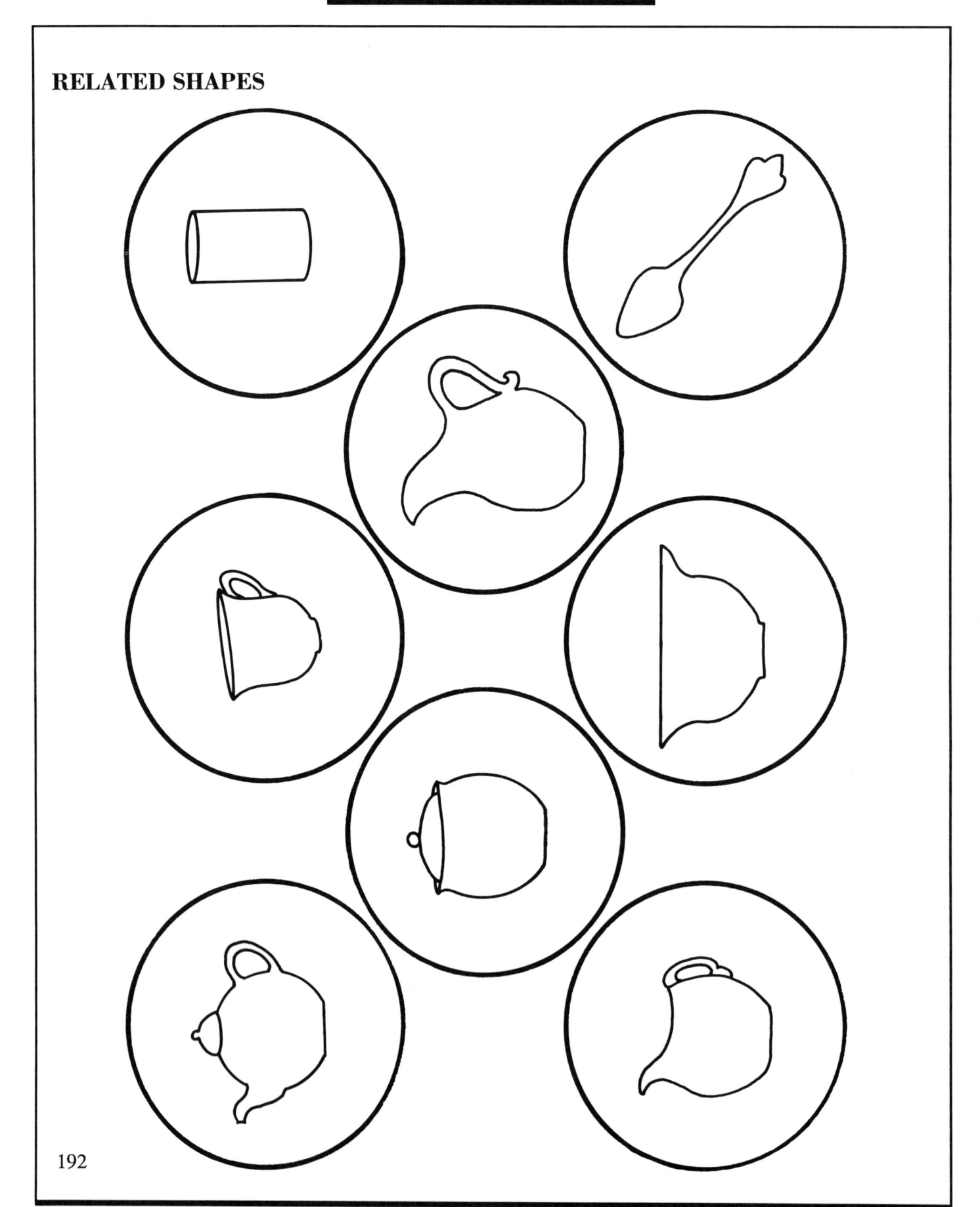

TRANSPARENCIES

RELATED SHAPES

192

TRANSPARENCIES

RELATED SHAPES

193

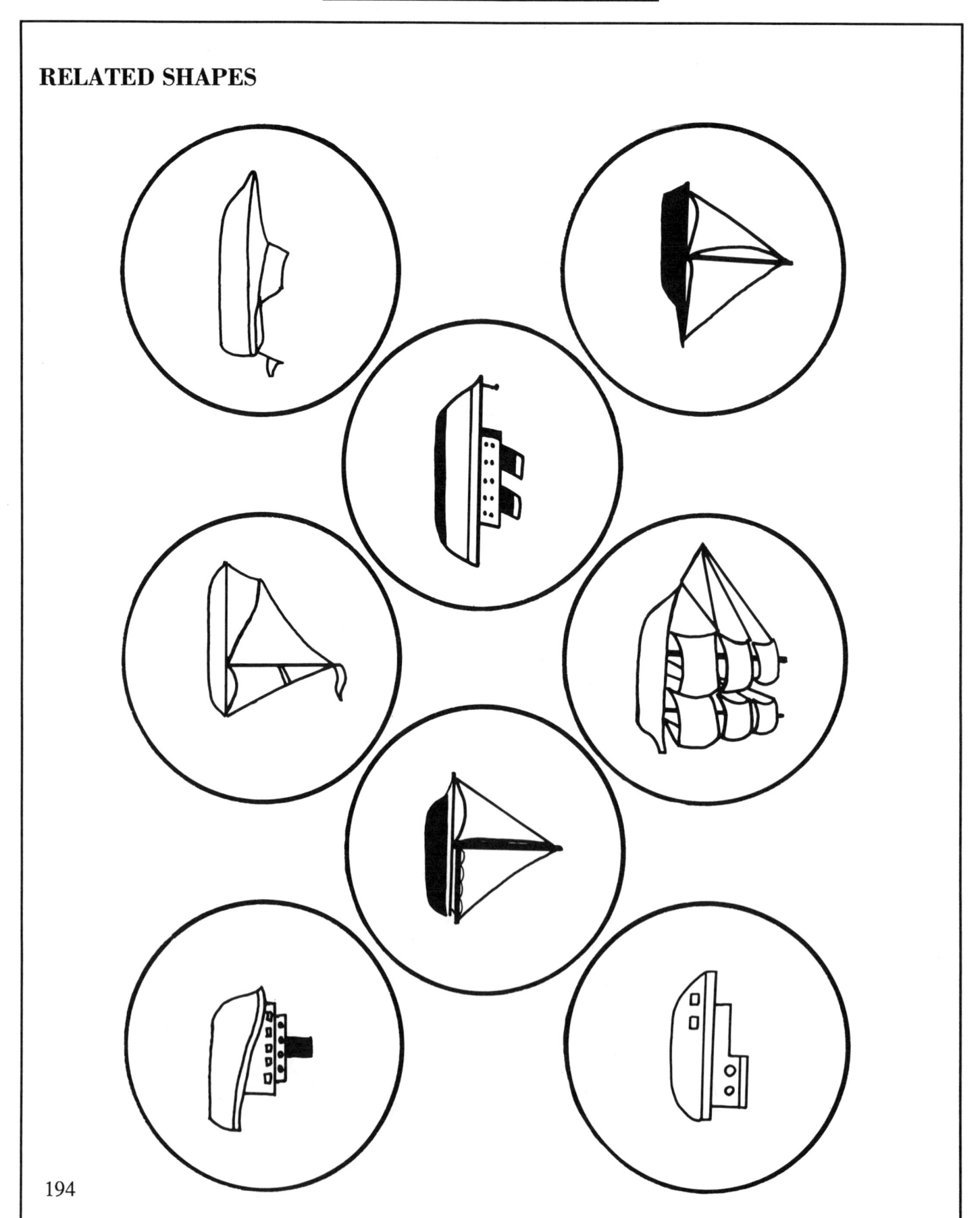

TRANSPARENCIES

RELATED SHAPES

194

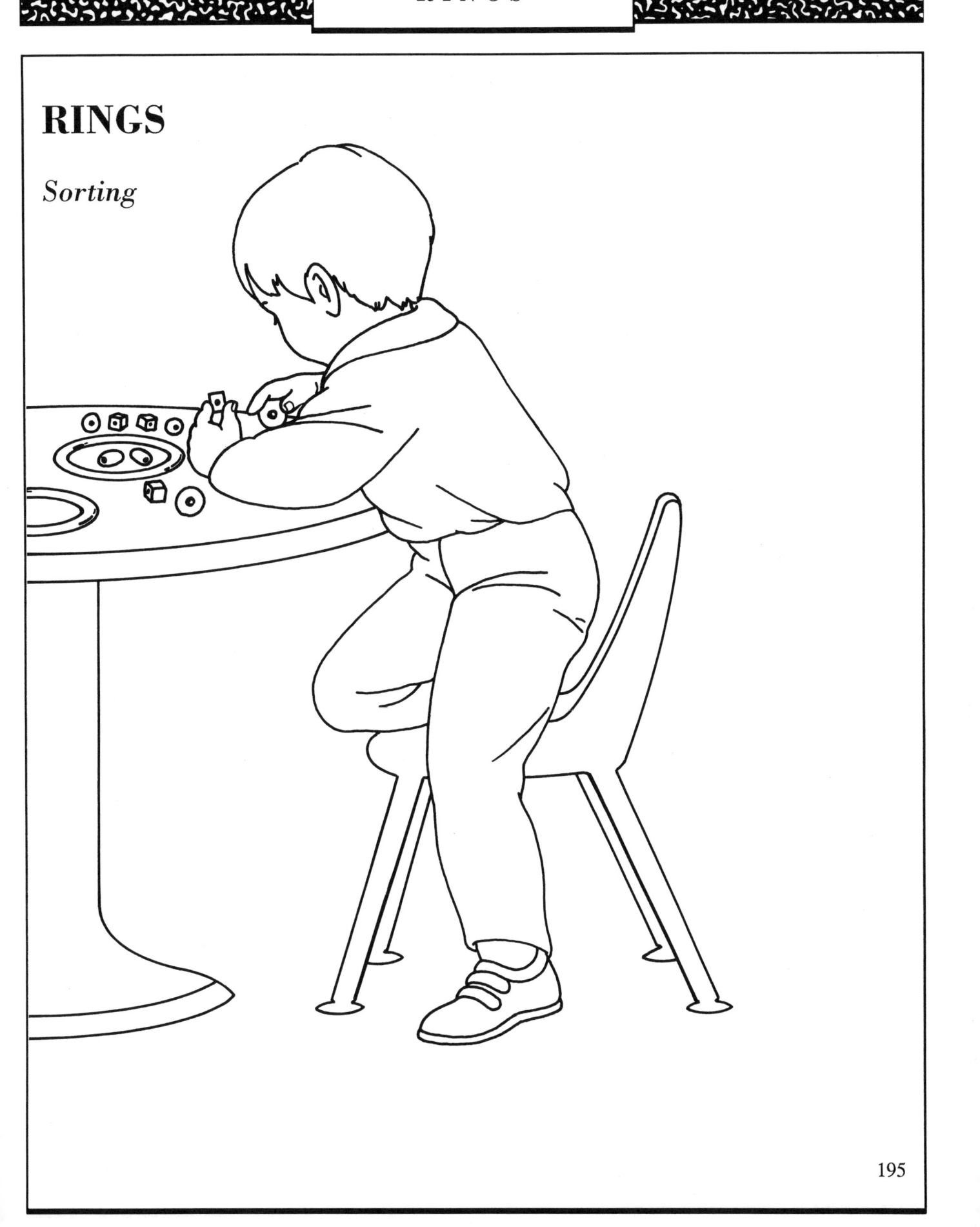

RINGS

Sorting

RINGS

What kids do

Sort small objects, by putting them in rings to define and separate them. The rings can be arranged in a semi-circle which makes a continuous line, without taking up as much workspace as a horizontal line. However, if space is no problem, there is no reason children can't arrange them to suit—horizontally, vertically. Flexibility and creative thinking, as always, are encouraged.

What teachers do

Collect interesting items for the sorting activities. Good things for sorting will begin to jump out at you from everywhere. When you're on vacation, you may see a package of assorted sea-shells at a resort shop, for instance, and immediately think of your class and how much they would enjoy sorting them and examining their minute differences. You'll begin to think twice before discarding things—could these be used for sorting? Little miniatures of all kinds will fascinate you. Or, at least, I hope they will—it's been endless fun for me, and the children I work with get as excited as I do about my new finds.

Think of the objects in these activities as starters, to lead you to make your own discoveries. Allow the number of RINGS activities to grow as much as they will—let it be an ongoing process. Ready-made learning materials abound—they're literally ours for the taking.

Rings can be made of plastic, metal, or wood, and may be found in hobby, handicraft, and variety stores. Macrame rings are perfect; embroidery hoops (separate them into two rings) can be used, and, in a pinch, girls' bracelets will work, although they are a bit small for some of the objects. Rings 4" to 4 1/2" (10 to 11 cm) across work best. You will need six rings per set for all activities except two, CORKS/NOT CORKS and CORNERS/NO CORNERS, which require only two rings; two of the six rings used for the other activities can be used if the sorting objects are very small, or you can provide two larger rings approximately 6" to 8" (15 to 20 cm) in diameter if the size of the sorting objects requires larger rings. For a small class one set of six rings can be used for all the activities. Provide more sets for larger classes. Six different groups of objects to sort, with two or more things in each group, for each activity is the ideal; however, some things such as play money don't have that many classifications, or you may be unable to obtain six different groupings of some things. Simply use the number you have

RINGS

and explain to the children that in some ativities some rings may be left empty, and that in others there may be different numbers of things in the rings. Storage of the sorting objects is very important because of their small size. Please refer to the book's introduction for ideas. Pint-size, self-sealing (freezer-weight) plastic bags are one way to store the items; small baskets and margarine tubs also work well.

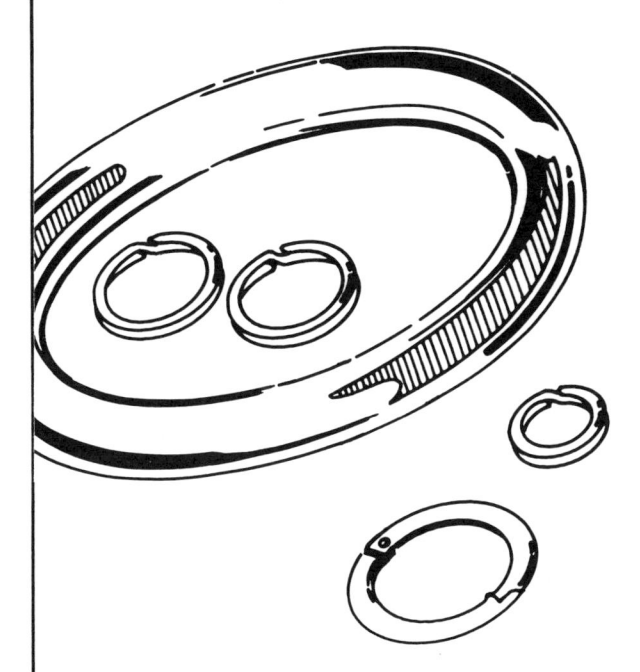

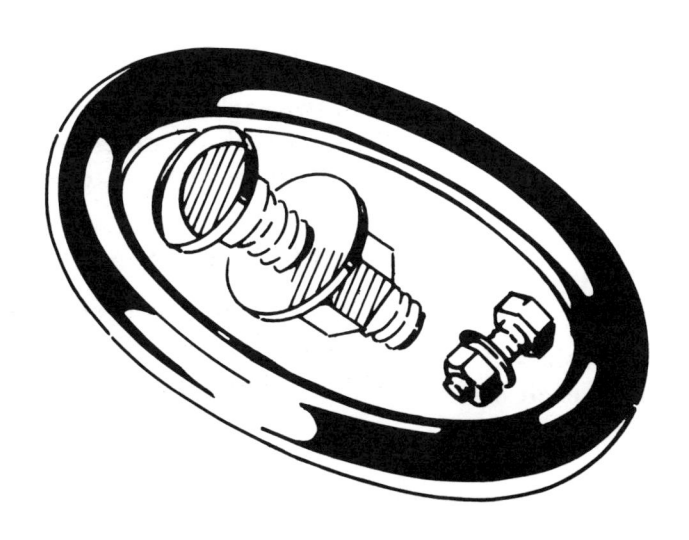

RINGS

FARM ANIMALS

Sorting plastic farm animals by type in rings

LEVEL:
Beginning-Advanced

SKILLS:
Classification by shape; other classifications such as color, characteristics

MATERIALS:
Set of six rings

Plastic farm animals such as cows, horses, pigs, chickens, etc.—2 or more of each kind, 6 or fewer kinds

What kids do
Sort the animals the first way that comes to mind. Then look for other ways to sort them.

What else kids can do
Find other ways to sort these animals—by color, size, name, the type of body covering each has, for example, whether fur, feathers, etc.

CORKS

Sorting corks by size in rings

LEVEL:
Beginning-Advanced

SKILLS:
Classification by size

MATERIALS:
Set of six rings

6 or fewer different sizes of corks, 2 or more of each size

What kids do
Find two corks that are the same size, and put them in a ring. Do the same with the other corks. They may put them in order from small to large or large to small.

What kids and teachers can do
Talk about the way corks are used. Are both ends of these corks the same size? Are corks ever another shape? Put one in water and see what happens.

RINGS

METAL KEY RINGS

Sorting metal key rings by size in rings

What kids do
Find key rings that are the same size and put them into a ring. They may want to put them in order from large to small or small to large.

What kids and teachers can talk about
Talk about how these rings are used. Try to figure out how keys are put on them. Why are they useful?

LEVEL:
Beginning-Advanced

SKILLS:
Classification by size

MATERIALS:
Set of six rings

6 or fewer sizes of metal key rings, 2 or more of each size

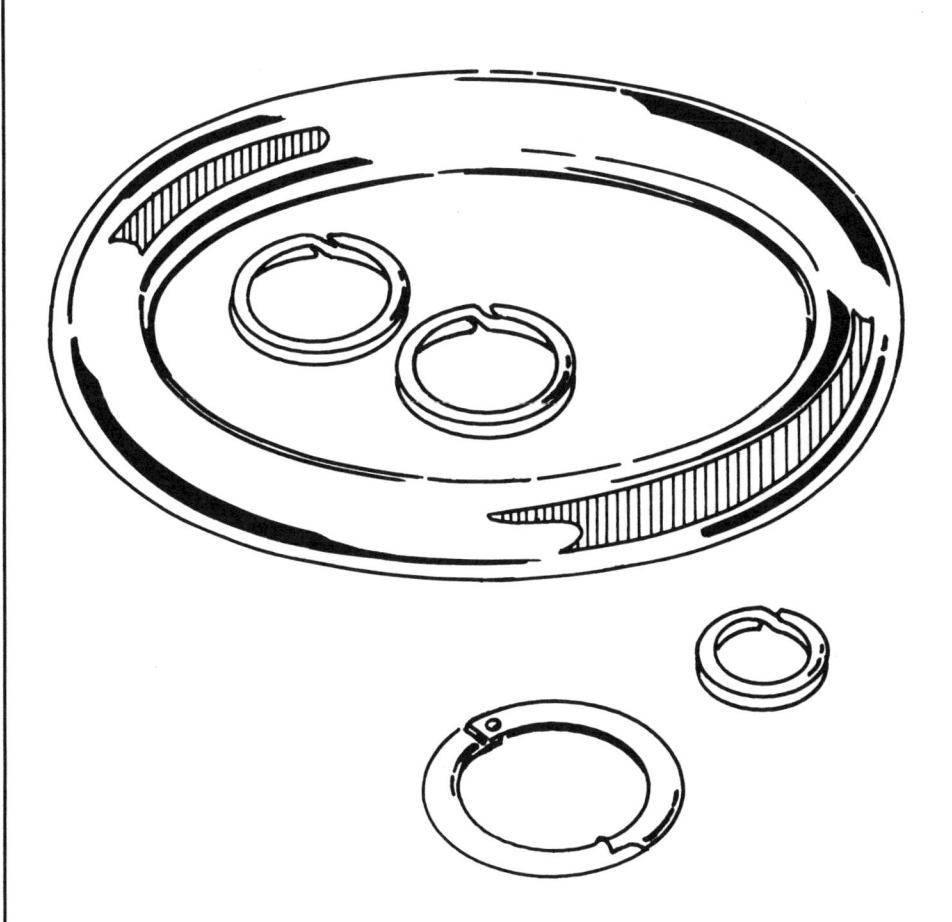

199

RINGS

LEVEL:
Beginning-Advanced

SKILLS:
Classification by color

MATERIALS:
Set of six rings

40 to 50 fringe balls in 6 or fewer different colors, all the same size; use 18 to 24 for BEGINNERS. These fluffy yarn balls, or pompoms, are sold in handicraft and fabric stores.

FRINGE BALLS (POMPOMS—BY COLOR)

Sorting yarn balls by color in rings

What kids do
Sort the balls by color as they put them in the rings; can they be sorted any other way?

What kids and teachers can talk about
Talk about the colors with beginners.

LEVEL:
Beginning-Advanced

SKILLS:
Classification by size

MATERIALS:
Set of six rings

6 or fewer different sizes of fringe balls, all the same color, approximately 40 to 50 for INTERMEDIATES and ADVANCED, fewer for BEGINNERS. These are available at handicraft and fabric stores.

FRINGE BALLS (POMPOMS—BY SIZE)

Sorting yarn balls by size in rings

What kids do
Sort the balls by size in the rings. Can they be sorted any other way?

What kids and teachers can talk about
Talk about why the fringe balls can't be sorted any other way than by size.

RINGS

LARGE/SMALL

Sorting large and small toys and discards by size in rings

What kids do

Put two things that are alike, except for their size, in a ring. Each ring will hold a pair of objects, one large and one small.

What kids and teachers can talk about

Talk about the names of and uses for all the items. Why are they made in two different sizes?

LEVEL:
Beginning-Advanced

SKILLS:
Classification by size, recognizing similarities

MATERIALS:
Set of six rings

6 or fewer pairs of things in a large and small size: large and small crayons, spools, corks, marbles, plastic paper clips, plastic caps or lids, washers, etc..

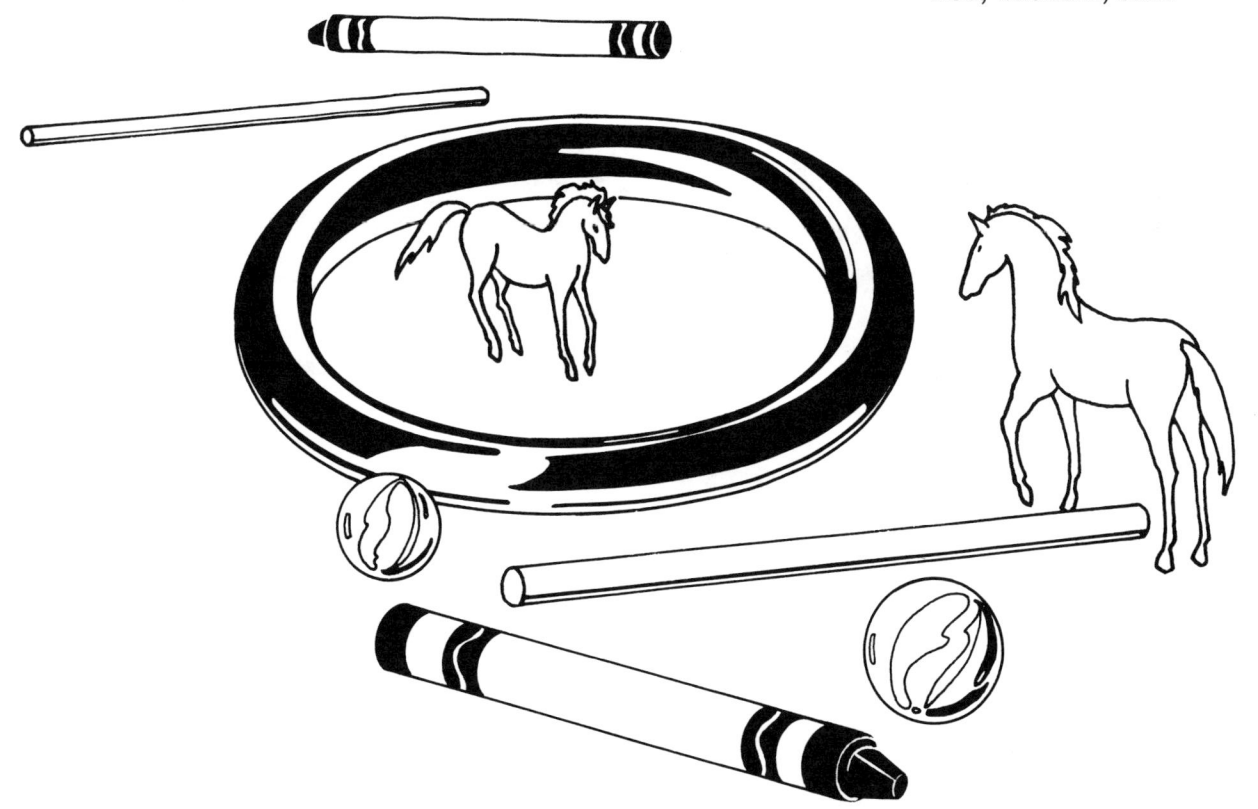

RINGS

BUTTONS (ASSORTED)

Sorting buttons several ways in rings

LEVEL:
Beginning-Advanced

SKILLS:
Classification by color and other features

MATERIALS:
Set of six rings

50 or more assorted buttons. For BEGINNERS, use large buttons only and approximately 25 of them.

What kids do
Sort the buttons as many different ways as they can devise—for instance by color, by size, by shape.

What else kids can do
Find other ways to sort these buttons—for instance, by the number of holes they have. Separate the ones that have shanks. If some are metal, place them together.

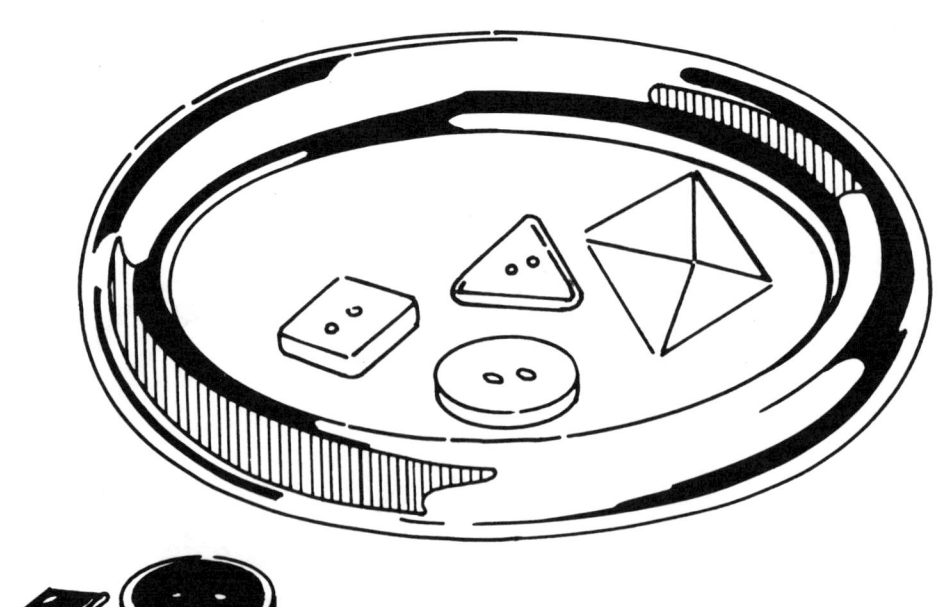

RINGS

PLASTIC EGGS

Sorting plastic eggs by size or color in rings

What kids do
Find eggs that are exactly alike and put them into a ring.

What else kids can do
Try sorting the eggs by color and by size.

LEVEL:
Beginning-Advanced

SKILLS:
Classification by size or by color

MATERIALS:
Set of six rings

6 or fewer sets of hollow plastic eggs that differ by color and/or size. Glue all eggs together to prevent breaking.

WASHERS

Sorting metal washers by size in rings

What kids do
Find washers that are exactly alike and put them into a ring. Then put the rings in order from small to large or large to small.

What else kids can do
Can the washers be stacked from large to small to make towers?

LEVEL:
Beginning-Advanced

SKILLS:
Classification by size

MATERIALS:
Set of six rings

6 or fewer sizes of metal washers, 3 or more of each size or kind

RINGS

NUTS

Sorting different kinds of unshelled nuts in rings

LEVEL:
Beginning-Advanced

SKILLS:
Classification by size and by features

MATERIALS:
Set of six rings

Different kinds of nuts in the shell— walnuts, pecans, Brazils, filberts, almonds—3 or more of each kind

What kids do
Find nuts that are exactly alike and put them into a ring.

What kids and teachers can do
Talk about the kinds of nuts, their names, whether you have eaten them, etc.. Crack some like them one day and see the insides.

RINGS

WILD ANIMALS

Sorting plastic wild animals in rings

What kids do

Sort the animals by their shapes.

What kids and teachers can talk about

Can the animals be sorted any way besides shape—by color for instance? Talk about the names of the animals, their habitats, etc.

LEVEL:
Beginning-Advanced

SKILLS:
Classification by shape

MATERIALS:
Set of six rings

6 or fewer kinds of plastic wild animals—2 or more of each kind

BOTTLES

Sorting bottles by size in rings

What kids do

Find bottles that are exactly alike and put them into a ring. If there are matching caps, snap them on before or after they put the bottles in the rings.

What else kids can do

Order the bottles in two sets on the table in graduated order.

LEVEL:
Beginning-Advanced

SKILLS:
Classification by size

MATERIALS:
Set of six rings

6 or fewer different sizes of plastic medicine bottles (available from a pharmacy), 2 or more of each size

bottles may be used without caps; if caps are used they should be the snap-on kind, not the safety kind

RINGS

BUTTONS (BY COLOR)

LEVEL:
Beginning-Advanced

SKILLS:
Classification by color

MATERIALS:
Set of six rings

Buttons in 6 or fewer different colors, all the same style and size

Sorting buttons by color in rings

SAFETY NOTE: Do not use very small buttons. This activity is not safe for children who might put the buttons in their mouths.

What kids do

Sort the buttons by color in the rings. Do they see any other ways to sort them?

What kids and teachers can talk about

Talk about colors with BEGINNERS. Talk about why the buttons can't be sorted any other ways with INTERMEDIATES and ADVANCED.

BUTTONS (BY SIZE)

LEVEL:
Beginning-Advanced

SKILLS:
Classification by size

MATERIALS:
Set of six rings

Buttons in 6 or fewer different sizes, all the same color—fabric and handicraft stores often sell broken sets of buttons inexpensively.

Sorting buttons by size in rings

SAFETY NOTE: Do not use very small buttons. This activity is not safe for children who might put the buttons in their mouths.

What kids do

Sort the buttons by size in the rings. Do they see any other ways to sort them? Order the sorted rings according to size—large to small or small to large.

What kids and teachers can do

Talk to BEGINNERS about largest, smallest, etc. Combine these buttons with those from the previous activity. Now what are the possibilities for sorting?

RINGS

BEADS

Sorting beads by color, size, or appearance in rings

Note: Only large beads are safe for BEGINNERS to use.

What kids do
Find beads that are exactly alike and put them into a ring.

What else kids can do
Sort the beads by color, by size, and by any other characteristic they may have in common, such as design.

LEVEL:
Beginning-Advanced

SKILLS:
Classification by size, color, feature

MATERIALS:
Set of six rings

6 or fewer kinds of large wood or plastic beads, in varying sizes and colors, 3 or more alike

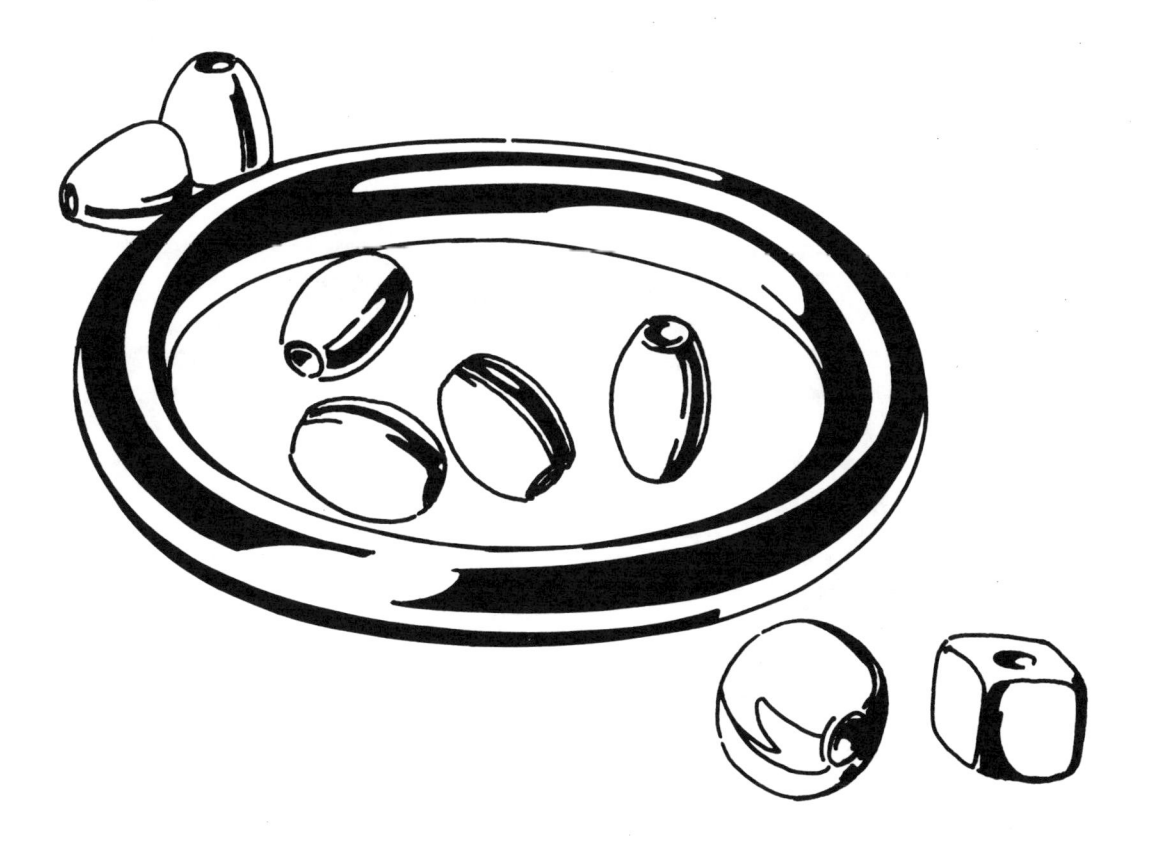

RINGS

DINOSAURS

Sorting plastic dinosaurs in rings

LEVEL:
Beginning-Advanced

SKILLS:
Classification by shape

MATERIALS:
Set of six rings

6 or fewer kinds of plastic dinosaurs—2 or more of each kind

What kids do
Sort the dinosaurs according to their shapes. Then look for other ways to sort them.

What else kids can do
Find other ways to sort the dinosaurs—by color, name, etc.. Children may be inspired to look at picture books of dinosaurs and to learn the names of some of them, so have some relevant books on hand.

RINGS

TOYS

Sorting small toys in rings

Note: Make several TOYS activites if you like, using different kinds of toys for each activity.

What kids do
Sort the toys in the rings, placing those which are the same together.

What kids and teachers can talk about
Talk about the names of the toys.

LEVEL:
Beginning-Advanced

SKILLS:
Classification by function

MATERIALS:
Set of six rings

Tiny toys (these come packaged in toy and variety stores, priced inexpensively—look for tea sets, tools, etc.) The package should contain 2 or more of each kind of toy, 6 or fewer different kinds.

MEASURING SPOONS

Sorting measuring spoons according to size in rings

What kids do
Sort the spoons into the rings according to size.

What kids and teachers can talk about
Talk about sizes—largest, smallest, etc.. Talk about how these spoons are used. Can they be nested together?

LEVEL:
Beginning-Advanced

SKILLS:
Classification by size

MATERIALS:
Set of six rings

2 sets of measuring spoons, 6 sizes (tablespoon, one-and-one-half-teaspoon, teaspoon, half-teaspoon, fourth-teaspoon, eighth-teaspoon) if possible

RINGS

THREAD

Sorting spools of thread by color in rings

LEVEL:
Beginning-Advanced

SKILLS:
Classification by color and color families

MATERIALS:
Set of six rings

Spools of thread, in six or fewer colors—2 or more of each color, though not necessarily the exact same shades—for instance the red group could include red, red-orange, rose, and pink.

White glue

What kids do
Sort the spools by color or color families in the rings, putting all shades of red together, all shades of blue together, etc.

What kids and teachers can talk about
Talk about the colors and color families—light and dark shades of the same color, etc..

NOTE: Put a generous drop of glue on the end of the thread on the spool, to prevent its being unwound

COLORS/OBJECTS

Sorting objects by color in rings

LEVEL:
Beginning-Advanced

SKILLS:
Classification by color

MATERIALS:
Set of six rings

Miscellaneous objects—toys, discards—in 6 or fewer colors, 2 or more of each color

What kids do
Put the objects of the same color in one ring.

What else kids can do
Look for other ways to sort the objects.

RINGS

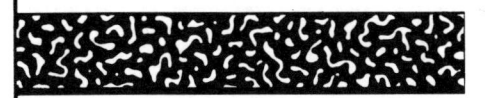

ET CETERA

Sorting miscellaneous objects by similarities in rings

What kids do

Look at the objects carefully and put the ones that belong together in one ring.

What kids and teachers can do

Work together to sort the objects if some children have trouble seeing the similarities.

LEVEL:

Intermediate-Advanced

SKILLS:

Classification by function or character

MATERIALS:

Set of six rings

Miscellaneous items that are related or alike—2 of each. These can be discards of all kinds, such as spools, office supplies, jewelry, etc.—6 or fewer different kinds.

211

RINGS

METAL, PLASTIC, WOOD, PAPER, FABRIC, RUBBER

Sorting objects according to their material in rings

LEVEL:
Intermediate-Advanced

SKILLS:
Classification by material

MATERIALS:
Set of six rings

3 or more objects of each kind of material:

metal: keys, hardware, jewelry

plastic: toys, bottle caps, small discards

wood: burned match, twig, lollipop stick

paper: wrappers, cardboard, paper scraps

fabric: scraps of different kinds of cloth

rubber: hose washer, pencil eraser

What kids do
Sort the objects according to the kind of material they're made of. Each ring will contain similar materials.

What kids and teachers can talk about
Talk about the different materials and where they come from.

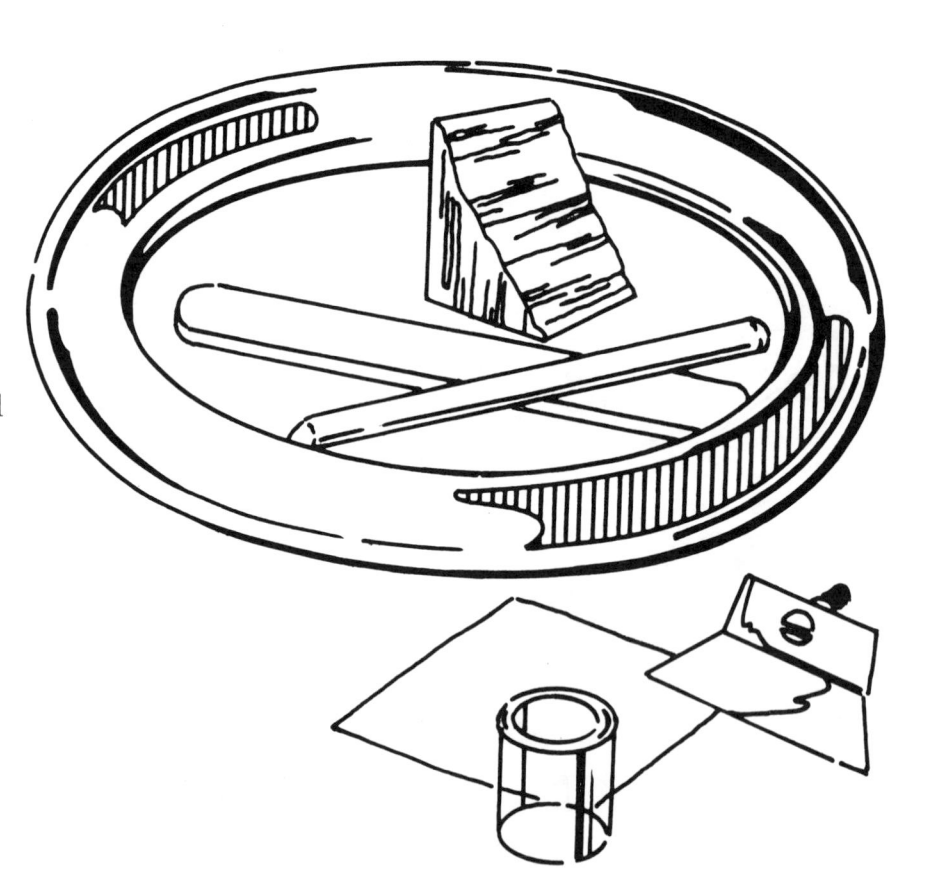

RINGS

LACE

Sorting strips of white lace by pattern in rings

What kids do

Find three pieces of lace that match exactly and put them in one ring.

What else kids can do

Lay the three matching lengths of lace end to end to make 18" (46 cm) lengths.

LEVEL:
Intermediate-Advanced

SKILLS:
Classification by pattern

MATERIALS:
Set of six rings

6" (15 cm) strips of white lace in 6 or fewer different patterns, 3 of each

COINS

Sorting play coins by denomination in rings

What kids do

Find coins which are exactly alike and put them in one ring.

What kids and teachers can talk about

Talk about the names and denominations of the coins.

LEVEL:
Intermediate-Advanced

SKILLS:
Classification by denomination

MATERIALS:
Set of six rings

Play coins of different denominations such as penny, dime, nickel, quarter, etc., made of plastic or metal, 3 or more of each kind

RINGS

HARDWARE

Sorting hardware of matching sizes in rings

LEVEL:
Intermediate-Advanced

SKILLS:
Classification by size

MATERIALS:
Set of six rings

6 or fewer sets of matching bolts, nuts, and washers, each set consisting of a bolt, nut, and washer of the same size—for example: 1/4" (6 mm), 5/16" (8 mm), 3/8" (10 mm), 7/16" (11 mm), 1/2" (13 mm), 5/8" (16 mm)

What kids do

The only way to find a matching set is to put them together. Put the washers on the bolts they fit, and then put the matching nuts on the bolts. Put matched sets in the RINGS, and order the rings from small to large or large to small. Take the pieces apart when they're finished.

What kids and teachers can do

Talk about the names of these pieces of hardware. Some children will appreciate help putting the sets together; it takes practice to learn to avoid crossing the threads.

RINGS

FABRIC PATTERNS

Sorting squares of fabric by pattern in rings

What kids do

Find the squares that are exactly alike and put them into one ring.

What kids and teachers can talk about

Talk about the patterns using descriptive words such as dots, flowers, plaid, stripes, etc..

LEVEL:
Intermediate-Advanced

SKILLS:
Classification by pattern

MATERIALS:
Set of six rings

2" squares of fabric in 6 or fewer different patterns, 3 or more of each pattern (apply iron-on interfacing to the backs for stiffening if desired)

MARBLES

Sorting marbles according to coloration in rings

What kids do

Look carefully to find the marbles that are colored alike and put them in one ring.

What kids and teachers can talk about

Talk about marbles as toys and the games children sometimes play with them. Pictures in encyclopedias will show marbles with many different designs.

LEVEL:
Intermediate-Advanced

SKILLS:
Classification by pattern and color

MATERIALS:
Set of six rings

Marbles of 6 or fewer different colorations (differences may be subtle), 3 or more of each

RINGS

LEVEL:
Intermediate-Advanced

SKILLS:
Classification by denomination

MATERIALS:
Set of six rings

Paper play money in several denominations, such as twenty, ten, five, and one dollar, 3 or more of each

PAPER MONEY

Sorting play currency by denomination in rings

What kids do
Sort the play money in the rings according to denomination.

What kids and teachers can do
Notice that the money looks different on each side. Compare it with real money if possible. Talk about why the play money does not look exactly like real money.

LEVEL:
Intermediate-Advanced

SKILLS:
Classification by texture

MATERIALS:
Set of six rings

2" (5 cm) squares of sandpaper of different textures, from coarse to fine, all of the same color—2 or more of each texture (glue the squares to cardboard squares for strength if desired)

SANDPAPER

Sorting squares of sandpaper by their texture in rings

Note: If only three or four different textures in one color are available, the activity is quite adequate with that number.

What kids do
Find the sandpaper squares that feel alike. Place them in one ring.

What else kids can do
Try matching the sandpaper squares with eyes closed, by touch only.

RINGS

SHELLS/ROCKS

Sorting shells or rocks in rings

Note: Shells and rocks should not be mixed in an activity; make one or the other or both.

What kids do
Find the shells or rocks that are exactly alike and put them in one ring.

What kids and teachers can do
Look up pictures of the shells or rocks and learn the names of some of them.

LEVEL:
Intermediate-Advanced

SKILLS:
Classification by feature or shape

MATERIALS:
Set of six rings

6 or fewer kinds of shells or rocks, 3 or more of each kind

217

RINGS

PEGBOARD HOOKS

Sorting metal pegboard hooks by shape in rings

LEVEL:
Intermediate-Advanced

SKILLS:
Classification by shape

MATERIALS:

Set of six rings

1 package of pegboard hooks containing 2 or more hooks of each shape—available at hardware stores—use hooks of 6 or fewer different shapes

What kids do
Find hooks that are exactly alike and put matching hooks in one ring.

What kids and teachers can talk about
Talk about the way these hooks are used.

RINGS

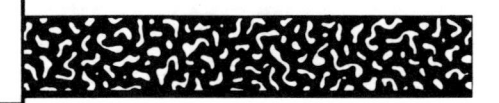

PRICING

Matching toys marked with prices and coins in rings

What kids do

Match the priced toys with appropriate value coins and put them in the rings together.

What kids and teachers can talk about

Talk about money and the names of these coins.

Note: Make several different sets, if you want, each to be used separately. Make prices appropriate for your age group, using small numbers such as 6 cents, 11 cents, 3 cents, etc.

LEVEL:
Advanced—possibly Intermediate

SKILLS:
Counting, price matching

MATERIALS:
Set of six rings

6 or fewer little toys or trinkets with a price written on each (use a white paint pen to make a 3/8" (1 cm) dot on the toy, and write the price on the white dot in black ink)

Plastic or metal play coins to exactly equal the total of the prices of the set of toys

CORKS/NOT CORKS

Sorting corks and miscellaneous items in rings

Note: The activity can be varied by substituting large beads or other like objects for the corks.

What kids do

They will use only two rings to sort these things. Look carefully at the objects and try to find a way to sort them into two groups. Put each group in one of the rings.

What kids and teachers can do

Work together to find the one way to sort the objects—by placing all the corks together, and all the remaining things, which have no common features, together.

LEVEL:
Intermediate-Advanced

SKILLS:
Classification by elimination

MATERIALS:
2 rings

10 to 15 corks of the same size or different sizes, and 10 to 15 miscellaneous, unrelated things—(there should be no two things alike in the unrelated group)

RINGS

FABRIC TEXTURES

Sorting fabric squares by texture in rings

LEVEL:
Intermediate-Advanced

SKILLS:
Classification by texture

MATERIALS:
Set of six rings

2" (5 cm) squares of 6 or fewer different fabrics in one color, 3 squares of each: corduroy, satin, felt, burlap, velvet, vinyl, fake fur, etc.

What kids do

Sort the squares into rings by feeling them. Those that feel the same go together.

What kids and teachers can do

Describe how the different fabrics feel. Use words like smooth, soft, rough, ridged, etc. Talk about the names of the fabrics and where you may have seen fabrics like these.

COLORED PENCILS

Sorting colored pencils by length in rings

LEVEL:
Intermediate-Advanced

SKILLS:
Classification by length

MATERIALS:
Set of six rings

12 or fewer short, approximately 4 1/2" (11 cm), colored pencils, sharpened to 6 or fewer different lengths, 2 of each length

What kids do

Find the two pencils that are the same length and put them in one ring. They may want to put them in order from small to large or large to small.

What else kids can do

They can arrange the pencils on the table in graduated order, or sort the pencils by color.

RINGS

CORNERS/NO CORNERS

Sorting discarded objects by their form in rings

What kids do
They will use only two rings to sort these things. They should look at them carefully, find a way to divide them into two groups, and put the groups in the rings.

What kids and teachers can do
This activity is ideal for sharing. Help the children see that there are really only two categories of things—those with corners and those without.

LEVEL:
Intermediate-Advanced

SKILLS:
Classification by form

MATERIALS:
2 rings (see the reference to rings for this activity in the introduction to this section)

2 sets of objects: those with rounded edges, and those with angles or square corners, such as balls, bottles, caps, and boxes, square and rectangle-shaped cardboard, etc.

INDEX

SKILLS INDEX

Abstraction 20, 25, 49, 64, 66
Accuracy 66, 107, 108, 110
Advanced Skill Level 13
Alternation 67
Attention to detail . 20, 27, 30, 35, 95, 98, 133, 138, 139, 168, 170
Beginning Skill Level 13
Classification by color . 200, 202, 203, 206, 207, 210, 215
Classification by character . . . 211
Classification by denomination 213, 216
Classification by elimination . . 219
Classification by features . . 204, 207
Classification by form 221
Classification by function . 209, 211
Classification by length 220
Classification by material 212
Classification by pattern . 213, 215
Classification by shape . . 198, 205, 208, 217, 218
Classification by similarities . . 201
Classification by size . . . 198-201, 203-207, 209, 214
Classification by texture . 216, 220
Clean-up 104, 106
Color differences . . . 95, 120, 215
Color distinction 21, 24, 29, 48, 54, 123, 124
Components 94, 100
Construction 62, 105
Counting 38, 39, 103-105, 107, 109, 111-115, 121, 122, 124, 126, 132, 138, 139, 219
Creative thinking 44, 196
Critical judgment 137, 168
Crosswise 21, 27, 46-50, 52, 54, 57, 58, 62, 63, 86, 88
Demonstrations 12, 46, 104
Design recognition 37, 95
Exploration 9, 44
Eye-hand coordination . . . 61, 108, 158, 159, 162, 163
Fantasy 160
Fine-motor control 104
Flexibility 196
Graduated Size 28, 60, 122, 168, 170
Graduation 26
Independent learning 78
Intermediate Skill Level 13
Laminate 31, 49, 59-61, 64, 66-68, 70, 72, 75, 78, 80, 90, 91, 95-101, 133, 135, 136, 143, 145, 168, 170
Left/Right pairing 96
Lengthwise 21, 41, 47, 49, 50, 52, 54, 57, 58, 60, 62, 63
Letter recognition . . 17, 40, 72, 75
Light/Dark 135
Lower case letter recognition . . 40
Manual dexterity . . . 48, 49, 53-55, 83-86, 88, 147-152, 158-162
Matching 16, 18-22, 24, 25, 27, 31, 34, 38, 40, 41, 72, 75, 78, 80, 87, 88, 94, 98, 100, 117-139, 168, 170, 205, 213, 214, 216, 218, 219
Money awareness 119, 128
Money denomination . . . 119, 128, 213, 216
Number distinction 24, 129
Ordering 40, 45, 50, 75
Organization 67
Pairing 15, 16, 90, 94, 98
Pattern duplication . . . 68, 48, 66
Pattern comparison 121
Pattern distinction 24
Perception 20-22, 31, 63, 66, 136
Precision 61, 107, 110
Progression 26, 52
Sequence . . 20, 27, 40, 72, 75, 78
Sequencing 27
Shape distinction 125
Shape identification 127
Shape perception 63
Sharing 221
Size differences . . 95, 99, 123, 134

MATERIALS INDEX

Baker's clay . . . 142-145, 147-154
Brazil nuts 111
Broad-tip marker 16
Card stock . . . 45, 90, 91, 168, 170
Cloth sponge 44, 45, 66, 67, 87
Colored card 91, 168
Colored water 107-110
Cone-tip marker 16
Copier 31, 47, 90, 143, 145, 168, 170
Cutters 144, 146, 147
Dry one-cup measuring cup 155, 157
Embroidery hoops 196
Fine-line marker 16
Flotation 161
Flour 144
Geometric shapes 23, 37, 68
Glue 34, 45, 50, 88, 120, 121, 131, 143, 145, 163, 203, 210, 216
Grid card 80, 90, 91, 95-99
Handicraft stores 16, 206
Hobby stores 16, 155, 196
Hookboard 91
Knife 144, 146, 150
Laminating machine 45, 90
Large, dried beans . . 106, 110, 132, 155, 158
Large serving spoon 160
Letter card 148
Liquid one-cup measuring cup . . 160, 162, 163
Liquid two-cup measuring cup . 110, 162, 163
Macrame rings 196
Magnet-backed card 91
Measuring tablespoon . 104, 107, 109
Measuring teaspoon 107, 109
Name card 153
Nation/Ruskin brand sponge . . . 45
Number card 145, 154
Numeral 36
Office supply stores . . 16, 124, 168

223

INDEX

Outline card 58-61, 63, 66
Overlays 168-170
Paper money 128, 216
Pecans 104, 111, 204
Permanent marker 41, 59 107-110, 112, 169
Plastic sandwich bags 143, 144
Plastic self-closing bags 118
Playdough 142, 144, 148
Polyester (polyfoam) sponge 44
Rice 104, 106-110
Rolling pin 144
Salt 144
Samsill brand 118
Sand 113, 142, 155-160
Sanford's Sharpie Permanent Marker 16
School supply catalogs 90
Scoop 104, 105, 110, 155, 159
Slotted spoon 155, 161
Small dried beans 106-110
Small eating spoon 106, 144
Solo Company 104
Spatula 144, 146, 147
Sponge cellusose 44
Squeeze bottle 156, 164
Static electricity 47
Stickers — Hallmark 90, 93
Stickers — Dennison 90, 93
Stickers — Mrs. Grossman's . . . 90, 93, 94, 100
Stickers — Eureka 90, 93

ACTIVITIES INDEX

CUPS
1-10 (fringe balls) 113
1-10 (toys) 112
Advanced numbers (two digit) . . 114
Dots 107
Graduated fill lines 108
How many clips? 114
How many nuts to fill 111
Money 115
Numbers 109
Same fill lines 110
Sets 113

GADGETS
Clay/Hands 148
Cutters 147
Flat beads 151
Floating Things 160
Funnels/bottles 162
Funnels and Tubes 163
Letters 148
Measuring cups and spoons . . . 157
Molds 160
Names 153
Numbers 154
Round Beads 152
Siphon and Suction 165
Squeeze, Spray, and Sprinkle . . 164
Stamping tools/Knife 150
Stamping tools/Pastry wheel . . . 150
Strainer/beans 158
Village 160

POCKETS
Beans 132
Buttons 129
Cards 136
Clips (assorted and plastic) . . . 124
Clips (metal) 134
Coins 119

Color shades 135
Counters 121
Dominoes 139
Erasers 125
Fabric textures 131
Felt shapes 127
Flags 133
Flowers/leaves 135
Lace 129
Magnets 122
Paper money 128
Pegs 128
Poker chips 126
Ribbons 121
Rings 123
Rubber bands 133
Sewing trims 120
Spangles/beads 138
Spices 137
Stamps 136
Textures 130
Washers 122

RINGS
Beads 207
Bottles 205
Buttons (by size) 206
Buttons (assorted) 202
Buttons (by color) 206
Coins 213
Colored Pencils 220
Colors/objects 210
Corks 198
Corks/not corks 219
Corners/no corners 221
Dinosaurs 208
Et cetera 211
Fabric patterns 215
Fabric textures 220
Farm animals 198
Hardware 214
Lace 213

224

INDEX

Large/Small 201
Marbles 215
Measuring spoons 209
Metal key rings 199
Metal, Plastic, Wood, Paper,
   Fabric, Rubber 212
Nuts 204
Paper money 216
Pegboard hooks 218
Plastic eggs 203
Pricing 219
Sandpaper 216
Shells/Rocks 217
Thread 210
Toys 209
Washers 203
Wild animals 205

SPONGES

Alphabet (lower case) 75
Alphabet (upper case) 72
Beginner puzzles 49
Building blocks 62
Color stacks 53
Cutouts (round) 87
Cutouts (square) 88
Feeling shapes 57
Fractions—circle 83
Fractions—rectangle 86

Fractions—triangle 85
Fractions—square 84
Graph 80
Length Bars 52
Lotto 70
Numbers 78
One-color puzzles 63
Outlines 66
Patterns 68
Positive/negative bars 60
Puzzles 64
Shapes for intermediates
   and advanced 54
Shapes for beginners 48
Squares 67
Towers 55
Two-color puzzles 58
Vertical puzzle 61
Width bars 50

STICKERS

Categories 101
Components 100
Large/small 99
Left/right 96
Orientation 97
Paring 98
Sorting 95
Types and Brands 93

STICKS

1-20 39
1-10 38
Alphabet (upper case) 40
Alphabet (lower case) 40
Arrows 22
Colors 36
Dots 22
Geopuzzles 23
Geoshapes 37
Halves 25
Hearts 24
High-Low 28
Ice cream cones 27
Lines 24
Measurements 41
Music Notes 35
Names/faces 34
Numbers 36
One-color 18
Patterns 21
Puzzles 31
Smiles 29
Stars 30
Steps 26
Stripes 27
Two-color 19
What's Missing 20